EXPANDING
ASTROLOGY'S
UNIVERSE

OTHER BOOKS BY
ZIPPORAH POTTENGER DOBYNS, PH.D.

The Asteroid Ephemeris Calculations by Astro Computing Services. Positions of Ceres, Pallas, Juno and Vesta given for years 1883-1999. Introduction and delineations by Zipporah Dobyns offer a discussions of philosophical issues, astronomical information, mythological background and psychological principles associated with the asteroids.

Distance Values, 1971-1980 Percentages of distance based on smallest and largest distances of the Sun, Moon and planets from Earth for use in astrological research and chart interpretation.

Evolution Through the Zodiac A discussion of the twelve-letter alphabet of astrology. This view also presents the zodiac as an evolutionary spiral of human development.

Finding the Person in the Horoscope The essentials of psychological delineation of a horoscope. The horoscope as a mirror helps us to see our own nature more clearly and grow toward an infinite potential.

God's World Inspirational poetry offering philosophical insights in verse form. May be used as brief spirit lifters or as topics for depth meditation.

The Node Book Includes tables of geocentric positions of the planetary nodes for 1950 with corrections for an entire century! Nodes of Ceres, Pallas, Juno and Vesta are also included. Dr. Dobyns discusses the meaning of the positions of the planetary and asteroid nodes as well as the nodes of the Moon in the six zodiacal polarities, with examples.

Progressions, Directions and Rectification Finally. . .A way to begin the difficult process of **determining an unknown birthtime** without guessing or grasping at straws. Easy to understand explanations of the major current pattern systems and how they can be used in the rectification process. A **MUST** for the serious student and professional.

The Zodiac as a Key to History This beautifully illustrated volume explains the confusion over the timing of the Aquarian Age and presents a theory of sub-ages with suggestive correlations with history including help in understanding present day trends.

All available through:

TIA PUBLICATIONS, P.O. BOX 45558, Los Angeles, CA 90045

Cover Design: Nebula by Hale Observatories; Chichen Itza pyramid by Mike Carroll; Composition by Laurie Ortiz

International Standard Book Number 0-917086-49-X

Printed in the United States of America

Published by ACS Publications, Inc., P.O. Box 16430, San Diego, CA 92116

EXPANDING
ASTROLOGY'S
UNIVERSE

by
Zipporah Dobyns

Also by ACS Publications

CONTENTS

CHAPTER 1

Basic Premises

Astrology, humanity's key to cosmic order: what is it, when was it discovered, who uses it and for what purposes? We can say that astrology is the study of correspondences between earth and sky. Saying anything more throws us immediately into controversy between differing theories. We do not know who discovered astrology. Marshack suggests that scratches on reindeer bones dating back to neolithic hunters around 20,000 years ago were representations of the phases of the Moon. Humans may have already associated the Moon with fertility in animals and people. Certainly we know that astrology is found wherever there is civilization: a group sufficiently advanced to have specialists with time to study, where total time and energy are not required to gather enough food for survival.

Astrology is found throughout history, even in areas with relatively primitive cultures. Apparently, the sky has been used by humans in almost all areas as a way to orient themselves in time and space. The sky has been our clock and calendar, our map and compass. But its most valuable use for thinking humans is as a key to meaning in the cosmos. Modern, materialistic science accepts the use of the sky as a key to time and space. Even birds can use the constellations to find their way across the trackless oceans. The sky marks the seasons for farmers who need to know when to plant. But materialistic science denies the possibility of a meaningful or purposeful world. The theories of materialism assume a world of chance (probability theory), which presumably started with a big bang and which may eventually fall into a black hole. Despite the evidence of evolution, inherent purpose is denied and growth in complexity is credited to survival of the fittest. So long as science clings to such theories, it cannot deal with astrology as a key to meaning.

Of course, scientists are not the only materialists in the world. The vast majority of astrologers also implicitly or explicitly accept physical forces as the primary reality and power in the cosmos. They believe that the planets create character at the moment of birth, and that the planets cause events to happen to people. Having accepted the role of innocent victim, subject to destructive cosmic forces, such astrologers offer a system of "good" days and "bad" days. When the planets are well configured, one can theoretically do what one wishes. When there are conflict patterns in the sky, one stays in bed, or at least does as little as possible. If you prefer to maintain such a belief system, this book will be of no assistance to you. Lists of good and bad days can be purchased from a variety of rip-off advertisements.

The theories offered in this book suggest that life rather than physical matter-energy is the final reality and power; that life is continuous (some form of reincarnation); that we return to Earth to continue growing, coming to parents, environment, heredity and horoscope that fit the character we ourselves have already created in past lives. If we have held in our energy in the past, we may come to a defective body to learn to use our energy constructively. If we have lacked trust and tried to carry too much in the past, we may come to parents who "let" us be responsible for ourselves early in life. They may die, be ill, be incompetent or be indifferent. Results in the life are not "punishment," as is suggested by many theories about karma. Results are simply consequences. Character (habitual attitudes and actions) creates destiny — the consequences in the life. When we change our character, our attitudes and actions, we change our Karma or destiny. The past only explains how we got where we are. What we do right now determines what happens to us tomorrow.

Suggested Exercise: Write out your own beliefs. What is the nature of Truth and how can we test our idea? What is the nature of ultimate reality? Can humans change their lives and, if so, how? Rank your value hierarchy: most important good or goal, next most important, third most important, etc. What or whom do you trust most, or do you lack faith in anything, including yourself? How do you think astrology works if you do accept it as a valuable way of understanding yourself and life? There are no final answers to these questions but this exercise may help you to become conscious of your beliefs. Our beliefs shape our lives, determining what we think is possible and desirable. Conscious beliefs can be examined, and either supported by evidence or discarded. Unconscious beliefs rule us without our ability to question them, and many people respond to a challenge to their beliefs as they do to an earthquake; with panic. A lack of clear beliefs may lead to a lack of direction and difficulty in making choices. Increased awareness is a central goal in this book.

CHAPTER 2

Psychological Theories

Chapter 1 offered a brief statement of my own personal belief system, but I do not consider any such system to be final or total truth. I think that what we call the "laws" of nature are basically observed regularities, and that a major part of our explanations of these regularities are constructs: abstract concepts created by the conscious minds of humans. Another useful word for these concepts or constructs is **models**. In general, models are simplified imitations or representations of a more complex reality, but they can be very helpful in dealing with the more complex situation. A road map is a simplified diagram of a network of roads, but it is highly useful in unknown territory. The blueprint of a building is also a model, and also helpful if we wish to remodel the building.

Systems for conceptualizing and describing personality are metaphorically similar to maps and blueprints though they deal largely with abstract ideas and only rarely attempt graphic designs of their subject matter, human nature. Psychologists have created a large variety of personality systems within the past hundred years during which psychology has sought to become a science. Such systems range from the relatively simple one devised by Freud, largely from observations of his neurotic patients, to factor analysis with the aid of computers drawing from a pool of thousands of questions, using a relatively "normal" subject population as in the work by Cattell. But, regardless of the complexity and sophistication of the techniques and the results, the end product is just another model. There is no one "right" model, and the rest wrong. There are a variety of more or less useful models. You can photograph a tree from different positions, with different types of film and cameras, at different times of day and seasons of the year, and all of the pictures are still representations of the tree. The picture is not the tree!

The road map is not the road. The blueprint is not the building. The model of the personality is not the person.

Roots of Astrology

Astrology is the oldest known model of human personality. As was indicated in Chapter 1, astrology is found in all civilizations for which we have records, including many that are preliterate and apparently had little in the way of a specialized class as guardians of knowledge. As was stated earlier, humans have used the sky as a map and compass and as a clock and calendar, to orient themselves in time and space. But the evidence of archaeology and of writing after 3,000 BC suggests that humans went beyond use of the sky as a key to time and space. Humans apparently discovered thousands of years ago that the patterns in the sky also offered psychological meaning.

Since modern science has almost totally ignored astrology, we have very inadequate information about the early stages of its development. We know that a few hundred years BC there was a system of personality types in general use. The Greeks may have been the first to democratize astrology, to apply it to ordinary people. Prior to that period, it may well have been reserved for priests and kings, and especially for mundane purposes, i.e., to keep track of the seasons for planting, to warn of eclipses, war, famine or storms. Even after the Greek period when astrology apparently went popular, it was still used for divination most of the time. Predicting the death of the current ruler and the identity of his probable successor became such a popular sport in Rome that the Caesars would sometimes ban astrology, except for their own private seer, of course. Astrology survived, naturally, going underground to the extent that it had to. The personality types and terms remain in the general speech to this day. We still refer to people as martial, jovial, mercurial, and speak of venereal disease, of lunatics (dating to the time when insanity was associated with the Moon) and of saturnine individuals.

Astrology seems to have grown over the years from observing the positions of the heavenly bodies and the earthly events which followed them closely in time. Especially in recent years, new tools and techniques have been added to the ones found useful so that astrology today is vastly more complex and sophisticated than even a few dozen years ago. It remains to be seen how many of the new theories and techniques will survive the test of time and of modern scientific research which is finally being applied to astrology. The theories offered in this book are distilled from twenty-five years of experience with astrology. They tie together a multitude of specifics which have accumulated over the millennia into a systematic set of constructs, a model of the personality which hopefully will prove useful though it will undoubtedly be superseded or revised in time.

Twelve Sides of Life

The personality model offered in these pages consists of twelve key principles which can be conceptualized as twelve sides of life or twelve ways of "being in the world." The twelve primary constructs or archetypes (to use Jung's word) can be thought of as twelve types of people, much as popular astrology does when it classifies individuals by their Sun sign. But they also offer a useful concept of twelve stages of development within a single life: childhood, adult dealings with people immediately around us and concerns with society, larger issues, the universe. Such a longitudinal approach to astrology is similar to the Indian stages of child, adult householder and renunciate, except that astrology's last four stages of life can be important throughout the life, not just at the end. A real understanding of the complexity of astrology discloses that all twelve of these primary life urges are present in everyone, though to differing degrees. So a third use of the twelve sides of life permits a unique profile for each individual, each having varying strengths in the twelve motivational drives.

Since astrology offers a variety of factors which all seem to symbolize these same twelve basic principles, the metaphor of an **alphabet** offers a useful analogy. Everyone is familiar with printed capital letters, lower case letters and with handwritten script, and we can recognize and use a letter in any of these forms. In astrology we have planets, signs, houses, nodes and other forms of the alphabet; other factors which symbolize the same twelve key sides of life. If a student is familiar with the basic concepts, it is relatively easy to use logic to combine them.

A basic part of the conceptual system offered here is a view of life as a verb rather than mostly a collection of nouns, as an ongoing process rather than a set of objects. Each of the twelve sides of life seeks some function, some form of action whether it takes place on the physical, emotional, mental or spiritual level. The same primary desire may be manifested in many different details in the life. Astrology does **not** spell out the details; it does not tell us **what** will happen, but **why** it is happening in terms of the basic psychological motivations or goals of the person. When we know the reasons behind an action, we can often find a better way to achieve the desired goal. Not that insight alone is always enough, but it is at least a helpful first step.

Let's hammer once more at the idea of conceptual models. We are offering a description of life as composed of twelve primary drives or desires. The drives are **real**: desire is the essence of life and life does not function without it. The drives are real, but my description of them is a construct, a conceptual model. We might find in time that a model with less or more than twelve archetypes could be even more useful than the twelve traditionally formulated in astrology. The drives would remain as real and as powerful, but we would simply be dividing them and describing them in different ways. By definition, a model is a selection of what we think are fundamental and more important parts of a more complicated reality. Different scholars will select different fundamental principles. It is up to the user of the model to test it for personal usefulness. If the model helps you to understand a little better why you and others act as you do; why events happen to you as they do; and especially if you are helped to discover more effective ways to satisfy your basic desires, then the model is worth using.

The basic goal of this chapter is a brief discussion of some psychological concepts which are potentially useful in astrology. Psychology seeks to understand humans, partly in order to assist them to achieve more fulfilling lives. Self-awareness or insight into one's own basic nature is usually considered a valuable first step. If astrology is valid, it offers an enormously valuable tool to accomplish this insight. Following this first step of self-awareness, psychology often suggests we should seek self-actualization and integration. Self-actualization is defined as some sort of successful (satisfying) manifestation of the individual's full basic nature, as discovered through the insight. The concept of integration suggests that most of us have natures which include some degree of inner conflict and that we have to work out some sort of balance between our conflicting desires. We can't just "do our thing" if we want to do contradictory things. We either have to take turns with these conflicting desires in our nature, or we have to find a compromise position in the middle where we can experience a little of both.

Freedom vs. Closeness

An obvious example of such inner conflict is one which is very widespread in the Western world today: the **freedom-closeness dilemma**. We are being urged to an unprecedented degree to "do our own thing," to be ourselves, not to allow anyone else to put their trip on us. At the same time, we are pressured to find an ideal relationship. Romance sells almost everything in modern ads. Individuals not desperately seeking a personal relationship are considered strange and probably psychologically unhealthy. An ideal relationship to someone insisting on total self-will would call for the other person to do all the compromising. Since few self-respecting individuals will settle for the latter position, a great many relationships are very short-lived. Yet the quest goes on. The "magic" right person may be just around the corner, in the next singles bar. Integration might be attained by having some areas of life (hobbies, etc.) for total independence and being willing to compromise with the home and family. For others, integration might mean an open relationship, such as living together without the constraint of legal marriage. Another couple might resolve the issue by being married but open to affairs with others. The integration is not successful unless the solution is acceptable to all individuals concerned. Since most people are living in hope that tomorrow will be better, integration might be thought of as a goal we seek but never reach. But the more we understand the nature of our conflicting desires, the better are our chances for finding a relatively satisfying solution.

Defense Mechanisms

In addition to the concepts of inner conflict and integration, modern psychology offers the theories of the unconscious and the defense mechanisms. Freud did not invent the idea of the unconscious, but he did formulate its role in life more clearly than most of his predecessors. He also recognized its potential power in human lives and described some of the ways in which it operated in his concepts of defense mechanisms. In my work with astrology, the three Freudian concepts I have found most useful have been **repression**, **projection** and **displacement**. Freud felt that most people were unaware of some of their deep desires, usually because the desires were in conflict with more conscious wishes or with moral principles. If the desire was completely buried in the unconscious, the action was called **repression**. In such cases, the person was theoretically completely unconscious of this part of himself or herself. In Freud's concept of **projection**, instead of the individual completely burying the desire, it was imagined in other people. **Displacement**, according to Freud, involved acting out a desire but doing it in inappropriate ways. A familiar example of displacement would be the man who is put down by his boss but then takes out his anger on his wife. The wife in turn might scold a child, the child kick at the dog, the dog chase the cat, etc. Each is displacing the anger against a supposedly "safer" target.

As already indicated, the concept of astrology being presented here involves twelve sides of life. All twelve basic desires are present in everyone to some degree. All of the planets are somewhere in every horoscope. Also, all twelve parts of life are potentially constructive. In fact, they are all necessary if we wish to be a whole person. But as they are conceptualized here, some parts of life are mutually contradictory. We cannot manifest all twelve at the same time to their fullest extent. As was suggested in the discussion of integration, we have the choice of taking turns in our expression of the twelve "ways of being in the world," or we can maintain a compromise position where we have smaller amounts of the conflicting desires. For example, we can go in and out of relationships, and as long as we enjoy being independent while we are doing that, and enjoy being close while we are doing that, we have achieved integration. But if we are feeling lonely while we are independent and feeling trapped while we are emotionally close to someone, we have not achieved integration. We may also achieve integration by maintaining a commitment which includes some space so that neither person feels confined. That would represent a compromise solution. In any conflict, the solution requires some expression of both sides of the individual. "Either-or" will not do. Life is an "and."

When integration is not achieved, some of the defense mechanisms may come into play. If one of the conflicting desires is **repressed**, totally buried in the unconscious, a characteristic illness is likely to manifest as the desire takes physical form against the conscious will of the individual. For example, if we repress our normal desire to do what we please, to assert ourselves vigorously, we may create problems ranging from lack of energy (feeling tired all the time) to headaches, fever, accidents and surgery. If we deny our desire for pleasurable human companionship, we may manifest difficulties with our skin, kidneys, or our body's capacity to handle sugar.

Continuing with the same common dilemma, if we **project** rather than repress, we look for the blocked part of ourselves in others. Freud suggested that we imagined our own blocked nature in others, but more often I see people being attracted to individuals who actually manifest the conflicted desire, often in excessive forms. For example, projection of our desire for independence may attract very "free souls" unwilling to make any commitment, or very selfish people unwilling to compromise. In extreme blocking of our right to defend our own needs, we may even attract violence against ourselves. In effect, the more we deny a part of ourselves, the more we are unconsciously encouraging the other person to overdo some form of the principle. As with a seesaw, the further down we go, the more our partner has to go up. Another metaphor for projection could be feeding someone when you are hungry yourself. Unconsciously, one's desire is saying, "Eat some more. I'm still hungry." We do get some vicarious satisfaction from the manifestation of our desire by another person at the start of the game, but it becomes increasingly more uncomfortable as it escalates in vigor, and it can lead to very destructive consequences, including the use of our own power against us in attacks by others. The other end of the same seesaw, excessive self-will, can produce what psychology calls a **sociopath** or **psychopath**.

Obviously, the solution to our desire to do our own thing is to do it in constructive ways. Healthy self-assertion can include competitive games, sports, business, fighting for a cause, or just being very strong and self-reliant without imposing our will on anyone else. Astrology's concept of twelve sides of life carries us from the **self-will in action** of stage one to the potential saint in the final stage of life. But if the saint thinks s/he is "beyond" stage one, or s/he has simply forgotten how to deal with stage one, the consequence is likely to be a dead saint rather quickly. As already indicated, we need all twelve parts of life to be a whole person.

Balancing Drives

On the other hand, if we simply do all twelve sides of life equally, we may be quite normal and quite undistinguished. If we are to be outstanding in any way, we have to be unbalanced. We have to put much more time and effort into one or a few of the basic areas of expression. Even within one general area, we are likely to have to specialize if we wish to develop high skill, to achieve noteworthy results. Since there is a limited amount of time and energy available in any one lifetime, a desire to be above average in one area means other parts of life must receive less attention. I like the metaphor of life as a juggling act. We are juggling twelve different motivational drives or desires. We need to express at least a little of each of the twelve, because any desire that is totally denied a healthy, normal expression is likely to manifest in unhealthy and painful ways. But we can consciously choose to do less of some of the twelve potentials. Some are really less important to us, and that frees time and energy to do more with the important drives.

If astrology is a valid part of the cosmos, an individual horoscope offers a blueprint of the relative strength and importance of the twelve key desires of the individual. Each horoscope is unique, unless two babies are born at the same moment at the same place. Twins are born at least a minute or two apart, and even that short an interval produces measurable differences in the horoscopes, though there will obviously also be many similarities. If we are able to understand our basic drives, including the natural conflicts (desire to express parts of life which cannot be manifested to their fullest extent simultaneously), we can choose more effective ways to manifest the drives. To repeat, the solutions include alternating between the two conflicting urges, remembering to enjoy each while we are doing it, or finding a compromise position which permits a moderate degree of satisfaction of each of the urges by means of some sort of blend.

Where excess rather than conflict is a problem, diversity may offer a solution. Remember that each of the twelve primary sides of life can be manifested in a large variety of ways. By understanding the primary motivation, we can frequently find more successful ways to satisfy the desire, or can at least vary our expression. For example, the basic urge of stage two is the search for physical pleasures. If we have been overeating, drinking or smoking too much, we may be able to substitute an active creation of beauty, which gives us pleasure, for some of the passive indulgences. We might take up dancing, gardening, gymnastics or swimming, and find less craving for the sensual indulgence. Of course, if the indulgence was motivated by security needs (stage four in our twelve-step system), other forms of satisfaction of the desire might be required. Insight is the first step toward a solution, but action must follow for there to be any real change in the life. Using sensual pleasure activities (eating, collecting possessions) to try to satisfy the need for emotional security is an example of displacement. An action which does not fully satisfy an urge leaves us unfulfilled, so that we are apt to overdo the action hoping that doing more will reduce the tension. Another risk in displacement is the likelihood that the misplaced action will create problems in other areas of life. The displaced anger mentioned above would certainly lead to tension in family relationships. Recognizing the real essence of our desires should help us to satisfy them in more effective ways.

SUMMARY:

Desire is the force that moves life. Astrology offers a conceptual system of twelve primary desires or motivational drives: twelve sides of life. Everyone has some capacity for all twelve and needs to express them all to some degree, but some are more important (to a given individual) than others. Each person is a unique combination of the same twelve primary urges, and the horoscope (map of the sky at birth) is a blueprint of that unique mixture. By understanding the nature of our own drives, we can find effective ways to satisfy them. We cannot manifest all twelve sides of life at the same time to their fullest extent, so we have to either take turns with them or express mixtures which present compromises of various sorts. If we fail to find one of these solutions to the conflicts which are inherent in the nature of life, we may repress part of our own nature and become ill. Repression is total self-blocking, so the resultant emotional tension is forced to express through the physical body. Or, we may project our own drive and find others who will act it out for us, but that usually means the others will overdo it to make up for our deficiency and the end result is not fulfilling. Or, we may displace the drive and express it where it does not fit and does not work well. We may also have problems through sheer excess in any part of life, or we may have to put extra attention and effort into developing the ability to handle a part of life which we have neglected in the past. All of these potential problems can be solved if we understand the problem and want to work it out. The horoscope offers the understanding. The action is up to us. Deep-rooted, habitual reactions are not changed easily. Life is like climbing a sand dune: two steps up and slide back one. But when we want to change, we can. Desire is the force that moves life.

CHAPTER 3

Astrology Groupings

In our first two chapters, we have been exploring some ideas that may seem strange and unfamiliar to many readers. It is possible to earn a Ph.D. in a variety of fields of science without a single course in philosophy or psychology. It is possible to be highly successful in business, science, government or homemaking without ever questioning the issues we faced in these first chapters. Probably the vast majority of people in the world take for granted that they know what is real and what is not real. Most people only start realizing that such a decision might be a problem when they are exposed to philosophy. They find that science defines reality as physical or material, affecting our physical senses or the instruments we create to extend the range of our senses. In contrast, many philosophies and most religions define reality as an Ultimate which exists independent of time and space, is undetermined by anything outside Itself, absolute or self-existent as opposed to what is derivative or dependent. The Ultimate is seen as more closely related to mind than to matter.

Let's look at an example. Is this table "real?" Or is what we see an

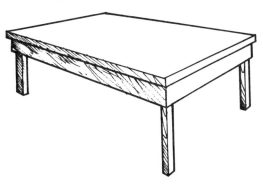

illusion, created by our physical senses while the reality is almost inconceivably small charges of energy operating in mostly empty space? Science assures us that this latter statement is the reality. Or, is the idea of the table the "real" reality? After all, nearly anything can be a table if we choose to use it as such: a cardboard carton, a chair, the back of an elephant, a ledge of rock, a tray on one's knees. Are they all real tables when we use them as tables, each useful under different circumstances? Is the object more real, or the process of using it? Is the world really nouns (objects) or do verbs (actions) define and create the nouns?

The last statement is my preferred hypothesis at this time. As humans, we seem quite unable to just accept the world as it is. We are driven to try to understand it, hoping to make it better. We start with physical sensations; for example, a sound. But almost immediately, we turn the sensation into a perception by identifying and labeling it, assigning meaning to it, which means we deal with it with memory and the conscious mind. The simple sound becomes "the bell of St. Francis Church ringing for the 11 AM Mass." One of the meditation exercises taught by some Eastern religions involves noting sensations (sights, sounds, smells) without labeling them, doing a "mind trip" on them. Most people find it very hard to do this. Our labels may range from very general to quite specific; a visual sensation may be color, yellow, a flower or a daffodil, partly depending on our background and interests and experience with the target. Of course, if we are totally absorbed in a "mind trip," we may not even see the color which is directly in front of our eyes. The goal of the meditation is to experience the world without immediately "thinking" about it, naming and explaining it. It is a difficult exercise for most intelligent people, and helps us to realize how much we live in our heads.

Believe me, I am not putting down the head! This whole book is a head trip. Astrology is largely a head trip. We just need to be clear that we are doing what we are doing, working with abstract (nonmaterial) ideas or concepts. Animals have memories and dreams which replay memories, but as far as we know, only humans rearrange ideas to create new constructs, and sometimes live more in the construct than in the physical sense world. We may call these "ideas about the world," theories, hypotheses, premises, assumptions, beliefs, and we use them to guide us in our interactions with the world. We hope that they are "true" and that they will permit effective interactions. I suggested in the first chapters of this book that all of these mental constructs were only partly true. They are models, or simplified representations of the more complex reality of the world. I also suggested that the usefulness of the theory may be more important than its "truth" in terms of someone's theory of absolute Truth. Different theories and models are useful under different circumstances, depending on our needs and goals. Our goal in this book is to show how we can use astrology as a helpful model of the human mind. Astrology offers a personality system with twelve key principles which can help us to understand the more complicated variety of actions and reactions which we express ourselves and which we observe in our fellow humans. Even if astrology is only one of many potentially useful models of human nature and life, it may help us to deal with life more effectively. To find out whether something is useful, we have to try it. Let's go.

The twelve key principles of astrology symbolize twelve sides of life, or twelve ways of being in the world. Chapter 4 will discuss the twelve individually, but first it might be helpful to look at what psychology would call "higher level constructs," or simply, more general principles. The twelve sides of life, or **alphabet of astrology**, can be grouped in three different and useful ways. Such grouping helps us to see what the members of the groups share in common, as distinct from the members of other groups. Two of the groups come down to us from ancient astrology: **elements** and **qualities**. The third way of grouping the twelve basic parts of life (motivational drives, or to think of them as verbs, processes) divides the twelve into thirds. The first four stages of life can be described as **personal needs**, the second four as **interpersonal relationships**, and the last four as **transpersonal concerns**.

Elements

Turning first to astrology's concept of the elements, the suggestion that the world is composed of four elements, **fire, earth, air and water**, is credited to Heraclitus and Empedocles. Philosophy is unaware that the concept came originally from astrology. Although we no longer think that the world is literally composed of those physical substances, the association of an element with each of the primary tools in astrology (planets, signs and houses) provides a beautiful metaphorical feeling for the tool under consideration.

Fire symbolizes the initiation of action, energy pouring out in a free, spontaneous way. It is the essence of creativity, doing something new or more than has gone before. It is eager, enthusiastic, dynamic, dramatic, refusing to be contained by anything outside its own desire and will. It marks the zest and excitement of life, a recuperative power that can bounce back from anything. It represents faith or confidence in one's own will and power with the first two fire **letters**, (whether planets, signs or houses), and for the last fire "letter," there is an instinct to reach for something higher and more absolute.

Earth logically follows fire. After we have poured out our creative energy in some new or expanded way, we meet and deal with the tangible world of physical matter. Earth applies the new outreach to achieving a tangible, lasting result in the world. It symbolizes being practical, realistic and productive, coping with the material world. The first earth letter represents our capacity to enjoy the world of the physical senses. The other two earth letters mark our capacity to work successfully, so they are concerned with all the Puritan virtues: being competent, thorough, well-organized, handling details, finishing what we start, being conscientious and responsible.

Air logically follows earth. After we have experienced the world of physical sensation, we try to understand our experience. We use the conscious, reasoning mind. We move into perception. We assign meaning to our experiences. We make up models in hopes that these simplified representations on the abstract (non-material) level will help us to deal more effectively with the earth experience. Reading a book, talking to someone, thinking, trying to "figure something out," are all air actions. Science alternates between air (ideas and words) and earth (testing the ideas or theories on the physical world). Actually, all humans do this, though not usually in as systematic and thorough a way as professional science. It is important to realize that the experience must come first. Words can only point to previous experience, saying, "This is like that and unlike this other experience." If you doubt that statement, try to explain music to someone born deaf and color to someone born blind. If I want to describe to you the taste of a cherimoya, I can say, "It is something like a combination of peach and guava with the texture of custard." If you have never eaten those fruits or custard, we have a problem in understanding and communication.

Another way to get a feeling for air is to think of backing away after an experience and literally putting air (space) between yourself and the experience. With distance, we can see the broad perspective and not get hung up in the details. Air symbolizes the capacity to "take things lightly." It is also symbolic of peer relationships with other people: people as equals, where we see them objectively but just try to understand and accept them, not change them.

Water logically follows air. Water symbolizes the unconscious mind as air symbolizes the conscious mind. Water represents the process of absorbing and digesting the experiences we have accumulated to date through the other three elements. Water includes the storage of memories from which dreams are drawn, accumulated habit patterns, or actions we do without stopping to think whether or how to do them. It includes the body processes which are handled by the unconscious such as digestion of food, healing breaks in the skin and breathing. Sometimes we can alternate between directing the action consciously and letting the unconscious part of the mind handle it. Sleep is a water action when we turn off the conscious part of the mind and temporarily turn everything over to the unconscious. We need such intervals when the other three elements are relatively quiescent and water can be undisturbed in its job of assimilating all the varied inputs from the other three types of activity.

The instinct of water is always to enclose or to be enclosed, always to turn inward, to focus on the inner depths. Another metaphor for water is the cow chewing its cud, swallowing it, bringing it back to chew some more, until it is thoroughly assimilated. With water, the rest of our experiences are either absorbed to become a permanent part of ourselves or (especially with the second water letter) they are eliminated as no longer helpful. With the last water letter we learn to give whatever is too big for us to a Higher Power. Where there was a clear sense of our separateness from the rest of the world with earth and air, water is connected. It flows into, permeates, blends. The personal unconscious merges with the collective unconscious (as conceptualized by Carl Jung) so we are open to the rest of the world through the unconscious. Water is the sensitive or psychic element. There are no barriers. No wonder the strongly water people need to retreat at times, to protect themselves from the intense bombardment from the world as well as to focus on the inner process of absorption and assimilation.

The division of life into four parts is obviously a model, a conceptual system to help us to understand and deal with life. In "real" life, we function in all four elements at the same time, though one of them may be the primary focus. As with the concept of the four levels of life (physical, emotional, mental, spiritual), the four-element model is just one way to describe life, but it can be useful. The four elements have some similarities but also some differences from the four-level model. There is a lot of overlap in the two concepts, but they are far from identical. The physical and intellectual levels correspond rather well to earth and air. We run into problems trying to match the less objective and rational elements and levels. Many people interested in Carl Jung's psychology and also interested in astrology have tried to equate Jung's four functions with the four elements of astrology, and they have run into the same problem. Earth and air correlate nicely with sensation and thinking. But different experts reverse the assignment of feeling and intuition to fire and water. The reason for the uncertainty is obvious enough; it is much harder to be conceptually clear and precise when we deal with the emotional parts of life.

Yet Jung was quite explicit that feeling was opposite thinking and intuition was opposite sensation. "Feeling" is an English translation of a German word, and does not simply mean "emotion." A better translation of the word might actually be "valuing." Jung apparently was describing an immediate, gut reaction of "I like it" or "I don't like it," which is quite close to the response of fire — a spontaneous emotional expression out of our own center. Jung described intuition as seeing into the depths, beyond the surface appearance. Water certainly symbolizes such inward searching, as well as the psychic or intuitive capacity to be aware beyond the limits of physical senses (earth) and logic (air). Plus, of course, in astrology, air is always opposite fire and water is always opposite earth in the twelve sides of life drawn as a circle. It would seem, then, that the four elements of astrology are conceptually quite close to the four functions of Jung. But it is true that the description of the nonrational functions in Jung lacks the clarity of the rational ones, and the associations with the elements are less obvious.

We run into a similar situation in comparing the four elements with the four levels of life. Earth in astrology corresponds well with the physical level, and air matches the intellectual or cognitive level. But there the correspondence between the models ends, and people who insist on trying to force correspondences between every set of four concepts can produce a great deal of confusion and sloppy thinking. In astrology, both fire and water are emotional, but fire instinctively expresses the emotion, lets it out. Water instinctively holds in the emotion, needing to take time to run it through the assimilation process, and needing to be sure that it is safe to express it. The last letter in both the fire and the water series is spiritual, and the preceding fire and water parts of life are not. At least they are not spiritual if we define "spiritual" as concerned with the absolute rather than the immediate; with the whole rather than with the parts; with the eternal rather than with the ephemeral. The preceding discussion offers a good example of how we can create two different models of the same subject and both can be useful. As has been said repeatedly, models are not final and total truth. They are more or less useful ways to simplify a more complicated reality, to help us to deal with it more effectively. The model is not "the same as" life, or a substitute for life, but it helps us to "get a handle on life," to use a phrase from the vernacular.

Element Combinations

Once we are clear about the basic meanings of the four elements, we can draw some logical conclusions about how they might mix. The actual physical elements are so metaphorically appropriate that we can get a good sense of such mixtures by envisioning combinations of the physical elements. A molten lava flow is a combination of **fire and earth**. I call this combination the **steamroller** in contrast to simple steam which results from combining fire and water. We could also think of a tank for fire and earth, or a Mack truck. The earth will slow down the fire, make it more careful, but it will also add persistence. Fire is a great starter, but it tends to say, "Now I've done that, now what can I do?" Earth symbolizes the urge to keep going until something solid is accomplished. When they are integrated, working together and not fighting each other, things happen and the world is different. People with strong earth-fire combinations have an impact and are usually highly visible. Just don't get in the way of a good steamroller. The action is out there in the world, fueled from the inner creative drive and the confidence of the fire but made practical and productive by the earth. The person feels strong and is usually perceived as strong, with exceptional endurance. Earth-fire people are still going when the rest of the world has fallen by the wayside. Of course, if the earth and fire sides of the person are fighting, it is another matter. The fire says, "Do something new and exciting." The earth says, "Be careful, stay practical, you haven't finished what you were doing or done it well enough." If the fire is stronger, we get scorched earth. If the earth is stronger, it may smother the fire. Integration means finding ways in which they can cooperate and work as a team.

Fire and air give us **hot air**, the stereotype of the traveling salesman and life of the party. Where this mixture is strong, we find a tremendous sense of humor and high verbal fluency. Such people talk a lot, laugh a lot, keep moving and flowing. They hate anything repetitive or routine and tend to be somewhat impractical but clever enough and persuasive enough to live well by their wits. They are the popular teachers, never dull but sometimes superficial. They are delightful in small doses, but not so much fun to live with since they like to stay in their "high," and if you are looking for sympathy, they are likely to leave. They keep life lively.

Fire and water produce **steam**, as already noted, and it can be scalding. These two elements are both emotional, so the combination is intensely emotional, but the natural conflict is also greater than with any other two elements. Fire wants to express out and water wants to hold in. Fire says, "Do it now. I should have had it yesterday already." Water says, "Wait. I have to be sure I am safe or that it won't hurt anyone else" or "I just need more time to work it out." If integration is not achieved by making peace between these two sides of our nature, a heavily fire-water person may be subject to strong mood swings from euphoria, when the fire is getting out, to depression, when it is held in. I call this expression the **emotional roller coaster**, or **yoyo**. An alternate manifestation is the explosive or **pressure cooker** type, of person, where the water holds back the fire until it builds up enough pressure to explode. If the fire has the edge in strength, the explosion expresses out into the world and may shock or startle anyone in range. If the water is stronger, or if it is supported by earth, the explosion may be contained and hit the physical body in some form, leading to illness, accidents or surgery. It is important for people with strong fire-water combinations in their nature to keep in touch with the emotional intensity and to see that it has a healthy outlet which will not disrupt their associations or their bodies. There is often a sort of "firecracker" feeling about such people, and you never know when the firecracker is going to go off. Hyperactive kids often have a lot of this mixture. It is not just the level of their activity; it is the spasmodic and disruptive quality of it that adds to the tension. But the combination also produces the really warm, caring people of the world. Few of us would want to live in a world without feeling. As usual, we need to avoid too much, too little, or doing it in the wrong place.

Earth and air actually produce the relatively "unfeeling" combination, seeking to be practical and logical except for the Venus-ruled letters (Two and Seven) which do not fit quite so well into the construct when it is strictly defined. Venus is always looking for pleasure, so is less detached about things. As with the other combinations, an air and earth mixture **(dust)** is valuable when expressed in the right place. Bookkeepers, accountants, tax lawyers, computer programmers, researchers; anyone who has to take things apart, use logic and experience to calculate the source of a problem or just the optimum procedure for desired results, can profit from some earth and air. Modern science prides itself on being an earth-air enterprise though of course this construct is unacceptable because it is associated with astrology. Earth-air is a very useful combination for dealing with the physical world.

　　Earth and water give us **mud**, rather like wading through a swamp. Yet it is this combination which produces the **father-mother-savior(s)** of the world. Water alone can be either dependent (absorbed into something bigger) or nurturant (absorbing others into itself) in its concern for preservation. When the strength and responsible conscience of earth is added, the mixture tends to become nurturant. (Again, the Venus earth letter, Taurus, is more concerned with personal pleasure, so less likely to be sensitive to the needs of others.) But, in general, if you have problems, take them to the strongly earth-water person. She or he may bitch about it, but they will often take your load on their backs along with their own, and carry it. I call this combination the **Atlas Syndrome**, though we need a little fire for added confidence and strength. But too much fire would tend to be more self-centered. Earth and water alone are a heavy combination, needing some of the air and fire to give the light touch and humor. People with too much earth and water tend to take themselves and life too seriously. Security and the *status quo* are values for both earth and water, so their instinct is to save everything. As a result, their houses are usually full of clutter, especially so because with their strong instinct for staying where it is familiar and feels safer, they move less often than people with more fire and air who are looking for variety. Earth and water provide the stable, dependable base which makes a society possible.

　　Air and water produce **mist, fog, vapor**. The air-water combination lives in the head, the conscious and unconscious aspects of the mind. Where this mixture is too strong, we get floaters, drifters, dreamers who are basically spectators of life. But it is a marvelous combination for psychotherapists and psychics, indicating the ability to become conscious of the unconscious; the ability to connect the two aspects of the mind. Psychic inspiration can also be used in writing or in other creative endeavors. This combination shows maximum ability to empathize with others, to really enter their space, but this talent can also make it the most vulnerable combination unless the person can use the air to detach. The combination marks the widest expansion of awareness in general, the capacity to understand people and life and to communicate this under-standing: a truly valuable gift.

As is obvious from the preceding descriptions of the elements, they are all valuable and all necessary. Serious imbalance, too much or too little of any element, can create problems. People with too much fire tend to feel that they should always have exactly what they want immediately. They often live at a dead run and may burn out early. In contrast, those with too little fire often lack confidence, courage, initiative, the zest for living. They may do the work and miss out on the fun. Individuals with an overemphasis on earth are often successful but their lives may be very prosaic and routine. Weakness in earth may indicate a person with much talent who never does much with it. Earth is needed to produce in lasting form. Those with an air preponderance may stay a superficial spectator and commentator on life, but also may take it all lightly and enjoy it. People with too little air are apt to be too intense, and they can be over-whelmed by the intensity unless they learn more detachment, how and when to thumb the nose. An excess of water marks a danger of being too sensitive. Such individuals may retreat into a shell for protection. Those who lack water may have difficulty empathizing with others. They may be quite successful but have little patience with the problems of others, and they are best given a wide berth by the thin-skinned heavily water people. Of course all elements are present in all people; the issue is one of degree and of the repeated combinations. As indicated earlier, all the basic factors of astrology: planets, signs and houses, have their own ele-ment associations. Judging the respective emphasis of elements in a chart is a complex job and I have not yet found an adequate weighting system. Simply counting occupied signs, as is still taught in some astrology text-books, is highly inadequate and often highly misleading.

Qualities

The twelve key principles of astrology can also be grouped into qualities: cardinal, fixed and mutable. The last quality was once called "common." These names are normally applied to the signs of the zodiac, and sometimes to the planets, while the houses were traditionally named angular, succedent and cadent. The meanings are basically the same though the names were not used interchangeably in the past. The **cardinal** or **angular** parts of life are associated with overt changes in the life, whether or not we produce or invite these changes by our own deliberate action. We may change jobs, homes, relationships, personal action or health, the basic areas of life associated with the cardinal or angular letters of the astrological alphabet. Where the cardinal factors are earth or water, the elements concerned with security, we may be dragged kicking and screaming into change, but cardinality is associated with alterations in the basic structure of the life. The changes may be the result of past actions or elicited from the world unconsciously, or simply reactions to the actions of others, but in general, the more cardinality, the more likelihood of basic changes in the life structure.

The **fixed** or **succedent** quality symbolizes "enduring self- will." This phrase does not mean unchanging. Fixed planets, signs and houses represent parts of the character which (when fire and air especially) may seek and initiate change, but they do it on their own terms, when they are ready. They will not be pushed into changing, at least, not if they can help it. If you want to induce change in a person with a heavy fixed emphasis in the horoscope, you have to plant the idea almost casually and then let them alone. After they have considered it long enough to be convinced that it is really their own idea, they will change. In general, the fixed urge is to keep on to the end. Fixed earth and water may never feel that they have reached the end.

The **mutable** or **cadent** quality (formerly called "common") represents different aspects of the mind, so people with a strong mutable emphasis in their horoscopes live a lot in their heads. If they also have strong earth, they will use their minds to produce tangible form in the world, but they will still be highly mental. It is easier for the mind to change and adapt, so a mutable emphasis is also associated with flexibility and versatility. Strongly mutable people bend and bend back. They observe the world, seek to understand it, and learn vicariously. Cardinal and fixed types tend to learn with more head knocking. But the mutable types can also try to create their own world and retire into it if fire and water are strong. The ancient word "common" indicates the disdain felt for such mental and flexible people in a culture where will and force were more highly valued. Cardinal and fixed people tended to try to put their own will on the world while mutable people adapted to the world. Then there were the mutables who proved that the pen was mightier than the sword when their ideas proved more potent for change than the weapons of the warriors. Our current values have shifted from the Arian Age, when the astrology we have received from the past was being formulated. There is less inclination now to consider people who "live in the head" as inferior and ordinary.

As with the elements, we need all the qualities. Balance can be helpful, and knowing "when to do which." We can also conceptualize combinations of qualities and draw logical deductions about them. Individuals with the fixed and cardinal qualities emphasized and with minimal mutability, tend to live in a perpetual power struggle with the world. Such a life can be constructive or destructive, depending on whether we compete in the right places. Military service, competitive business, sports and games, fighting for causes can be positive expressions of the mixture. Fighting members of one's own team, inability to compromise or recognize the rights of others can bring an uncomfortable life. People with more of the cardinal-mutable mixture tend towards lives with little stability, just constant change. This result is especially likely if there is also an emphasis on fire and air. In general, the elements sometimes seem a little more important than the qualities. The fixed-mutable combination is harder to characterize. The life may be relatively stable but with constant "headtripping." For example, the person might have a stable home but travel a lot, or constantly study or work with the mind, new ideas, and a variety of people. As mentioned with elements, techniques for weighting elements and qualities are more complicated than is realized by many astrologers. Simply counting occupied signs is not at all accurate. It is not possible for any element or quality to be totally missing since the planets are the most important factors in astrology and they each have at least one association with a quality and an element. Planets which **rule** two signs complicate the situation. I consider the primary nature of the planet to be similar to the "personal" sign it rules: Aries for Mars, Taurus for Venus and Gemini for Mercury.

The third grouping being offered here comes from my own experience rather than from traditional astrology. I have not found any way to define and use the quadrants or quarter divisions of the horoscope. I mentioned, in the discussion of the elements and Jung's four functions, that there was a reasonably good correspondence between the two constructs. But I also indicated that assuming that any set of four constructs could be equated with any other set of four was apt to lead to confusion and sloppy thinking. Precisely this has been done by some astrologers who have tried to equate Jung's four functions with the four quarters of the horoscope. Different functions have been associated with different quarters by different experts, but the whole enterprise seems fallacious to me. I do not think there is any such association or relationship, nor have I been able to develop any other clear construct for the four quarters.

Major Thirds of the Horoscope

However, I do think we can divide the horoscope into thirds and use these groups as a valuable construct, noting what they have in common and how they are different from each other. The first four sides of life, as it is conceptualized by astrology, are symbolic of the child side of our nature. I like the term **personal needs** for this part of ourselves. We never outgrow our personal needs, no matter what our age, and if we deny them too much, we invite illness or other forms of self-destruction. We have a right to be ourselves, to enjoy ourselves, to satisfy our curiosity, and to find some form of emotional security, so long as we do not deny the same rights to others. In the second section of the twelve parts of life, we deal with **interpersonal relationships**, the face-to-face interactions with other people in our lives. Such people include family, mate and work associates that we see regularly. We learn to be an adult, to work and do our share with the other adults around us, to compromise and cooperate (or to compete fairly). The last third of the twelve astrological ways of "being in the world" involves us in the "big scene." The **transpersonal concerns** include the search for Truth (a faith to guide our choices and direct our lives); the confrontation with universal and cultural laws and limits, the rules of the game; expansion of our recognition of the rights of others to include everyone, not just close associates; and finally the experience of connectedness with the Whole.

A person who is too caught up in personal needs may be uncomfortably self-conscious or self-centered. Too much focus on the interpersonal area leaves us highly vulnerable to the attitudes and actions of those around us. Overdoing the transpersonal area may mean we cannot be close to individuals: the "I love humanity but I hate people" syndrome, or we may neglect our personal needs. As with all of our models, we need balance and to be able to express each of these basic human drives in its own proper place. Mixtures of the three basic sections of life can take a variety of forms, depending on our handling of the urges. For example, it is common to find helping professionals (teachers, social workers, psychologists, nurses) whose horoscopes feature mixtures of the interpersonal and the transpersonal. In effect, they are doing the "close, emotional sharing" of the interpersonal side of life in their work in the world, the transpersonal area. They may do this work instead of marriage and children, or in addition to the latter. Where the primary emphasis is on personal and interpersonal, there may be little attention paid to the world at large, or to intellectual pursuits beyond curiosity about the people right around the individual. Someone with a mixture of personal and transpersonal may work effectively and satisfy personal needs, but be disinclined to make the compromises necessary to maintain a lasting close relationship or to raise a family.

The primary goal of astrology, as of other ways of understanding life, is to assist people to achieve self-awareness. If there is really very little interest in one of these major areas of life, there is no need to force ourselves to invest major time and effort in it. The problems come when we really desire the neglected part of life but repress or displace or project that part of ourselves. Astrology can help us to recognize our basic nature in order to avoid such problems.

CHAPTER 4

Astrology's Twelve Sides of Life

Earlier chapters have suggested that the world is both orderly and meaningful and that the sky is part of the cosmic order and therefore a useful way to see the meaning, even though the sky does not create the order. In the theory offered in this book, life is the creative power; life continues in a series of bodies and worlds, always evolving toward expanded potentials. We come into each new chapter of life to parents, heredity, environment and horoscope which fit the character we have developed in the past and which give us a chance to go on growing. Self-awareness helps us to grow more effectively. One of the most useful keys to self-knowledge is given to us in a horoscope, a map of the sky at our date, time and place of birth. The sky offers us a mirror if we have the wisdom to understand its symbols.

We can divide the sky in many ways, and there are many objects which may all offer us part of the meaning of any moment in the unfolding of the cosmos. The conceptual model offered in this book suggests that dividing life into twelve parts provides a very helpful way to understand life and humans. In keeping with the idea that action is the primary cause and objects are the results, we can think of life as composed of twelve basic motivational urges or drives. As an alphabet with twelve letters, each of these basic desires is symbolized by many different factors in astrology. The planets seem to be the most important of our tools, the actual bodies in the sky which circle our Sun along with our own Earth. Another important tool is offered by the zodiacal signs, 30-degree divisions of the Earth's path around the Sun. The signs begin at the intersection of the Earth's path (the ecliptic) and the circle around the center of the Earth (the equator). These two great circles intersect at two points, and it is the northern hemisphere spring crossing that marks zero Aries, the start of the seasonal or Tropical Zodiac. In addition to the signs of the zodiac as a division of the space around Earth, the same space is divided into houses of the horoscope with the first house normally beginning at the intersection of the ecliptic and the eastern horizon. Opposite the Ascendant (where planets appear to rise in the east as the Earth turns over) is the Descendant, or beginning of the seventh house of the chart. The houses are numbered in counterclockwise order from one to twelve.

It was mentioned earlier that humanity has used the sky as a clock for thousands of years, and the horoscope can be conceptualized as a complex clock: one with two dials and many hands. The house dial, derived from the rotation of Earth around its axis in 24 hours, turns in front of the sign dial, derived from Earth's movement around the Sun in a year. The planets are the many hands of the clock, each moving at its own speed with our Moon which moves around Earth the fastest. So the planets move in front of the signs (the Earth's path projected against infinity and divided into twelve parts) while the houses turn past both the planets and the signs. Each planet is said to be in a sign and in a house, but in a single day, each planet will have passed through all twelve of the houses (as the Earth turned over) while it might stay in a zodiacal sign for many years. Pluto, the slowest known planet in our solar system, can remain in a sign as long as 30 years.

In the astrological model presented in this book, each of these tools symbolize the same principles. The first house of the chart, the first sign, Aries, and the planet which rules Aries, Mars, all symbolize the same one of the twelve basic life desires or goals. I am not saying that planets and houses and signs are the **same**, but that each in its own way symbolizes one of the same drives or parts of life. The planets are clearly the most important. The houses seem to be the next most important, and the signs come in third. The research by Michel and Francoise Gauquelin has strongly supported this order of emphasis. The Gauquelins have achieved statistical significance with odds up to a million to one against chance associating certain planets with vocations and with character traits. They have also achieved significance in work with houses, finding the ninth and twelfth houses especially important as keys to vocation and character. But they have not yet been able to get significant results in work with signs. In my experience, individuals seem to act out a combination of the planet and house, with the sign operating as an adverb, coloring the action. There is some truth in saying that the planets show what we will be doing, the houses show where we will be doing it, and the signs show how we will be doing it. But all three of these major tools are part of what, where and how, and should be considered. In Chapter 5, we will look at some other forms of the astrological alphabet: additional ways to divide the sky; additional intersections of great circles; ways to combine the primary factors and relationships between them; but the balance of this chapter considers the foundation principles: the twelve drives of life.

Twelve Letter Alphabet

Letter	Planet & Glyph		House	Sign & Glyph	
1	Mars	♂	1	Aries	♈
2	Venus	♀	2	Taurus	♉
3	Mercury	☿	3	Gemini	♊
4	Moon	☽	4	Cancer	♋
5	Sun	☉	5	Leo	♌
6	Mercury Ceres Vesta	☿ ⚳ ⚶	6	Virgo	♍
7	Venus Pallas Juno	♀ ⚴ ⚵	7	Libra	♎
8	Pluto	♇	8	Scorpio	♏
9	Jupiter Chiron	♃ ⚷	9	Sagittarius	♐
10	Saturn	♄	10	Capricorn	♑
11	Uranus	♅	11	Aquarius	♒
12	Neptune	♆	12	Pisces	♓

Letter One

Drive One, or **Letter One** to continue the metaphor of an alphabet, includes the planet Mars, the first house of the horoscope and the sign Aries. The primary urge symbolized by all of these is to be free to do what we please, and to be able to do it right now. We could want to do anything in the world, including just to be let alone and not have to do anything. In some periods of history, the urgent desire might have been to avoid slavery. For some young men during the Vietnam era, it included escaping the draft. If Letter One dominates the chart, the **self-will in action** may be highly aggressive or simply very self-absorbed. Normally, there will be self-confidence, self- assertion, energy, risk taking, spontaneity and need for variety. The motto of Letter One could be: "I know what I want and I have the right and power to do it right now," or just, "I do my thing."

If other parts of the nature block our faith in our ability to get what we want in life, we experience the opposite of the qualities listed above. The self-blocking individual lacks self-confidence, spontaneity, willingness to take risks, courage to try something new. Since there are several keys in each chart to each of the twelve basic drives, it is necessary to consider all of the different forms of each letter. Mars is only likely to be in its own (first) house about one twelfth of the time, and its own sign, Aries, for a few weeks out of every two years. So normally, we will have to look at the house in which Mars is placed, all planets in the sign of Aries, and all planets in the first house as well as all planets ruling all signs in the first house. All of the preceding factors will be part of the picture of Letter One in the chart; that is, all will be part of the individual's instinctive self-expression. Quite often, some of these keys to personal action will be in conflict with each other. Unless such inner conflict is integrated, the individual is likely to engage in self-blocking or to swing from one form of action to another contradictory type of action.

In discussing each of these twelve basic desires or urges, I try to give operational definitions; that is, to describe a basic goal and some of the ways the individual may seek to achieve it, rather than to simply use a word like individuality, personality or character. But we can assign one convenient word to Letter One. It marks our instinctive sense of identity. Most people identify with the actions that they perform naturally and automatically. But it is also common to identify with other people in our early lives, and to use such people as **role models**. Role models can be either positive or negative. When positive, we wish, consciously or unconsciously, to imitate the other person. When someone is a negative role model for us, we try (again either consciously or unconsciously) to do the opposite of what is done by the other person. Parents are often role models, and this potential can be seen in the chart by mixtures of the keys to parents (any form of Letters Four or Ten) with a form of Letter One. For example, Mars might be in the fourth or tenth house, or Saturn or Moon might be in the first house. Mars might be conjunct Saturn or Moon. Any ruler of the first house might be in the fourth or tenth house or vice versa, tenth or fourth house rulers might be in the first. One of the tenth or fourth house rulers (including Saturn or Moon, the natural rulers) might be conjunct the Ascendant (within a few degrees) even though it was in the twelfth house. The identification with the parent would still exist in such a case, but it might be more unconscious with the planet in the twelfth (water) house. With a ruler of the third house in the first house or vice versa, we could have a sibling or other relative as role model and key to identity. With the fifth house connected to the first, we may identify with one of our children, or we may value our freedom to the extent that we do not have children.

The primary issue is the need to see where all keys to Letter One are placed in the chart, and to consider them all a part of the basic identity, the natural self-expression. Where these factors are associated with other areas of life, the individual is likely to be active in those areas. For each of the factors, there will be a planet and a sign and a house to consider. The other primary tool of astrology, aspects, or angular distances between the planets, will be considered in Chapter 7. All forms of Letter One carry the fire element and the cardinal quality in addition to any other they may have through their own nature being blended with other planets, signs and houses. For example, if Pisces is rising, Neptune is a ruler of the first house. If Neptune is in Virgo in the seventh house, we have all four elements represented in the mixture. Neptune is a water planet; Virgo is an earth sign; the seventh house is an air house (the natural house of Libra with the same meaning); and the ruler of the Ascendant carries the fire principle of instinctive self-expression. In such a case, the individual would instinctively want to function with others rather than alone (seventh house), would be pulled between the Neptunian search for an ideal and the Virgo awareness of flaws, and would need to work out a balance between the urge to defend personal rights (first house ruler) and the desire for companionship, approval from others, (seventh house placement). If other keys to Letter One in the chart presented a similar message, we would have some very useful information for the individual to aid in his or her personal growth. We could say, for instance, "There aren't any perfect relationships, but you can handle your desire for one by finding a mate who shares your ideals. To avoid being too critical of the mate, or picking one who is critical of you (if you project that part of your nature), you might want to work with others, and keep the Virgo where it belongs, concentrating on getting the job done well, not looking for flaws in other people. And it is important for you to be aware of your own needs and not surrender them in your desire to have others like you. Also, if you would like to save people, choose a helping profession, but don't marry victims."

To summarize, Letter One (Mars, planets in Aries, all rulers of the first house) indicates where we will naturally try to express ourselves. If several of the different keys to our instinctive identity are in conflict with each other (usually shown by stress aspects to be considered later), it is highly important to become aware of the type of conflict and to try to work out a compromise and inner harmony.

Letter Two

Letter Two of our astrological alphabet symbolizes our desire for pleasure in the physical sense world. The major forms of Letter Two include the planet Venus, any factor in the sign Taurus and all rulers of the second house of the horoscope. If Taurus is rising, the individual will instinctively act to gain physical pleasure and comfort, feeling that he or she has the right and power to enjoy life. Of course, if there are conflicts shown to other keys to natural self-expression, the person will have to integrate these conflicting parts of the nature. For example, if Mars in

Aquarius is square (90 degrees from) the Ascendant, the Taurus desire will be for stability, security, comfort, relaxed pleasure, while the Mars side of the nature will be saying, "Get out of the rut, I'm bored, I want a new challenge. Let's go visit some friends, do something!" If the individual is conscious of the inner conflict, it is quite possible to resolve it, to maintain some stability and permit some risks, for instance. Problems arise if the person is only conscious of one side of the nature. The other desire is then pushed into the unconscious and the unconscious always wins by producing some form of the buried desire. But often the form produced is distinctly unpleasant. Repression of the desire will eventually lead to a characteristic illness. Projection will attract another person who will overdo the blocked desire. Or, the individual may alternate between the two parts of the nature and stay unhappy all the time, always wanting the unavailable expression instead of enjoying what is actually being done. To use the Taurus-Aquarius example, the person might feel stuck and bored when doing the Taurus part of the nature, and adrift and anxious when doing the Mars in Aquarius. Alternation between the different sides of our nature is a good solution **IF** we enjoy each side while we are expressing it.

There are always many different forms of expression for each of the twelve basic life desires. Letter One is absolutely unbounded. We might want to do anything in the world with our personal action. Letter Two can gain pleasure from making money, from collecting possessions of all types, from indulging the appetites (eating, drinking, smoking, sexing, etc.), or from creating beauty in any form that will give pleasure (gardening, writing, decorating a home, playing the stereo, dancing).

If the chart suggests an excess of Letter Two with a stellium in Taurus or the second house (a stellium is three or more factors such as planets or angles of the chart in the same area), one solution is to diversify: to express several different forms of that part of life. An individual with a Taurus emphasis can make money and collect possessions and enjoy the appetites and be active in artistic hobbies. We are less likely to carry one action to excess if we have a variety of outlets for the desire. It is important to be clear about what we really want, and we can usually find a number of ways to meet our needs.

Although Letter Two does not involve the work ethic found in the other earth letters (Virgo and Capricorn, to give their zodiacal sign form), Venus, Taurus and the second house are reasonably practical and grounded. Mainly, they want life to be pleasant and comfortable and attractive and easy. Naturally, when you mix them with other elements such as fire, you alter the situation. For example, Mars, Sun or Jupiter in Taurus, or in the second (Taurus) house, will indicate a much greater energy investment in the search for physical pleasure. Mars, with its penchant for spontaneous action, may love gardening, play a musical instrument or dance. The primary goal of this chapter is to present a clear concept of the twelve

sides of life, remembering that in "real" charts (and real life), we normally see mixtures. To have **pure** Letter One, we would need Mars in the first
2½ degrees of Aries in the first house of the horoscope. I have yet to see
it in the thousands of charts I have interpreted. Pure Letter Two would
similarly be Venus in the first 2½ degrees of Taurus in the second house,
and so on. (See the section on dwads in Chapter 5 for an explanation
of the emphasis on the first 2½ degrees.) My favorite metaphor for a
relatively unmixed Letter Two is Ferdinand the bull, sitting in the field,
smelling the flowers.

Letter Three

With our first two stages of life we are centered on our own will and
our own pleasures, and these concerns must always be remembered if
we are to survive in this world. But we also have to realize that there are
other people in the world seeking to meet their needs. With **Letter Three**
in our astrological alphabet, we begin the process of socialization. Mercury, Gemini and the third house of the chart give us our first air letter,
so here we move into the conscious mind. We look around, notice other
people in our vicinity, and begin learning how to learn and how to communicate. Initially, we can practice on anything that is handy. There is
no need to discriminate, so the tendency is to be superficial and scattered. Individuals with a strong emphasis on Letter Three are often marked
by an insatiable curiosity about everything, plus an enthusiastic eagerness
to talk about it all. At this stage, we are learning to be aware of other people, to understand them, and to accept them; all part of air in astrology,
and all initially learned with early relationships, including siblings, cousins
and neighbors. If peers (equals) carry out part of the socialization process, parents have a much easier time.

Letter Three is also associated with finger dexterity, with eye-mind-
hand coordination. Recent discoveries in anthropology have established
the fact that early hominids (evolving to become human) developed
upright posture before they enlarged the brain. It is possible that freeing
the hands for the manipulation of objects (which also occurs to some
degree in monkeys and apes) combined with use of the eyes for the
manipulation, may have contributed to the development of the mind
associated with the enlarged brains of humans. Letter Three is symbolic
of this whole process as we leave the pure sensation of Letter Two and
move into perception, assigning words and meaning to our experiences.
Such action is so automatic for most people that they find it hard to stop
labeling experiences. The meditation exercise mentioned in the Chapter
3 discussion of air in which one can occasionally try to suspend all "thinking about" sensations, helps one to find out how much time is actually
being spent in the head. We live in our ideas about the world and they
in large create our world. Astrology, at least as I practice it and as it is

being taught in this book, is almost totally a conscious mind trip. A large proportion of most people's problems stem from unconsciousness, and can be resolved if we can become conscious. The exercise of suspending thought for a time is actually one that will strengthen consciousness, bring it more under personal control. The exercise demonstrates how automatically (which means mostly unconsciously) we operate most of the time. It is easier to change what can be consciously understood and communicated.

Many varieties of communication come under Letter Three, including newspapers, magazines, telephone, letters, teaching. Where primitive peoples in the past learned mostly through imitation, we now have explicit techniques to facilitate teaching. It is certainly easier to learn if a clear explanation can be given. Experience precedes the assignment of words which can only point to the previous experience and say, "It is like that and not like this other." The discrimination of sex in baby chicks can illustrate the difficulty in learning by imitation which is required when an action is not clearly consciously understood and therefore cannot be clearly communicated in words. Right up to the twentieth century, the only way to learn to tell a male from a female newly hatched chick was to stand beside someone who could do it and watch him or her say, "That's a male, that's a female," until the apprentice somehow, unconsciously, discovered the clues which the "expert," also unconsciously, was using.

So Letter Three is an enormously important step in becoming fully human. Its symbol is the twins, our first people in the zodiac (the word means "circle of animals"). There have to be two so they can learn to relate to others, and they do want someone they can talk to. One of the greatest gifts of a fully developed Letter Three is the capacity to take things lightly. When we can see the whole perspective, it is easier to be objective and detached. Where there are conflicts in the chart involving Letter Three, the person may be trying to learn to say, "So what?" or "Is it going to be important in a hundred years? Then don't worry about it." Remember that the factors in the chart show the **issue** in the life, not the details of how the person is handling them. Always, the manifestation of the principle depends on the person's choices. There are always positive and painful potentials.

Letter Four

Letter Four completes our first section of the twelve parts of life. After we have initiated action with fire, applied the new outreach to the material world with earth, detached and learned to understand our experience, to describe it with words with air, we digest the experience with water. Letter Four includes the Moon, the sign Cancer and the fourth house of the chart as its major forms of the astrological alphabet. It symbolizes the need for emotional security which is typically expressed in the baby-mother relationship. The instinct of water is always to absorb or to be absorbed; to be dependent and cared for, or to be nurturant, caring for others. If we achieve a healthy balance, we become interdependent, doing both.

Some of the basic forms of security associated with Letter Four are food, home and family in general. Most people look to close human relationships for the needed reassurance, but if they are unattainable or unacceptable, pets may be substituted, one can talk to one's plants, and as a last resort, objects may be saved, producing a home full of clutter. We never totally outgrow the "baby" side of ourselves, so somewhere in life, we need to satisfy the hunger for a protective emotional matrix. Studies, especially some carried out in England, have demonstrated that older people live longer and stay healthier when they live with other people or have pets. Even a goldfish, which can hardly show much affection, is better than living alone.

Letter Four normally symbolizes one's mother (or mother-figure if someone else takes over the role) while Letter Ten represents the father. But there are frequent reversals of the fourth and tenth houses, and occasional reversals of Moon and Saturn. Basically, Letter Four symbolizes the parent who cares for the helpless infant. Unless the baby is given extra care, it cannot survive. Letter Ten is the parent who disciplines, holds the power, and determines the family status in the society by his or her role in it. In traditional families, these parental roles were clearly assigned. Nowadays, in the Western world, they may be reversed, or more commonly, one parent may be playing both roles. When the same planets rule both the fourth and tenth houses, or the ruler of one house is in the other house, the parents may be similar in some basic ways, or one parent may be handling most of the job.

Remember that everything in the chart represents the individual's experience. The keys to the experience of the mother may give you only limited understanding of the actual mother as she appeared to others and to herself. It is fascinating to note the charts of several children in a family to see how differently they saw the mother. One of my early examples of this fact came from the charts of my mother and her sister. My mother's Moon was in Capricorn, and she saw her mother as critical and controlling. My aunt's Moon was in Pisces, and she idolized her mother. But when Grandmother was widowed, it was my mother who did the responsible duty thing and provided a home and support for Grandmother, while my aunt sent her loving letters and a very small monthly check for "special treats."

Traditional psychology has tended to "blame" the parents, especially the mother, for the character of the children. But it is being increasingly realized that interaction is a two-way street: that the child elicits behavior from the parent and is not simply a helpless victim. Character produces destiny, or invites it from the world, and character (habitual attitudes and actions) exists from the beginning of life. As we mature and learn to change our attitudes and actions, we become able to change our destiny.

In time, we normally shift from the role of child to become parent. Anthropology has a convenient phrase to describe our 'two families." We are born into a **family of orientation** which teaches us the cultural traditions, helping us to fit into our world. As adults, we marry and establish a **family of procreation**. If we choose not to make such a commitment, and increasing numbers of individuals are making that choice today, we still need some sort of emotional support system and may look to friends, pets, possessions or food to provide it. Obviously, there is some danger of excesses if we look for all our needs from too limited a source. The stronger the emphasis on Letter Four in a chart (several planets in Cancer or in the fourth house or a prominent Moon), the greater the need for the person to satisfy the security urges in a variety of ways so no one source has to carry the whole load.

As mentioned earlier, water letters symbolize the unconscious as air represents the conscious side of the mind. Earth and air are clearly separated from the world, but at the unconscious level, we are connected. Jung wrote of the collective unconscious and our link with it through the personal unconscious. Water is, therefore, the psychic element, open to the world, and sometimes we have to learn to shut the psychic doors to avoid being too sensitive and vulnerable. Initially, for most people, the sensitivity is centered on personal needs. As self-confidence grows with maturity, people can become more sensitive to the needs of others. But the issue is always the degree of faith and consequent feeling of security, so it is not possible to know whether water in a chart will indicate a self-centered, clinging person or a highly nurturant, giving person. Another complication associated with water involves its inherent contradictory need to be alone some of the time to do the inner processing that fulfills its nature but, at the same time, to have a sheltering matrix to provide security while the inner work takes place. One of the ways that we all retreat from the conscious world of outer directed activity is through sleep — a water phenomena. Both Letter Four and Letter Twelve are possible keys to dreams which are produced by the unconscious aspect of the mind as it seeks to assimilate the challenges of life. It is important to be clear about both the value and the challenges inherent in the unconscious. It handles a large number of vital body processes such as the digestion of food; the healing of damages (cuts, burns, bruises); keeping us breathing while we sleep; directing a variety of inner activities. It also handles a large amount of activity that was once conscious. Once we have learned to walk, to tie our shoelaces, to drive a car or ride a bicycle, the unconscious manages much of the action and frees the conscious mind for new learning or other simultaneous activity that requires attention. We would truly be lost without the aid of our unconscious. Yet often, we program it with negative feelings that produce highly uncomfortable consequences. We push into it the desires we prefer not to acknowledge and then are upset when the unconscious provides them for us. The horoscope is one of the most helpful tools we possess to permit us to become aware of our unconscious desires. But dreams are also a very useful method for contacting and working with our unconscious. Remember, our unconscious is part of us. If we make friends with it, listen to its (our) emotional needs, we are less likely to be saying someday, "Why did this happen to me?"

Letter Five

With each of our three water letters in the astrological alphabet, we close a chapter, and with each of our three fire letters, we make a new beginning. Letter Four maintains a leg in two camps. It is both part of our personal needs (the baby side that must be fed) and part of our interpersonal urges to the extent that we play parent and learn to nurture others. But **Letter Five** (Sun, Leo and the fifth house) symbolizes our really dramatic thrust out into the adult world. Although we lump Sun, Moon and planets for convenience in astrology, we know that our Sun is really a star, the center of our solar system, and the source of life, which depends on its radiating energy. Similarly, wherever Letter Five falls in our chart, we would like to be a star, a center of radiating energy that will affect the world and will get a response back from the world.

The creative outpouring may take many forms. We may love and be loved; Letter Five is associated with the heart. We may procreate children as extensions of ourselves into the world, hoping we can be proud of them. Or, we may work with children: the teacher in front of the class with the class looking up. We may gamble, speculate or invest, hoping for a larger return on the output. We may become a salesperson or promoter, persuading others to do what we want. The ancient prototype of Letter Five is the king on the throne and the lion as king of the jungle. Whatever our choice, somewhere in life we have to feel proud of ourselves, gain a sense of self-esteem and power. Where Letter One simply wanted to be left alone to do what he or she pleased, Letter Five wants to do something bigger and to be noticed for it. Letter One is our instinctive identity. Letter Five is our ego, using the word in the popular rather than the Freudian sense.

The Sun is a natural leader. The overfocus on Sun signs that is so common in astrology is a source of the frequent lack of clarity about the different parts of life. Aries is often associated with leadership, but Aries is really a pioneer. Letter One in all forms wants to be in front but doesn't care whether anyone is following. The Sun is the leader, so Sun in Aries will both want to be in front and want a follower. When the Sun is placed in any sign, we are adding Leo to the sign, so there will be an enlargement or exaggeration of the area of life that is symbolized by the sign. We become ego-involved in the area.

Many people are highly ambivalent about the ego, including a variety of Eastern teachers who advocate "killing" the ego. But we need a healthy sense of our own power and worth. It is more likely to be the people with a weak ego who have to put others down in order to build themselves up. Individuals who are sure of themselves do not have to prove their worth. In my experience, the supposedly religious people who claimed that they had given their ego to God had only driven it underground into the unconscious where it totally ruled their lives. One of the Leo exercises in my daughter, Maritha Pottenger's book, *Encounter Astrology*, asks participants to stand up in front of a group and say three complimentary things about themselves. I have seen people freeze and be unable to say even one good thing about themselves. Others were unable to say anything without discounting it; e.g., "I think I am intelligent, but sometimes I do really stupid things." Leo, the Sun and the fifth house have the reputation of arrogance and overconfidence, but sometimes what we see is a front to hide the emotional vulnerability. Though different than the Cancer sensitivity, Letter Five is highly sensitive in its need for love, approval, admiration, recognition from others. Sometimes a major lesson for people with an emphasis on Letter Five is to learn to like themselves even when they are not being noticed and approved of by others.

Of course the other side of the coin is also possible. Individuals with several planets in Leo or in the fifth house or with a strong Sun, may be too focused on their own importance, unable to share the limelight with anyone else, driven to assert their power over the world. A number of possible activities have been listed as Letter Five outlets. One of the destructive expressions is sex without mutual pleasure, i.e., rape. The association of sex and power is very ancient. Traditionally, kings had the right to the first sexual contact with any female subject to whom they were attracted. The king's sign of power, the scepter, is a phallic symbol. Properly handled, Letter Five wants a positive response back from the world and will not use power for purely personal ego gratification.

Excesses are another potential problem for any fire letter. Fire is exciting, enthusiastic, eager, confident, the most fun of our four elements, and usually the one most likely to be overdone. Since many cultures put strong limitations on fire's spontaneous self-expression, there is some danger that the remaining outlets may be overused. An outlet for Letter One used to be war, but recent wars have been so terrible or so morally clouded, that few individuals in our country are tempted to seek satisfaction in battle. Those of my generation may still remember veterans of the First World War reminiscing about their effort to "save the world for democracy." For some of these veterans, that war period marked the only time in their lives that they were able to let their power out without restraint, convinced that it was for a good cause. For them, the war remains a high point of excitement and triumph in an otherwise drab and prosaic life.

The obsession with sex which is so marked in our culture may be due to the fact that for many people, sex is their only creative, exciting outlet. The orgasm is one of the basic activities associated with Letter Five. Though some religious leaders would like to see it limited to procreation, much as they advise killing the ego, too many people need its sense of unleashed power to permit celibacy becoming a popular fad. There are hazards to unrestrained sex since birth control methods still leave much to be desired and parts of our planet are already overpopulated. The problem would be lessened, though not solved, if sex were consistently paired with love. But so long as people remain limited in their Letter Five outlets, sex is likely to continue its dominant role in the world of entertainment. Traditional astrology has described the fifth house as one of entertainment and pleasure. I prefer to call Venus the planet of pleasure. The outpouring of the Sun is too vivid for that weak word. It marks our capacity for joy in some of its most intense forms.

Letter Six

As is always the case when we move from one stage of life into the next, there is a major shift of focus. After a fire outpouring, we must bring the new creative energy down to earth. With **Letter Six**, we learn to work, to handle the small details of a job, including all the Puritan virtues. In Virgo and the sixth house, we learn to be conscientious, responsible, practical, productive, thorough, well-organized and competent. We learn to do something well, and to follow through until we have the tangible results desired by all earth. Traditionally, Mercury is the ruler of Virgo as well as of Gemini, but it is a far more serious and careful Mercury here. It also seems possible that two of the asteroids, Ceres and Vesta, are keys to Virgo, but they will be discussed in Chapter 6. Even if Ceres and Vesta are accepted as symbolic of Virgo, we will continue to look at Mercury when analyzing any house containing Virgo.

We can describe the essence of Letter Six as "efficient functioning," including our ability to handle a job well and our ability to be healthy; to function effectively in our bodies. One of the common sources of illness is frustrations involving work. If we hate our job enough, our unconscious will produce illness that will free us from the job. Since most illness is accompanied by pain, the price for freedom may be rather high. It is sometimes wiser to change jobs even if it means a reduced salary, prestige or power, rather than to hang on and get sick. I have also seen accidents connected to a job the person hated. If there is no possibility of leaving a frustrating job, the individual had better find something likeable in the job and, if possible, also a pleasurable hobby to compensate for the job pressures.

Since the primary task of Letter Six is to do something well, the initial instinct is to look for flaws and to correct them. So long as this activity is limited to the job, the individual is highly valuable to society and usually fairly well rewarded for the effort. Virgo and the sixth house (and Vesta) get a bad press in astrology because of displacement. The search for flaws and the attempt to correct them can create problems if we do it to our kids, our mates, our parents or ourselves. Air is the astrological element for people: the ability to see others objectively, understand them and accept them. Earth is the element that tries to change the world and make it better (except for Taurus which just wants to enjoy it). Charts with mixtures of Letter Six and the rest of the interpersonal parts of life are particularly at risk of being critical of relationships or of choosing others who will be critical of them. The other danger in such a mixture is that the work will be so important that there is insufficient time and energy devoted to the relationships. Working with others may solve the problem. The critical attitudes can be kept focused on the job, and doing the job together keeps the people together instead of separating them.

When Letter Six is emphasized in a chart (several planets in Virgo or in the sixth house or a prominent Vesta), the individual strongly needs a sense of accomplishment, a sense of doing something that is worth doing and doing it well. Normally, homemaking will not be sufficient to satisfy such a need, and a job outside the home will be sought and is beneficial to the family. When a strongly Virgo or sixth house woman tries to fulfill all her needs by keeping an immaculate house and producing proper children, it is apt to be hard on everyone. Normally men are not permitted the option of being primary homemaker unless they are wealthy or ill. Even as a child, a person with a heavy emphasis on Letter Six needs to feel useful, to feel a sense of accomplishment. It is no kindness to overprotect such a child. The sooner he or she develops a sense of competence in handling the world, the sooner they will feel good about themselves, and they are also more likely to be healthy. It is common for a baby with the Letter Six emphasis in the chart to be ill in the early life; to become healthy with maturity after developing a sense of competence; and there is a danger of a return of illness after retirement unless the person has a hobby or other activity which maintains the sense of accomplishment.

Remember always that the horoscope points out the **issue**. It is possible for people with a strong Letter Six to be fighting their own desire for accomplishment, especially if there is strong water in the chart indicating a desire to be cared for by others, or strong fire showing a desire to simply do what they please. Such individuals may try to avoid the limitations of an ordinary job yet still feel guilty at some level of their beings, and consequently get sick to avoid the guilt. It is really not difficult to make peace with Letter Six. We can't do everything with painstaking care, but we should be able to do one or, at most, two things well. Then we can keep the rest of life for fun.

Letter Seven

Letter Seven of our astrological alphabet moves into a new stage of our developing adulthood. With both letters Seven and Eight, we are learning to establish lasting peer relationships. The first step in this process involves air, the capacity to see others objectively, to understand them, and to accept them as they are without trying to change them. Major forms of Letter Seven include the seventh house, the zodiacal sign of Libra and the traditional ruler of Libra, Venus. Venus, as already noted, is our key to pleasure. In Taurus, Venus seeks pleasure involving the physical senses, especially touch, but also including the other senses. Taurus savors the world. Venus as ruler of Libra enjoys the pleasure of people: the systematic, continuing interaction with equals in marriage, counseling, with business partners, or even with good friends, if a common activity and goal is shared such as a weekly bridge club or a weekly study group.

We started to become aware of the needs and rights of others with our first air letter, Gemini, but the focus there is on the immediate vicinity. As children, with limited power to roam, the vicinity is highly important. It becomes less important as we mature, and most people replace the strong ties with the family of orientation through marriage and the establishment of a family of procreation. If marriage is rejected, as is occurring more often now in the West, it is possible to continue to maintain ties with one's original family, or to substitute good friends for a more formal bond.

One-Seven Polarity

Letter Seven is not limited to legal bonds, but the closer the relationship, the greater the challenge and the greater the learning opportunity. It is harder to fully accept the people we live with than the people we only see occasionally. There is a constant confrontation between our needs and the needs of the other, which is symbolized in astrology by the opposition between Letter One and Letter Seven, between Aries and Libra, first house and seventh house.

One of the useful ways of conceptualizing astrology's twelve sides of life is in terms of six polar oppositions. Each of these oppositions is a natural partnership. They have much in common and they need each other. But some attention and effort is still required to work out harmony between the opposing ends of each polarity. As we discuss the remaining parts of life, we will refer in each case to the polarity principle involved. As already indicated, the One-Seven principle involves integrating our own will, desire, rights, needs, with those of another person. If both individuals care about each other and enjoy each other's companionship, it may be possible to make the necessary compromises that are required. But it is not easy for equals to live together. In fact, a truly equalitarian marriage may represent a really new venture for humanity, and only time will tell whether the attempt will be successful.

In addition to the Libra focus on peer relationships, Letter Seven is also associated with the Venus pleasure in aesthetic activity. Libra is instinctively looking for balance, and is especially connected to the graphic arts such as photography, designing and architecture. The sense of line and form, the handling of space, are part of the Letter Seven potential. The desire for harmony and balance is usually strong whether it manifests as activity in the arts or as a strong sense of social justice and fair play in the arena of human interactions. It is also important to recognize that Letter Seven can be competitive as well as cooperative. The issue is doing things with others, rather than alone, whether we are compromising in teamwork or competing in sports, games or business. When Letter Seven is strongly emphasized in a horoscope, the issue is central in the life whether the individual is learning to be an equal, learning to compromise, or learning to compete fairly.

Letter Eight

Letter Eight, including Pluto, Scorpio and the eighth house, continues the concern with lasting, peer relationships. Mars, the traditional ruler of Scorpio, is still considered a co-ruler of the sign. When working with co-rulers in a chart, the planet is more like its primary sign, but it is considered part of the picture in the house where the other sign is found. So Mars is basically more like Aries, an indication of one's natural self-will expressed outwardly in action. Of course, if Mars is in an earth or water sign or house, or strongly aspecting an earth or water planet, this spontaneous self-expression is usually restrained in some way. When considering the houses where both Aries and Scorpio fall, one will again look at the position of Mars as a clue to how and where the individual will manifest the parts of life symbolized by those houses.

The essence of Letter Eight is the need to deal with lasting, peer relationships, with the primary focus on shared money, material possessions, appetites and really intense emotions. With Letter Eight, we are learning to give, to receive and to share for mutual pleasure. Some people with a Letter Eight emphasis (several planets in Scorpio or in the eighth house or Pluto in a prominent position) will be concentrating on learning to give, some on learning to receive, and some on learning to compromise and share. Letter Eight is associated with all joint resources and joint pleasures: partner's income or our obligations for others, inheritance, return on investments, royalties, debts, taxes, including public funds. I have seen the strong focus on Letter Eight in individuals such as social workers whose main job was disbursing public funds; in people who worked in fields such as bookkeeping, accounting, taxes, investments and insurance; in highly dependent people who were being supported by others; and in many other variations of the concern with joint resources.

Growth may also occur in the sharing of pleasures. As with all water parts of life, Letter Eight is seeking to absorb or assimilate preceding experience. The water stages of life complete the preceding cycle of four, which in this case symbolizes our effort to become a mature adult. With Letter Eight, whether the astrological factor is Pluto, planets in Scorpio, or in the eighth house, part of the goal is a thorough-going **closet-cleaning** of the unconscious. More than any other of the twelve sides of life, Letter Eight is associated with depth psychotherapy, probing the unconscious, deciding what to keep (of our past experiences) and what has been learned from, outgrown, and should be discarded. Hercules cleaning the Augean stable is the great Scorpio myth. Jung called it "facing the Shadow." It is possible to do this introspective analysis of the unconscious alone, but most people need some help. The help usually comes from caring people with whom we share our lives. We see ourselves in the mirror of the mate, whether the mate is a spouse, a therapist with whom we have a temporary partnership, or sometimes a good friend.

Two-Eight Polarity

After we have achieved the self-knowledge which is a primary goal of Letter Eight, the next step is a movement toward self-mastery. Again, a mate may play a major role. We learn to master ourselves partly out of respect for the rights of the other people who are close to us. We can see the polarity principle with Letter Two (Taurus, second house, Venus). In Letter Two, we are rightly concerned with our own possessions and pleasures. We earn them, own them, and can do what we please with them without regard for others. In Letter Eight, we are learning how to share possessions and pleasures with another, hopefully for mutual pleasure. In the process, we balance between the natural self-indulgence of Letter Two and the mastery over the appetites which is a goal of Letter Eight. Until we achieve successful integration, we may swing like a pendulum between the two extremes: excessive indulgence vs. asceticism and self-denial. Common forms of this pendulum swing include dieting one week and overeating the next; smoking and feeling we ought to stop smoking; drinking and going on the wagon; sex vs. celibacy; spending vs. saving. With integration, we learn to enjoy the physical senses without being their slave, and we learn how to provide part of our own material needs but still share with someone else.

Where an emphasis on Letter Eight highlights the issue but the individual has not learned to express the positive potential, we may find the types described in many astrology books: the gangsters, thieves, rapists (possible here as well as with Letter Five) and con men, and so on; people who gratify their own desires by force rather than giving up some desires to permit mutual enjoyment. But it is also common to find very dependent people with a Letter Eight emphasis; people who have projected all their power and feel they must persuade the world to take care of them. And it is possible to find individuals who are threatened by any kind of dependency so they unconsciously attract weak people who will let them keep all the power. It is also possible to project some of the power, to keep enough to avoid dependency, but to be too insecure to risk closeness. Such people may retreat from any commitment yet remain deeply unhappy because at some level they really want a mate. Properly handled, Letter Eight becomes the adept through self-knowledge and self-mastery. The imminent movement of Pluto into its own sign as this book is being written is a signal from the cosmos that humanity must confront the issue of Letter Eight and learn to share the resources of the planet in harmony, for mutual pleasure. So far, we are not doing very well in learning this lesson.

Letter Nine

With **Letter Nine**, we leave the interpersonal part of life to enter the transpersonal or impersonal area. Hopefully, we have learned to be a mature adult, to function easily with other adults in ongoing relationships without denying our own personal needs or those of our close associates. By now we should also have learned to handle a job, to do something well that can be our contribution to society to justify what we receive. With Letter Nine, we move to larger issues. The last four of our stages of life, as symbolized in the zodiac, are all concerned with a larger whole rather than a part, with the long range rather than the immediate. As always, we make a new beginning with a fire letter, having closed the old chapter with water. Letter Nine includes Jupiter, Sagittarius and the ninth house of the chart, and our goal here is nothing less than the **truth** with a capital ''T.'' We may call our version of the Absolute science, religion or philosophy, depending on our background. Whether we emphasize experiments and statistical probability, faith in a holy teacher or a holy book, or we put our trust in logic, we still function with a conceptual framework, a set of beliefs, theories or premises which are accepted on faith and rarely questioned. We also, regardless of the source of our fundamental world view, feel that our ideas are supported by our experiences. All scientific theoretical structures rest ultimately on unproven premises or assumptions. All deep (not limited to lip service or a desire for social approval) religious faith rests partly on personal experience. The experience is real though the explanation is often a myth.

Everyone has some sort of world view, though for many people the beliefs are largely unconscious. Yet our belief system may be the most important part of our lives. Based on our beliefs about the nature of reality, truth, morality; based on what we value, trust, desire as an absolute good and goal; we make our daily choices and set our long range course in life. If we have confused, contradictory or unrealistic values and goals, we are in trouble. Possible Letter Nine problems include a lack of faith, putting faith in a small part of life which then becomes an idol, and conflict between different values. In my dissertation, I quoted William James who was quoting Chesterton:

> . . . in the preface to that admirable collection of essays of his called *Heretics*, Mr. Chesterton writes these words: 'There are some people — and I am one of them — who think that the most practical and important thing about a man is still his view of the universe. We think that for a landlady considering a lodger it is important to know his income, but still more important to know his philosophy. We think that for a general about to fight an enemy it is important to know the enemy's numbers, but still more important to know the enemy's philosophy. We think the question is not whether the theory of the cosmos affects matters, but whether in the long run anything else affects them.' I think with Mr. Chesterton in this matter.
>
> (James, 1963; originally 1907, p.5)

All I can add is that I agree with both Mr. Chesterton and William James. Traditional astrology has understood Jupiter as little as they have understood Neptune, our other primary planet that symbolizes a search for the Absolute. Jupiter is frequently described as a sugar daddy that will give you what you want but with some risk of excesses. Obviously, if you have turned the Jupiter area of your life into an absolute, you are almost inevitably going to overdo it. And it will often wind up as a problem unless you can find a larger faith. In their study of highly successful individuals in a variety of professions, Michel and Francoise Gauquelin found the prominent Jupiter in three groups: actors, politicians and Nazi leaders. In the charts of these individuals, Jupiter was rising or culminating with high odds against it occurring by chance. Astrologers who do not understand the principle of Jupiter have jumped to the conclusion that the Gauquelins' results connect Jupiter with authoritarian tendencies. Yet the results clearly fit the concepts offered here. Jupiter in the first house or in the twelfth house conjunct the Ascendant (within 15 degrees) can manifest as "My will is God. I have the right and power to do anything I want." Jupiter in the tenth house or in the ninth house conjunct the MC (within 15 degrees) can manifest as a worship of power and a willingness to adopt any means to gain it. Jupiter in either of its houses (9th or 12th) intensifies the drive to discover an absolute and unfortunately, can lead to fanaticism and a belief that the worshipped "end" justifies any "means".

The Gauquelins have not studied religious individuals. It may be that we will find the other side of the coin there, with Jupiter manifesting as, "I ought to be perfect. I cannot let myself fail or fall short in any way." I have certainly seen both these forms of Jupiter in personal charts. One hallmark of a religious guru or teacher who is either quite sure he or she already has the **truth** or who is determined to personally find it, is a combination of letters One and Nine. Forms may include Sagittarius rising, Jupiter rising, Jupiter in Aries, Mars in Sagittarius or in the ninth house or conjunct Jupiter, and so on. Such convictions can be a problem if we think that we have really arrived at the Truth so we stop growing, or if we are so compulsively determined to find Truth ourselves that we cannot consider ideas from anyone else. The positive expression of the One-Nine combinations is the personal determination to keep looking for the Absolute, realizing we are always on the journey and not kicking ourselves because we have not yet arrived at either personal perfection or final answers.

Normally, an emphasis on Letter Nine (several planets in Sagittarius or in the ninth house or a prominent Jupiter) will indicate an individual with considerable faith, sometimes over-confidence and impracticality. It is very common for such people to feel, consciously or unconsciously, that God will take care of it and they really should have whatever they want immediately. But, as noted earlier, astrology shows us the **issue** in the life, not the details. It is possible for a strong emphasis on Letter Nine to manifest as perpetual frustration since life is never as perfect as we feel it should be. One such individual might blame God, another might blame parents, the culture or himself or herself. Letter Nine alone would tend to have the faith and hope to keep going anyway, confident it would work out eventually. But since all twelve parts of life are present in everyone (all the planets are in every horoscope), there may be heavy conflict between the high hopes and expectations and the reality of life. A common reaction to frustration is to leave the scene. Among its associations, Letter Nine symbolizes long trips and foreign countries. Somewhere over the next hill we may find the Absolute. A strong desire for freedom is also associated with Letter Nine. Freedom is necessary to pursue our quest for the Absolute wherever our journey takes us. Mixtures of Letter Nine and the interpersonal areas of life can thus present problems. Too high expectations are one danger: we never manage to be the perfect parents of perfect children, or to create the perfect marriage. An alternate danger is that the search for freedom to pursue something bigger may block willingness to commit ourselves to the domestic role.

Three-Nine Polarity

The polar partner of Jupiter is Mercury; Gemini opposite Sagittarius; third house opposite ninth house. With Letter Three, we learned to deal with the world right around us, the vicinity, the here and now, logically and objectively. With Letter Nine, we are searching for the Absolute, wanting something higher, better, more ideal. We are deeply, emotionally invested in our faith or in our need for a secure faith. People react to a challenge to their faith as they react to earthquakes: with panic. The foundations of our trust, our morality, our value hierarchy which determines our choices; surely our belief system is one of the most important parts of our lives, yet so many people hold it implicitly, largely unconsciously, put their trust in people, money, power, fame or some other fragment of life which will let them down in the end. I wince when I hear astrologers dismiss Jupiter as expansion, or the planet of money or good luck. Certainly if you trust and value something, you are likely to go after it and to have some success in the effort. Faith can move mountains. Just be sure you want the mountain moved.

Letter Ten

Where Letter Nine symbolizes our belief system, our final goals and the values that determine them, **Letter Ten** tests our faith against the laws of the universe. Saturn, Capricorn and the tenth house represent all forms of the **law**: natural law including time and gravity, the givens of the world in which we live; cultural regulations such as stopping for red lights and going through green lights; authority figures who carry out the law, usually including father, boss, policemen, teacher; and our conscience — our internalized law which punishes us with guilt if we go astray. On all these levels, Letter Ten represents what we can do, what we can't do, what we have to do, and the consequences of what we have already done in the past. If astrology had a single symbol for Karma, it would be Letter Ten. As we sow, so shall we reap. Science believes in cause and effect, in law and order, in action and resulting reaction. But the Eastern idea of Karma carries the consequences through a series of lifetimes. My idea, expressed earlier, is that character (habitual attitudes and actions, including unconscious attitudes and actions) creates destiny. Character continues through many lives, gradually changing as we grow. As we change our character, we change our destiny. As long as we go on doing what comes naturally, we go on getting the results of that character, and Letter Ten is the report card that lets us know how we are doing. It is pointless to be afraid of Saturn, but we should pay attention. When the consequences are unpleasant (the report card comes home with an "F"), it is an indication that we need to change our attitudes or actions. When we get an "A" on our report card, we are being told to keep it up, that we're on the right track.

Four-Ten Polarity

The polar partner of Letter Ten is Letter Four, so we are dealing with the traditional parents. The Moon, Cancer, and the fourth house normally symbolize the parent who cares for the helpless infant. Without extra care, the baby could not survive. Saturn, Capricorn and the tenth house symbolize the disciplinarian parent who says, "You're big enough now to take the consequences of your actions. That's the only way you can learn what you can do and what you can't do and what you have to do to be in this world and play by the rules of this game." It is easy to see how we can have problems with mixtures of letters Four and Ten, such as Moon or Saturn in each other's sign or house or conjunct each other. As always, there is more than one possible manifestation. Letter Four may dominate and the child may be overprotected long after he or she should have learned to take responsibility for personal conduct. Eventually, such individuals have to learn that the rest of the world will not treat them like an overindulgent parent. The other side of the coin is the case where the child never has the protective care. The parents may be ill, dead, too busy working trying to survive, basically harsh, punitive, indifferent, or critical and judgmental. Whatever the details of the situation, the child feels forced to be an adult without ever being a protected child. In one such case (Moon conjunct Saturn in Aries), I asked the individual if either of these two extremes fit her early life. She replied: "I guess the overprotective parents. I remember when I went away to college, I was very indignant that there was no one to wash my clothes."

It is quite possible to have a combination of seeming opposites. For example, children may be overprotected and at the same time be criticized for their dependency. Many different mixtures of details occur in a blend of two or more parts of life. Astrology clarifies the principles. It does not dictate the details, and we can change them as we grow.

Once we are grown, Letter Four represents our own home and family, our domestic role, while Letter Ten symbolizes our career in the world, our dealing with power figures and our own handling of power. Where Letter Six marked the details of the daily job, Letter Ten is our role in society, our place in the larger scene, our status and reputation. In charts with an emphasis on Letter Ten, there is a strong attraction to a power position, but it is quite possible to block or project the power. If we block, we usually end up with illness. If we project, we unconsciously attract someone to do the power trip for us. I have seen many charts, especially of women who are discouraged by the culture from seeking or using power, where the individuals were anxious, repressed, guilty, and almost totally unaware that they had any strength. One case involved a woman with Sun, Mars and the South Node of the Moon all conjunct (close together) in the tenth house. She was in her third miserable marriage, had never worked outside the home, and was living in terror that her husband would leave her while he used her fear to totally rule her. In other cases, I have seen serious illnesses until the individual got out into a career and discovered his or her potential strength.

The other side of self-blocking is overdrive, attempting to rule or carry the world. In one form this is the Atlas syndrome: the people who feel they must run the whole show, either because otherwise the world will "get" them, or their conscience will "get" them. Mixtures with the other letters concerned with power are often a clue to the danger of overdrive. For example, Mars, Sun, Pluto, or their signs in the tenth house, in Capricorn, or conjunct Saturn, can seek to make personal will into Law. Most of our recent presidents of the United States have had such combinations. Nixon had Sun in Capricorn in the fifth house, a combination of two counts for king and one for executive. Remember the proper use of Letter Ten is as the executive who carries out the Law but does not try to make personal will into law. When we overreach, beyond our capacity or beyond our rights, the Law is bigger than we are, and we are likely to be put down in some way. One of the traditional associations with Saturn connects it to falls. When we overreach, we are brought down to our knees, also associated with Saturn.

Letter Eleven

When we have properly internalized the conscience, accepted the necessary limits which are part of the rules of the game, and learned to be practical in our handling of the world, we are ready to move on to **Letter Eleven**. Uranus, Aquarius and the eleventh house symbolize the urge to go beyond any limits, the desire to get out of any ruts, the lure of the future, the widest possible expansion of the human mind and contact with fellow humans. If the conscience has been properly internalized, as already noted, it is possible to remove all the outer limits because we have built the necessary ones inside and accept them voluntarily. Then we can be free to do anything we please because we are committed to that same freedom for everyone else and would not deny the rights of anyone. Fritz Perls, founder of Gestalt psychotherapy, stated: "I do my thing and you do yours. I am not in this world to live up to your expectations and you are not here to live up to mine. I am I and you are you, and if by chance we meet each other, it's beautiful. If not, it can't be helped." This is pure Aquarius.

When Letter Eleven is handled well, we have democracy, tolerance, openness, acceptance, noncoercive relationships with purely voluntary cooperation. Friends are usually assigned to Letter Eleven, but it is actually the widest possible contacts with anyone and everyone. Of course, it is easier to accept casual acquaintances as they are, and not try to change them, than to accept people we live with. Yet it is one of the greatest gifts we can give anyone. "I accept you as you are." Traditional astrology also associates Letter Eleven with "hopes and wishes," but the primary themes I see are the need to be free of any constraint; the intellectual curiosity that may investigate "new age" subjects, including astrology (which is very old but currently out of favor with the establishment), or a fascination with new technology; and a strong potential for coolness and detachment. If the positive side of Letter Eleven has not been developed, the individual may simply rebel against the old without offering anything better to take its place. Or, there may be a demand for personal freedom without the corollary of respect for the same freedom for others.

Five-Eleven Polarity

The polar partner of Letter Eleven is Letter Five, so the Sun in Aquarius is part of the fixed dilemma. Where Sun, Leo and the fifth house want intense love and commitment, Uranus, Aquarius and the eleventh house want space and freedom. Letter Five is deeply emotional; Letter Eleven is highly rational and objective. Letter Five needs to feel superior somewhere in the life. Letter Eleven preaches democracy and equality. Yet they need each other. Life should be big enough for an intimate lover and a variety of casual friends, for heart and mind, for self-esteem and respect for the rights of others. The juggling act of life involves learning to manifest each of our twelve sides in its own proper place in harmony with the rest.

Letter Twelve

Letter Twelve completes our journey. Neptune, Pisces and the twelfth house mark the summing up of all that has gone before as we seek to assimilate the whole of life and develop the capacity to experience oneness. Letter Twelve symbolizes our hunger for the emotional Absolute, for infinite love and beauty, in contrast to the human affection, pleasure and beauty of Venus. We have three basic options with Letter Twelve, though each of them can manifest in a myriad of details. One choice is to be an artist, to create beauty in the world, whether we work with photography, music, gardening, poetry or many other media. A second choice is the savior, the healing-helping person who works to make the world a little better, a little closer to his or her ideal. The third choice is the victim who wishes the world were more beautiful or more ideal but who has not found a way to achieve the desires, and has either given up or is looking for utopia in destructive ways. Minor forms of escapism include daydreaming, TV or movies, reading romantic fiction and sleeping a lot. Major forms of escapism include illness, crime, psychosis, drugs and alcohol. The victim has the same beautiful dream as the artist or savior, but is running away, trying to find happiness in an easier way, or simply staying miserable and impotent. To get out of being victim, of course, we need to get into being artist or savior.

Six-Twelve Polarity

This is where the polar partner of Letter Twelve comes in. Letter Six symbolizes the ability to actually accomplish something, to handle the nitty gritty details that will move us toward the beautiful dream of a perfect world. Letter Six is the satisfaction from accomplishing a "bite-sized" goal, rather than waiting until it is all perfect to feel happy. But Letter Six needs

Letter Twelve as much as the reverse. Pisces alone is the dreamer who may do little except dream. Virgo alone may do a good job for the sake of doing a good job without any sense of what it is for in the larger view. Together, they mark the artist-craftsperson or the healing-helping person.

In the end, I think the most important principle of Letter Twelve is the capacity for faith in a Higher Power. I have repeatedly seen horoscopes with a strong emphasis on Letter Twelve (several planets in Pisces or in the twelfth house or a prominent Neptune) where the individual had a strong faith and was totally protected by life. In a striking pair of twins, both women had several planets in the twelfth house, but one of them had Jupiter-Saturn conjunct with the rest in the twelfth house while her twin had the Jupiter-Saturn combination in the first house. One twin had always been protected and was essentially problem-free: with a husband who loved and supported her, good health and a happy life. The other twin had to work at a job she disliked because her husband had been an invalid for many years and she had to support the family. She was frequently ill, partly because of the frustrations of the job, and not very happy. Right from the beginning of life, the twins had demonstrated a character difference. Pictures of them in high chairs showed one with a beaming face and her arms held out to the world while the other was looking down with a sad face and her arms folded over her chest. Character produces destiny. The twin with most of her chart in the twelfth house was born with faith and God always took care of her. The twin with Jupiter and Saturn in the first house was saying unconsciously, "I have to be God and Atlas and carry the load," and the world said. "Well if you want to, we'll let you."

Of course, God won't do it all. We have to do our share and then trust that a Higher Power will take care of the rest. Then life flows.

CHAPTER 5

Minor Forms of the Astrological Alphabet

The planets (objects in the sky circling our Sun as part of our solar system); the zodiacal signs (30-degree divisions of the Earth's path around the Sun); and the horoscope houses (irregular divisions of the sky based on the Earth's rotation in 24 hours) have been described as different ways to symbolize twelve primary principles in astrology. The twelve principles can be conceptualized as twelve sides of life, or as twelve primary motivational drives or desires. They provide a convenient way to understand life though they are only one of many possible models or simplified representations of a more complicated reality. A model is always selective, choosing the elements that seem more central, basic or useful out of the complex original. Models are never total truth; all we can ask of them is that they be useful, that they help us to deal more effectively with the complicated original situation. The astrological model has proven highly useful for thousands of years. The sky is part of the cosmos and its orderly patterns permit us to make more sense of the often confusing affairs of Earth, assuming that the same cosmic order also underlies the situation on Earth.

In this chapter, we will consider additional astronomical factors which can supplement the major tools of astrology, the planets, signs and houses. Personal experience suggests that these additional factors symbolize the same twelve parts of life. They are not essential for the interpretation of a chart, but they can be helpful to support the picture given by the major tools. Often, they will clarify, add emphasis, sharpen the picture. The number of details added to a chart will be limited by the time required to calculate them and the capacity of the astrologer to integrate a mass of data. With increasing access to computer calculations, and with the concept of the basic Twelve Letter Alphabet, both of these limiting factors can be handled. Still, few astrologers will want to use these minor keys on every chart. I have found them especially helpful in work with twins. Even a few minutes difference in time of birth can make radical changes in the chart when we look at all of our tools. Also, twins offer us a marvelous opportunity to test the principles.

Nodes of the Planets and the Moon

The **Nodes of the Planets** offer a minor but very useful form of the astrological alphabet. A **node** is the intersection of a planetary orbit with the extended plane of another planet's orbit (or path around the Sun). Normally, we extend the Earth's orbit, the ecliptic, and note where the orbits of the other planets cross it. Alternately, we can extend both orbits and visualize a "line of nodes" stretching out to infinity. The latter process will give a zodiacal position for the node which is the same for an observer on Earth and for a hypothetical observer on the Sun. If we take the node to be the spot in the sky where the planet crosses the plane of the Earth's ecliptic, this point will be seen in a different section of the zodiac if we look from Earth than if we calculate it from the Sun's position (giving its heliocentric position). The differences between the Earth's view and the Sun's are minimal for the outer planets. In the space of the solar system, the Sun and the small planets are close enough to share a related view of the outer planets. But when we look at the nodes of the inner planets (Mercury and Venus), Earth and Sun have very different viewpoints, so the geocentric and heliocentric positions for the nodes can be totally different.

In my experience, both node positions (Earth view and Sun view, geocentric and heliocentric) seem to be useful in a horoscope. In terms of pure theory, I originally reasoned that one should not use heliocentric positions in a geocentric chart. How can one use a map of Chicago with Washington, D.C. shown to the east and a little south, and then insert the view of Washington from New York, putting it south and a little west? But astrology is based on experience. When experience contradicts theory, I go with experience and revise the theory. Heliocentric positions do seem to be meaningful and useful in geocentric charts, based on the experience of myself and others. T. Pat Davis has recently published a book on working with heliocentric planetary positions in geocentric charts, and Astro Computing Services has published an ephemeris of heliocentric positions for those who want to test this new tool. After discovering that it is possible to combine geocentric and heliocentric positions, my theoretical explanation was easy: we have simply noted another support for the symbolic nature of astrology. To return to our metaphor of the map of Chicago, if there were actually forces coming from Washington, D.C. (who am I kidding with the federal government there?), they would come from the ESE and it would be pretty ridiculous to claim they also came from the SSW, the direction in which New York sees Washington. Of course, if we were born in Chicago and we move to New York, we will use the New York version of our chart in addition to the Chicago one, and will find that both charts are meaningful. Though none of us is likely to take up residence on the Sun, its perspective (its view of the solar system) may symbolize our growth potentials as does the natal Sun in our chart.

If we stop trying to materialize astrology and realize that it is symbolic, we can use any pattern in the sky as a potential key to the cosmic meaning. Since there are many more potential keys than we have considered to date, we can never exhaust the potentials though we might exhaust ourselves trying to cover the waterfront. I have found the Geocentric Nodes valuable, working with them since 1971. I have used the Heliocentric Nodes and planets more sporadically, but also found them useful on occasion. The primary issue is always the repeated message. Everyone has some potential for all twelve sides of life. Everyone has some inner conflict and some inner harmony. The basic themes that are repeated in the horoscope, said over and over again by all the different tools and techniques, are the important keys. They permit us to discover a real and unique person rather than a collection of fragments which may be confusing rather than helpful in our attempt to understand ourselves and others.

Lunar Nodes

Though use of the planetary nodes is fairly recent in astrology, and still limited to relatively few people, the **Nodes of the Moon** have been in general use for thousands of years. Ancient terms for the Moon's nodes were the Dragon's Head for the North Node and the Dragon's Tail for the South Node. Early observations had noted that eclipses only occurred when the Sun and Moon were near the Moon's nodes, although the reason for this fact was not known. As is usual, in an attempt to explain the observation, a theory (now less politely dismissed as a myth) was invented to account for the experience. A dragon was said to swallow the Sun or Moon during the eclipse. In ancient China, the populace would turn out *en masse* and bang on pots and pans to try to scare the dragon into releasing the heavenly body. Eclipses were feared in ancient times (and still are by some astrologers who think the planets are running the world), so it was important to be warned in advance of their coming. Looking again at ancient China, astrologers are reported to have been beheaded when they failed to give advance warning of an impending eclipse. So the nodes of the Moon have been an important part of astrology for a very long time.

At least one modern school of astrology omits the Moon's nodes, but experience confirms their importance and value. My theory of the astrological alphabet suggests that they represent another form of the Moon. If the Moon symbolizes the need for emotional security, however we seek to satisfy that need, the nodes may indicate additional areas of the life where we seek a sense of protection or offer protection to others. Most astrologers who have used the Moon's nodes in their work have observed that they are a useful key to relationships with other people. As indicated in the discussion of Letter Four in Chapter 4, it is true that the most common source of emotional security is close associations with other people. The nodes are almost always aspected in the progressed chart (to be discussed in Chapter 9) when individuals go in or out of important relationships. They are also highly valuable in comparing two charts, to understand the potentials in a relationship between the two people. When nodes, planets, or angles (such as Ascendant or MC) of one person fall in the same sign and close to the same degree of those of another person, there is a strong, emotional reaction. With water factors, the reaction may be partly unconscious and therefore even more powerful because it is partly out of conscious control. Theoretically, the nodes of the Moon can be considered to be water like the Moon, and therefore partly unconscious.

In addition to the natural meaning, element and quality of every factor in astrology, there are also the sign and house placements to be considered. The nodes are always opposite each other, so they present a sign polarity and a house polarity that needs to be integrated. Remember that integration means expressing the two ends of the polarity as partners, compromising and working as a team. Until we manage to make a partnership of the two ends, we run the risk of swinging from one extreme to the other and feeling the loss of the missing part of ourselves. Alternately, we may repress one end and become ill, or we may project one end, find someone else to do it for us, but find they are overdoing it. The ancient traditions suggested that the North Node was more like Jupiter, representing an area in life that flows more easily, while the South Node was more like Saturn, symbolizing a lesson where we have first something to learn and then something to give. We may both learn and give voluntarily, or we may be pushed by life circumstances into learning. We are not allowed to ignore the South Node, as is advised by some current astrologers. Above all the rest of the chart, we had better not ignore either Saturn or the South Node of the Moon. The lesson could involve a danger of doing too much, too little, doing it in the wrong place or manner; each situation must be judged individually, and always, in the end, we must look at the life to see how the person is manifesting the potentials. The horoscope shows the principle, the issue. The person determines (consciously or unconsciously) the detailed way the principle will manifest. There are always positive potentials in any combination in the chart. When we understand the nature of our basic desires, we can usually find more satisfying and effective ways to manifest them.

My experience suggests that the same principles hold for the planetary nodes. I interpret the nodes of Mars as another form of Mars in the chart;

the nodes of Venus as another form of Venus. A fuller statement about the meaning of the planetary nodes is presented along with an ephemeris of their geocentric positions, in our *Node Book*. But if you understand the basic principles of the twelve sides of life as discussed in Chapter 4, you do not need additional explanations. As with the Moon's nodes, the planetary south nodes sometimes seem more challenging than the north nodes, but there is always a positive way to express them when you understand what is being sought by the planet, the sign and the house involved. Remember, it is the repeated message that is important. If a node does not repeat a theme that is present in the major factors in the chart, it is relatively unimportant.

Dwads

Another minor form of the astrological alphabet is derived from a division of the zodiacal signs into twelve sections, each representing a subtle overlay of one of the twelve signs. In effect, we are seeing a whole zodiac in each sign. These divisions come from Hindu astrology and the Hindu name for them is *dwadasamsa*. Most Westerners abbreviate the name and call them Dwads. A division of 30 degrees by twelve assigns 2½ degrees to each dwad. One system for calculating the dwads involves beginning each sign with the Aries dwad and continuing through the zodiac signs in order to Pisces. The other system, which has been more effective for me, starts each sign with the dwad of that sign and then continues in order through the twelve signs. For example, the first 2½ degrees of Gemini would be the Gemini dwad. From 2½ to 5 degrees of Gemini would be the Cancer dwad, 5 to 7½ would be the Leo dwad, and so on. With a little practice, it is easy to mentally calculate the dwads. At 15 to 17½ degrees of any sign, we are in the dwad of the opposite sign. The last 2½ degrees of any sign is the dwad of the preceding sign. As with nodes, the dwads can be interpreted as symbolizing the same twelve sides of life; just another form of the same alphabet. They should not be weighted as heavily as the major factors, but they do show a subtle coloring, an overtone that can be helpful.

Fixed Stars

The so-called Fixed Stars were heavily used in ancient astrology but are less emphasized in recent work. Nothing in the universe is actually fixed or stationary, but the stars which are light years distant from us seem to remain as a backdrop for the rapidly moving planets and Sun and Moon. Traditions coming down to us from two thousand years ago suggest that the bright stars are associated with one, or sometimes two, planets. Thus a star might be said to have the nature of Mercury and Mars, or of Jupiter and Saturn, or of Venus. I have not personally worked enough with the stars to be sure of these assigned meanings, so mention them only as a possible indication that the stars may also represent a form of the Twelve-

Letter Alphabet. George Noonan, a San Diego, California mathematician, has worked extensively with a variety of ancient astrological ideas and techniques. Noonan feels that the stars do correspond with the seven traditional bodies of astrology: the Sun, Moon and five visible planets. He matches these bodies with seven spectral classes of astronomy in which stars are classified according to their material composition. (Three other spectral classes, R, N and S were added later by astronomy. Is it a coincidence that three new planets were discovered with the aid of telescopes?) In his system, Noonan matches the heavily oxygen stars (0 class) with the Moon. He assigns Jupiter to the next spectral class (B) and Venus to the next class (A), with these three bodies being rated "benefics" in ancient astrology. Mercury is put in the middle class (F) as a neutral, then the Sun follows as class G, Mars is class K, and Saturn is associated with the heavy metal class, M. Ancient astrology considered the last three bodies to be "malefic" in increasing order of danger. Interestingly, the Sun is a class G star. Noonan states that the associations of stars and planets made in ancient astrology agrees about 75% of the time with spectral class, using his system of matching planet to class. Since the early astrologers had only color and brightness as sensory clues for their classification, a 75% correlation would be remarkable.

The theory offered in this book denies that any part of life or astrology is inherently good or evil. Any principle can be manifested in constructive or destructive ways. If we are properly working with the rules of the game, Saturn can indicate some of our greatest successes, while if we are waiting for God to do it all for us, Jupiter can symbolize some major disappointments. Additional work with the stars is on my future agenda, but so far, I have not had the time, so this comment on the subject is purely theoretical, opening up the issues. One of the problems with the ancient work is its emphasis on the negative. Since astrology was based on observation and experience, there must be a grain of truth in the associations, but where once people would have lost their eyesight, now they have laser treatments and get glasses. Basically, I think that trying to guess the details in someone's life is far less helpful than aiding them to discover the basic motivations which are producing the details. As has been said repeatedly, when we understand what we really want, we can often find more satisfying ways to accomplish the goal. Most of the work I have seen with the stars has been hindsight. Writers have noted the negative details in someone's life and then looked for an appropriate star to fit the details. I find this approach to astrology highly unhelpful, to put it mildly.

Arabic Parts

Arabic Parts represent another ancient technique in astrology, and may also be considered an additional minor form of the Twelve-Letter Alphabet. These "sensitive points" in the horoscope are calculated by adding two factors and subtracting a third factor. For example, the most commonly used Arabic Part is the Part of Fortune, derived by adding the longitude of the Moon to the longitude of the Ascendant and then subtracting the longitude of the Sun. Points calculated in this way probably predate the Arabs, but the latter made extensive use of the technique during the Middle Ages when Europe was doing very little new thinking and the Arabs were maintaining the traditions of scholarship. The modern school of astrology which makes the greatest use of the technique is the Uranian school, founded in Germany by Alfred Witte and continued in the United States by Hans Niggeman of New York. The Uranians calculate all possible combinations, including eight hypothetical planets, so they work with hundreds of sensitive points which they call Planetary Pictures.

The most commonly used Arabic Parts are the ones using the same basic formula as the Part of Fortune but substituting other planets for the Moon. As I have said repeatedly, I think that once we are clear about our twelve basic principles in astrology, we can use logic to understand the combinations. To consider the formula just listed, if we add the Ascendant, which symbolizes automatic personal action to any planet, we are suggesting that we will take the form of action associated with that planet. If we subtract the Sun from the result, with the Sun symbolizing our urge to do bigger things, to expand our effect on the world, the formula implies that at the point of the Arabic Part we are likely to act out the principle of the added planet without embellishing it, without enlarging it, prior to or without the help of the growth potential of the Sun. A logical deduction would suggest that the Arabic Part is therefore potentially another form of the planet that was added to the Ascendant. If this is true, the Part of Fortune would be another Moon in the chart, symbolizing emotional needs and unconscious tendencies from the past. The English name is actually a mistranslation of the Latin word *Fortuna* which means "fate" rather than good fortune. If character produces fate and our own unconscious is a major power in our character, it makes sense to associate this Moon point with fate.

If we change the formula and add a planet to the Ascendant but then subtract the Moon, we would again be suggesting that at the designated point, we would act out the principle of the added planet, but we would do so without the emotional sensitivity or needs, the unconscious clinging to the past, of the Moon. The converse of the Part of Fortune has been called the Part of Spirit, and it is calculated by adding the Sun to the Ascendant and then subtracting the Moon. I associate the Sun with ego, not spirit, so I consider this last name misleading.

In general, I am not satisfied with the traditional names assigned to the Arabic Parts, and would like to see a less prejudicial type of nomenclature. If we simply used the most common formula, Ascendant plus planet minus Sun, we could call the resultant point the Part of the planet, whichever planet was being used. This class of Arabic Part does seem to represent another form of the same basic alphabet. When we add Mars to the Ascendant and subtract the Sun, we seem to have another Mars in the chart. Adding Saturn and subtracting Sun points to another place for Saturn; Neptune added to the Ascendant with the Sun subtracted gives us another Neptune. As usual, these minor forms of the alphabet are less important and only to be considered when they have close aspects and when they repeat the same message that is given by the major tools. But they often do just that: they say it again and again. The order of the cosmos is so totally there, no matter how we multiply and divide, add and subtract, we still see the same order again. So long as our treatment is systematic, we will still see the same order. I would also like to see a standard symbol for at least this formula for Arabic Parts: the planet which is added to the Ascendant with a circle around it, which can indicate clearly that the point is another form of that planet.

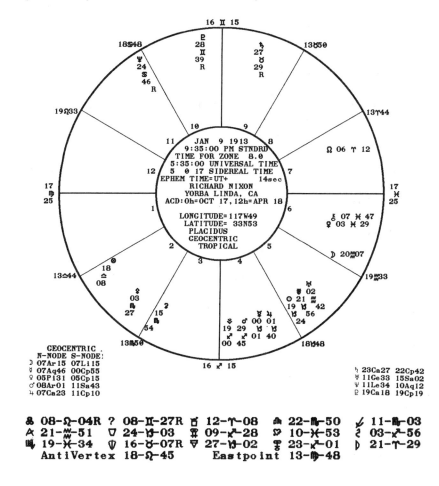

The horoscope of Richard Nixon, disgraced ex-president of the United States, is highly useful as an illustration of many of the new or less used factors in astrology. People who live dramatic lives with major events, especially when the life involves world events and issues, often provide "casebook" charts for the principles of astrology. As was mentioned in Chapter 4 during the discussion of Letter Ten, Nixon has his Sun in Capricorn in the fifth house. In this combination, we have two counts for the king (Sun and fifth house) and one count for the executive (Capricorn). When we add the Part of Saturn (Ascendant plus Saturn minus Sun), it falls conjunct (close to) the Sun, repeating the power theme. The nodes of Pluto fall conjunct and opposite the Sun, while the nodes of Saturn fall conjunct and opposite his natal Neptune and on his Washington, D.C. Midheaven and IC. [See pages 97-98 on locality charts.] Natal Pluto is in the tenth house and Mercury and Jupiter are conjunct in Capricorn as well as conjunct Mars in late Sagittarius. Saturn is in the ninth house in Taurus. Note the repeated themes connecting different keys to power to each other and to ultimate value when we include Jupiter, Sagittarius and the ninth house. All the power letters are connected in these patterns: Letters One, Two, Five, Eight, and Ten.

Another theme comes in with Letter Twelve. The move to Washington, D.C. put natal and progressed (current) Neptune on the MC. During the years of Watergate when Nixon sought to cover up his knowledge of the situation and lied continually, he also had his progressed (current) Sun in Pisces conjunct the Part of Neptune. Letter Twelve symbolizes our search for infinite love and beauty. If we fail to take practical action to make a more loving or more beautiful world, we can end as victim. Among the major dangers if we are not handling Letter Twelve is a lack of faith in a Higher Power and an attempt to play God ourselves. Both the Letter Nine and Twelve patterns in Nixon's chart show that danger. Secrecy and lies are often the aftermath when we have overreached, found that we cannot handle what we have attempted, and we are trying to escape the consequences. Again, faith is an issue. Lack of faith in ourselves and a Higher Power and fear of the world are the source of the secrecy and lies. Where there is faith and trust, there is openness. To repeat what has been said repeatedly: the chart shows the issues, not the results in detail. Nixon's chart shows the intense emphasis on power and faith, but his method of dealing with the issues was up to him. His ninth house Saturn, and Jupiter in the Saturn sign, Capricorn, both pointed to faith, morality, ethics as a lesson area. Neptune on the Washington MC (another form of Saturn), gives the message again. I wonder whether he has learned anything?

As already mentioned, it is possible to create Arabic Parts from every set of three factors in a chart. Since I have mostly only worked with the formula listed above, the rest remain to be tested some day. I suspect that the most important ones in any chart would be the ones created with planets which are prominent. At this point, the idea is purely theoretical, but it fits the repeated themes principle to have the major issues in the chart indicated by all the different forms of the letter in question. Thus, if the Saturn principle is the issue, all the possible forms of Letter Ten could repeat the message, reminding the individual to pay attention to his or her handling of the Saturn principle.

Midpoints

In contrast to Arabic Parts, which are calculated from combinations of three factors in the chart, Midpoints are (as the name suggests) the center point between two factors in the chart. One can use the midpoint or halfsum (to give an alternate name) of two planets, two angles (such as Ascendant, MC), a planet and an angle, a planet and a node, and so on. The sensitive points that are equidistant from two factors in the chart seem to represent a blend of the two factors. Strictly speaking, therefore, we cannot consider midpoints as representative of a single letter of the astrological alphabet. But we can logically combine the meaning of the two factors which are the source of the midpoint, if we are clear about the meaning of both. Certainly the midpoint is not as important as the planets themselves, but it seems to carry the combined nature as if the planets were both at that spot though in a weaker form. We will consider midpoints again in Chapter 7 when we discuss aspects.

Decanates

Another method for subdividing signs is in common use in astrology, but since I have not tested it to my satisfaction, I consider it still theoretical. Signs can be divided into three sections of ten degrees each, with the subdivisions called Decanates. I have mostly tested dwads (described above) on twins, and it is less common to find a difference in time sufficient to change the decanates of the angles. A further problem is that, as with dwads, there are two totally different sets of signs assigned to the decanates. An ancient system relates certain signs to each of the ten-degree sections but it makes little sense in terms of modern theory. Alan Leo, a well-known English astrologer around the beginning of the twentieth century, suggested that the three sections in each sign could relate to the three signs that shared the same element. For example, the first decanate of Aries would be pure Aries; the second ten degrees would be the Leo decanate; the last ten degrees would be the Sagittarius decanate. At this point, I have no faith in the technique and do not use it. It is on the list with stars and additional Arabic Parts to be tested some day.

Distance Values

One other minor and inadequately tested technique might be

mentioned in conclusion though it is not a form of the alphabet. German students of astrology, especially the Ebertins in the Cosmobiology School and Edith Wangemann of Wuppertal, have felt that the distances of the planets provided valuable information. I have not personally tested the technique enough to have any faith in it, but can present Edith's theory. She feels that when a planet is very close to Earth (within its possible range), the affairs symbolized by that planet are dealt with in a very concrete way, with much attention to detail. When planets are far away (again within their possible range), that part of life tends to involve a long range view, like a view from an airplane, with a broad perspective. The figures for what are called **Distance Values** are given as a percentage of the possible range of the planet. A high figure indicates that the planet is relatively close to Earth. A low figure means that the planet is relatively far from Earth. Edith says that unless the figures are over 80% or under 20%, they are not sufficiently emphatic to be worth noting.

To summarize the general principles that have been covered in this chapter, there are many possible techniques that may have some value in astrology if you have the time to work with them. One can do a good job with a chart without using them, but they do often repeat the message, add emphasis, clarity and focus.

CHAPTER 6

New Asteroids

Asteroids are small planets. Their name means "small star," and they should properly be called "planetoids," but the original name is firmly entrenched by this time. There are thousands of them in our solar system, mostly between Mars and Jupiter, though some range out as far as Uranus and some penetrate inside the orbit of Mercury. Sizes range from grains of dust to bodies as much as 350 miles in diameter. In 1801, an Italian astronomer discovered the first asteroid and named it **Ceres** for the patron goddess of Sicily. As more powerful telescopes have been developed, increasing numbers of asteroids have been observed in recent years. New ones are named by their discoverers, and as the supply of well-known mythological names was depleted, individuals began naming the little planets after living or historical people, cities, or sometimes, apparently for their own amusement. The result has been names like **Gyptis, Bilkus, Dembowska, Rockefellia, Pittsburghia, Dudu**, etc.

What can astrologers make of this proliferation of heavenly bodies? Could these tiny planets, some not much bigger than big meteorites, really be important enough to include in a horoscope? What can we do with the strange names? Aren't the familiar planets enough? Astrologers in India mostly endorse the latter viewpoint. They ignore Uranus, Neptune and Pluto, the planets discovered in modern times with the aid of telescopes. Most Western astrologers would be reluctant to give up the three outer planets, but might be willing to dispense with any more, and might rule out the asteroids on the basis that their small size suggests unimportance. But Pluto is now known to be very small, especially since it was found to be a binary with a moon almost as big as itself.

The only pragmatic way to judge whether the asteroids are meaningful or useful is to put them in a lot of charts and to watch the individuals involved. To test any new factor in astrology, we can watch for individuals who have the factor prominently placed in their charts and we can watch for times when the new factor is prominent in current patterns and see what happens. Prominence is shown by numerous, close aspects to other factors in the chart. To manage such testing, of course, we have to have the positions of the new factors, in this case the asteroids. Until recently, few astrologers had the knowledge or the facilities to develop accurate positions (ephemerides) for new planets. The advent of microcomputers has permitted a revolution in astrology, and it has barely begun. The years ahead will see a whole new world.

Eleanor Bach, a New York astrologer, was the first to suspect the potential of the asteroids and to publish an ephemeris offering positions for four of them. In 1972, **Ceres, Pallas, Juno** and **Vesta**, the first four asteroids to be discovered, were made available to astrologers for testing. The theory that the world is a mirror always reflecting us back to ourselves helps us to understand why the factors that are important in our own charts are also often important in the charts of people who come to us. Since all of the first four asteroids were prominent in my own horoscope, it is not surprising that I found them prominent and important in the charts of many clients and associates. I do a great many charts in the course of a year, and within a few years, I had come to regard these asteroids as nearly indispensable for a full understanding of the owner of the chart. As a result of that experience, I was ready to consider **Chiron** as soon as it appeared in an ephemeris, and was predisposed to look at any other small planets as they became available. At this point, they are being churned out on both coasts of our country though the East coast has a considerable lead on us. Only much time and effort will finally determine the real importance and meaning of these new asteroids. At the rate they are coming, we will need a computer to do the calculations and perhaps part of the analysis as well. As of this writing, I have ephemerides for twenty-eight asteroids, but positions have been calculated on the East coast for seven more which I hope to get.

Ceres & Vesta

My interpretation of the first four asteroids has been published in a number of my books, including the introduction of our *Asteroid Ephemeris* which offers their daily positions from 1883 to 1999. My experience suggests that Ceres and Vesta represent the personal and the impersonal sides of Virgo. Ceres is symbolic of the Great Earth Mother who works in order to help people. There are strong maternal overtones, so much so that I have found Ceres a key to the individual's experience of his/her own mother-figure and of the capacity to be a mother and care for others. Individuals with a prominent Ceres seem able to be a mother and also hold a job outside the home. Whatever the job, it is "for people." Vesta seems to symbolize the purest Virgo where the job is done for the sake of doing a good job. If Vesta is very prominent in a chart and not modified by softening factors, the job may be done at the expense of people, sometimes with a serious alienation from fellow humans. Jim Jones is a striking example of such a problem, with a first house Vesta-Saturn conjunction in Capricorn. Although he started out to help people in his religious ministry, he ended his life so alienated from any empathy for others that he could order the death of over 800 of his followers. On the positive side, Vesta shows the capacity for the total focus, concentration, tunnel vision that permits enormous success in the world. Einstein had it rising. Edison had it on the MC. Some of the most famous psychotherapists and spiritual healers had Vesta-Sun conjunctions, including Carl Jung, Alfred Adler, Fritz Perls, Katherine Kuhlman, and Josephine Sisson, who is probably the best of the psychic surgeons of the Philippines. The warning flag of the prominent Vesta reminds us not to let the devotion to one's job blind one to the consequences on the rest of life.

Pallas & Juno

Pallas and **Juno**, the second and third asteroids to be discovered, seem to symbolize the two sides of Libra. As was the case with the Virgo asteroids, Pallas and Juno mark a more personal and a less personal emphasis in the Libra need for continuing peer relationships. Juno is clearly the marriage asteroid. I find it emphasized in current patterns when individuals marry, divorce, or simply concentrate on their emotional desire for a partner. Juno seems very important in synastry (chart comparison). I have seen numerous cases of intense attractions between individuals with Juno conjunct planets or angles in the horoscope of another person. Mutual Juno aspects, especially with Venus also involved, often indicate the desire for marriage even when the individuals seem inappropriate (by reason of age differences, cultural or religious conflicts), or when the individuals have previously seemed resistant to marriage or had painful experiences in earlier relationships.

Pallas can want marriage when placed in relationship signs or houses (Cancer, Leo, Libra and Scorpio), but in personal or impersonal areas of the chart, it is more likely to seek less confining peer relationships. Pallas is often found prominent in counselors and consultants of all varieties: therapists, business advisers, etc. It often marks a concern with social causes, social justice, fair play, humanitarian issues. Both Pallas and Juno want equality, and both can be a key to artistic talent and activities. The Libra feeling for balance, harmony, grace, the sense of line and form and space, can be expressed in the graphic and other arts (such as photography) or in helping people to find harmony in their lives.

Message to World

If the theory is accurate that the universe is meaningful and purposeful, rather than controlled by chance (probability theory), it would follow that there is a reason for the asteroids coming into use in astrology at this time in history. If the patterns in the sky offer us a convenient way to see and understand the evolving cosmos, anything that happens in the sky or in our expanding knowledge of it could be meaningful. The increased emphasis on Virgo and Libra principles, on these two of our twelve sides of life, suggests that we need to pay attention to those principles. Virgo symbolizes the work ethic: the willingness to do a good job because we want to do something well, not for money, fame, power. The value once placed on craftsmanship, on the skill of the artisan, has been largely lost in an age of specialization and machines. Too often, work is carried out purely for survival rather than for any intrinsic satisfaction in what is being accomplished. We need a return to the positive potential of Virgo: personal satisfaction in doing something worth doing and doing it well.

The essence of Libra is pleasure in sharing activity with systematic, lasting peer relationships. Air symbolizes the conscious mind and the associations with people as equals with whom we learn to communicate and learn to see objectively, to understand and to accept others without trying to change them. Of the three air parts of life, Libra marks the systematic, continuing, more emotionally involved, deeper, more committed relationships. With the increased emphasis on individual rights, independence to do what we please, self-actualization, there has been a tendency in the United States to reject the compromises which are necessary if one is to work out a lasting, caring peer relationship. Aries and Libra are natural partners, as are all the oppositions in astrology, but to have a lasting partnership, both have to compromise to meet in the middle. The issue involves self-will vs. the need for others. If we need others too much, we lose our self-confidence and self-reliance. If we insist on too much self-will, we lose our ability to relate to others except in temporary and superficial ways. Pallas and Juno coming into use at this time in history suggest that we need to work both on true equality between partners (a major issue in the Women's Liberation Movement) and on ways to work out harmonious, mutually satisfying, lasting relationships. It is not easy to maintain close, equalitarian associations, but Pallas and Juno symbolize the rejection of anything less than full equality. The attempt to achieve equality in marriage may well be a new venture. Historically, males have normally been dominant through sheer physical strength. Even in so-called matriarchies, the female was simply trading overlords. In place of domination by her husband, her father continued in the role and when he died, her brother took over. Obviously, there have always been some strong women and some weak men where the power roles were reversed, but the achievement of equality was truly rare, partly because it is truly difficult. I think that Pallas and Juno are signals from the cosmos that humanity is now ready to attempt this monumental challenge.

Chiron

Chiron was the fifth asteroid to come into general use in astrology. It was discovered in 1977 by Charles Kowal of the California Institute of Technology. Not one but two ephemerides were in print offering its positions within a year of its discovery. Such prompt action had never before occurred in astrological history, as far as I know. Again, assuming that the universe is meaningful rather than controlled by chance, I suggest that Chiron is important, and that its symbolic meaning is a central issue in the world today. The most impressive evidence against a world controlled by chance comes from the names assigned to the asteroids. Newly discovered minor planets are named by their discoverers, and so far, the asteroids we have been able to study all seem to fit their names! This single fact, that astronomers have consistently chosen appropriate names for the new planets, including Uranus, Neptune and Pluto, should be sufficient to throw out the materialistic concept of a meaningless and chance-ruled world. Despite the decades of drawing on the well-known figures of Greek and Roman mythology, Chiron was still unassigned, waiting for the discovery of the little planet. Mythologically, Chiron was a teacher and healer who became the constellation of Sagittarius in the sky. If the name is appropriate, the small planet symbolizes much the same principle as Jupiter, our largest planet. So far, in the four years I have been watching Chiron in personal horoscopes, it does seem to share the Jupiter meaning, to indicate a search for the Absolute whether we look for Truth with a capital "T" or whether we try to turn some other part of life into an absolute. The latter becomes a kind of idolatry, and can lead to problems, but properly manifested, the Chiron principle indicates a love of knowledge. People with a prominent Chiron in their horoscopes are often driven by a lifelong hunger for knowledge. I have noted this intellectual drive even when the individuals were raised in families which discounted knowledge. The individuals (both male and female) might hide their reading, their time spent in libraries from their families in order to avoid being put down and laughed at by the family. Sometimes they have persisted in obtaining formal education, putting themselves through college. Sometimes they have just continued to read and study on their own. But knowledge has been a driving force in their lives despite families whose primary values were "horse racing and beer drinking," to quote one such person.

Once we have discovered that asteroids can be useful in a chart, that they can amplify, clarify and reinforce the messages spelled out by the traditional planets, where do we stop? Starting in 1980, Al H. Morrison (publisher of the *C.A.O. Times* and one of the Chiron ephemerides) and Janet Lee Lehman, Ph.D. of New York, began producing ephemerides for additional asteroids. The Morrison-Lehman team printed the positions of ten asteroids in 1980-1, including **Icarus, Pandora, Hidalgo, Urania, Psyche, Sappho, Eros, Lilith, Toro** and **Amor**. Al Morrison is currently (1982) working on **Apollo** and **Bacchus**, while J. Lee Lehman, in cooperation with the New York chapter of the National Council for Geocosmic Research has calculated and published ephemerides of **Diana** and five other asteroids that have been given female names. N.C.G.R. members are placing these asteroids in the charts of women who have the same names to see whether the asteroids are unusually prominent or helpful in such charts. Simultaneously, on the West coast, Mark Pottenger calculated ephemerides for four additional asteroids that were selected by Batya Stark of Denver. Batya has written a humorous book, *The Asteroid Ephemeris*, on the latter four: **Dudu, Dembowska, Pittsburghia and Frigga**. The positions of the asteroids are listed in the book.

Obviously, anything written about the new asteroids must be considered highly tentative until we have much additional evidence. Our quarterly journal, *The Mutable Dilemma*, is offering material on one of the new bodies in most issues, starting with the Gemini 1981 article on Icarus. Lilith was discussed in the Virgo 1981 issue, and Hidalgo in Sagittarius 1981. By the time this book is in print, Urania and Pandora are likely to have been covered, but at the rate at which new asteroids are appearing, we may have to shift to several asteroids per issue of the journal. Even though the names assigned to the asteroids have proved valuable as a key to their meaning in the ones tested to date, we cannot assume that this will always prove to be true. Each new small planet must be studied in many charts, watching for individuals who have it strongly aspected in their natal charts and for times when it is strongly aspected in current patterns to see what happens in the lives.

Icarus

Of the first ten asteroids calculated and published by Al Morrison and J. Lee Lehman, **Icarus** has proved the most dramatic so far.* Since I had felt fairly comfortable associating the first five asteroids studied with one of the twelve sides of life theorized as the conceptual system of astrology, I naturally had hoped that others would also fit into one of the twelve slots. Unfortunately, I have not yet succeeded in matching all of the new asteroids with one of the twelve "ways of being in the world." Additional work may resolve the problems, or we may find that some require a special category of their own. Icarus seems to be clearly fire, with some associations with Leo and the Sun, and we may actually find that it does represent another version of Letter Five in our astrological alphabet. I have numerous, dramatic cases in which individuals came crashing down as a result of attempting too much or too soon. The myth, of course, would fit such an interpretation. Icarus was the son of Daedalus who designed

*Due to its eccentric orbit, Icarus' positions are uncertain especially in ♈ through ♏.

the labyrinth in Crete. Both were later imprisoned in it. They escaped by building wings of wax and flying out to freedom, but Icarus developed what the Greeks called *hubris* (the pride that leads to a fall). He tried to fly too close to the Sun; his wax wings melted, and he fell to his death.

The unusual cases I have observed to date do point to Leo areas of life: love, sex, public performances, power, prominence and ego, which can include overconfidence. In a number of instances, there has been a kind of mutual reinforcement of risk-taking that led to two people doing something together that neither might have done alone. All of these cases involved individuals who had an Icarus conjunction with each other. One example was the well-known astrologer Marcia Moore and her husband Dr. Howard Altounian. Although Marcia was highly health conscious with a commitment to yoga, vegetarianism, meditation and spiritual seeking, and her husband was a trained anesthesiologist, together they experimented (sometimes daily) with a drug called Ketamine that created an altered state of consciousness. Marcia disappeared in January, 1979, and enough of her body was found for identification in March, 1981. Marcia and Howard had an Icarus conjunction in their natal charts; her progressed Icarus was on her Descendant, opposite her Ascendant when she disappeared and presumably died; transiting Icarus was conjunct her own and Howard's natal Icarus when the body was found.

Another case involved a mother and daughter whose charts were printed in Lois Rodden's book of charts of famous women, *Profiles of Women*. The daughter was 17 years old when the police interrupted a noisy party, found a number of men in various stages of undress, and arrested the mother for contributing to the delinquency of a minor. The mother and daughter had an Icarus conjunction between their charts, in Scorpio. In the mother's chart, it fell at the midpoint of her Mars in Libra and her Venus in Scorpio, all in her fifth house. For the daughter, Icarus was conjunct her twelfth house cusp, square Pluto in Leo in the ninth house and quincunx Saturn in Gemini in the seventh house. During the same month as her mother's arrest, the daughter shot a young actor in the head during a nude struggle in bed. During this period, progressed Icarus was sextile her Sun while transiting Icarus was square her Moon-Saturn opposition, first house-seventh house. At the time of the mother's trial, progressed Icarus was trioctile her first house Neptune and square her progressed Chiron, both suggesting monumentally poor judgment. Icarus was also aspecting natal Venus and Mercury. Transiting Icarus was square her natal Ascendant on the date of the trial.

Another interesting case involving personal acquaintances seemed to indicate the potential for intense attraction between two people with a mutual Sun-Icarus conjunction. The woman is an astrologer and teacher of yoga and meditation, much like Marcia Moore. The man is a very middle-class, straight American businessman. The woman had always said that one of her basic personal rules was to avoid any involvement with a married man. The man had been married for years and had never looked at any woman other than his wife. The two are now having an affair, both feeling guilty about it but irresistibly drawn together.

Another fascinating case involved a very different sort of attraction. President Ronald Reagan and the young man who shot him, John Hinckley, have an Icarus conjunction between their natal charts. Transiting Icarus was conjunct their mutual natal Icarus at the time of the shooting, and it was exactly on the Descendant of the shooting chart, opposite the Ascendant which symbolizes the life force in action. President Reagan also has Icarus widely conjunct his Sun in his natal chart, and it was conjunct the MC within two degrees in his inaugural chart. His presidency is thus connected to Icarus, and by the end of the term, we should know much more about the meaning of this small planet which comes closer to the Sun than any other object in the solar system except comets.

Before we leave the topic of people who share an Icarus position, we might mention that ex-President Richard Nixon's secretary, Rose Mary Woods, had her progressed Icarus conjunct Nixon's natal Icarus during the years of Watergate when she presumably erased the incriminating tape recording but insisted that it was an inexplicable accident. Despite her loyal efforts to save him, Nixon was forced to resign from the U.S. presidency. In passing, we might add that Nixon had a wide Icarus-Sun conjunction in his natal chart. Rose Mary Woods had natal Icarus opposite her Ascendant, in her seventh house and square her Mars in Virgo, but sextile her MC.

I have also found Icarus prominent in individual charts of people who overreach or who are very precocious. For example, a woman with Mars-Sun-Icarus conjunct in Sagittarius in the fifth house began playing the piano in public at the age of two years. After a family move, her public performance ended and she became precociously involved with sex. Immediately after high school, she married a man who was a good provider but quite uninterested in sex. She is now working with the spiritual and intellectual potential of her Sagittarius, to sublimate some natural frustration over the loss of the former Leo outlets — public performance and sex. In both areas, there was a premature flowering and then loss of that form of expression, much like the myth of Icarus who flew too high and fell.

Two other cases involved charts done personally for former child stars in Hollywood. One woman began singing in public at the age of two, and all through what would have been normal school years, she was singing and supporting the rest of her family—parents and two siblings. At 18, she retreated from the whole world, seeking a normal marriage and domestic life, but now, in her thirties, she realizes she had tried to lose her own identity in her husband and that it did not work. She is now

attempting a comeback in the theatrical world. Her natal Icarus is exactly conjunct her Mars and Eastpoint (like another Ascendant) in Sagittarius
in the first house. In both this and the preceding case, we can note the
overwhelming fire emphasis of Icarus in a fire sign, a fire house, and conjunct fire planets. The other recent case also involved an early career in
Hollywood. From the age of six she provided the main support for her
family. At 18, again when most individuals are just entering adulthood
and beginning a career, she "ran away," but more tragically than the
preceding case. She was not conscious of her need to escape the early
overdrive, and when an emotional conflict is buried in the unconscious,
the consequences are apt to be painful. She had a serious accident at
18 that left her partially disabled and unable to continue her career which
had centered around dancing. Her natal Icarus was also in Sagittarius,
octile (semi-square) her Ascendant exactly and widely conjunct her Antivertex, which symbolizes an auxiliary Ascendant. The solar arc-directed
Antivertex was conjunct natal Icarus when she began her career at age
six. When she ended it, progressed Icarus was quincunx Uranus and trioctile (sesquisquare) natal Vesta, which was conjunct the natal MC. Any
important principle in one's character will be shown repeatedly in a chart.
The Vesta conjunct MC indicates a potential for intense drive, commitment to success, and capacity for focus. I have found it repeatedly in individuals who can directly influence the physical world by their mental
concentration, whether they use it for "spoon-bending"*a la* Uri Geller,
or for spiritual healing. The individual just described had already
discovered that she had this power when I discussed her chart with her.

Another interesting group of charts includes politicians who overreached in a variety of ways. Eagleton was proposed for Vice President,
to run for office with George McGovern. When his mental history was
revealed, a record of depression and shock treatments, he was quickly
replaced as candidate for the office. Eagleton's natal Icarus was closely
conjunct his fifth house Saturn in Sagittarius and square his natal Moon
in Virgo, a classic mutable dilemma of wanting to achieve more in his
work than was possible. At the time of his rapid rise to public notice and
equally rapid fall, his progressed Washington MC was exactly opposite
Saturn-Icarus and square the natal Moon while his progressed Washington
Ascendant was conjunct the Moon square the Saturn-Icarus. His progressed angles from his birthplace were square and conjunct his natal Sun
at the same time.

Spiro Agnew, the initial Vice-President under Richard Nixon, was accused of taking bribes in business dealings in his native state of Maryland,
continuing the practice even after he had become Vice-President. As a
result of the scandal, he was forced to resign a short time before Nixon
had to follow the same course. Agnew's natal Icarus was in his first house
in Capricorn, trioctile his ninth house Saturn in Leo. At the time of his

forced resignation, his progressed Sun was conjunct natal Icarus.

Nixon followed Agnew out of office less than a year later, the first U.S. president to be forced to resign in disgrace. Nixon's natal Icarus in Capricorn in the fifth house was in a wide conjunction with his Sun and a closer one with Uranus which was in early Aquarius. Progressed Uranus had moved to put Icarus at the exact midpoint of itself and the natal Sun. On the day that he resigned, transiting Icarus was conjunct natal Venus, octile natal Sun, and trioctile Nixon's Washington Ascendant which was ruled by Venus. The combination symbolized the blow to his ego, self-esteem and personal happiness. His progressed Icarus was just reaching the square to natal Saturn, further supporting the picture of a power struggle involving bureaucratic structure or the Law in some other form. When we try to make our will into Law, we invite being put down.

Possible Meanings

It is not possible to do justice to all of the new asteroids in a general book on astrology, but the preceding may encourage readers to obtain the ephemerides and explore them in the charts of family and friends. The following list of asteroids with suggested possible meanings must be considered highly tentative, based on a very limited amount of actual work with the minor planets.

ICARUS (∇): attempt to reach the Sun or to be another Sun. When in fire signs or houses, or aspecting fire planets, a danger of overreach or premature action. There may be strong attractions, passionate feelings or indiscretions between individuals with Icarus conjunctions.

LILITH (⚸): a real asteroid, not the imaginary dark Moon. Seems to be another Pluto with a range of potentials, including strong will; interest in hidden matters including the occult and the unconscious mind; often involved in power struggles to maintain equality in relationships; wanting self-control but if not handled well, using power, money and sex to control others; marking the need to learn when is enough and how to let go, with death sometimes a form of permanent release. In terms of the basic alphabet of astrology, the Sun symbolizes our desire to do more than we have done before, to expand our power outward to affect others and to get a reaction from them. Pluto (and possibly Lilith) symbolize the capacity to turn our power inward to control ourselves with full respect for the rights of others. A stress aspect between the two principles shows a potential power issue needing attention: our ego needs and rights versus the power and rights of others. At the time of Watergate and Nixon's resignation, his progressed Sun was conjunct natal Lilith and his progressed Lilith was square natal Sun.

HIDALGO (⚜): may be a little brother to Saturn, found aspecting Saturn more often than chance in women who make it to the top to positions of power and success. Nixon had his natal Hidalgo octile his natal Sun and square his natal Venus (ruler of his Washington Ascendant), while it was also octile that local Ascendant. At the time of his resignation, his progressed Ascendant in Washington was conjunct progressed Hidalgo. Since the Ascendant is similar in meaning to another Mars, indicating our urge to do what we please, the Ascendant-Hidalgo conjunction is similar in meaning to a Mars-Saturn conjunction: self-will meeting the limits of self-will. At the same time, the progressed local Ascendant-Hidalgo combination was trioctile the Washington MC, with the latter similar to another Saturn aspect. Again the chart repeated the message: are you voluntarily living within the limits? How are you doing in handling the rules of the game?

PANDORA (▽): we might have another Gemini Mercury here, with the curiosity that killed the cat. I've been finding Pandora prominent in the charts of most astrologers checked since I started exploring these new little planets. Mostly, I've just found it an indication of an insatiable intellect willing to investigate anything. Occasionally it has fit the myth, suggesting the danger of opening up areas that we can't handle, or of taking action that is irreversible once it is started; no turning back. To continue with the chart we have been using, Nixon's natal Pandora was exactly opposite his Neptune, just three degrees from a conjunction with Icarus. At Watergate, his progressed Pandora was quincunx his Washington MC, and Neptune had retrograded to conjunct that local MC to be tied in to the aspect. Progressed Pandora was also octile and trioctile the nodes of the Moon indicating the problems with relationships and emotional security. Progressed Pandora had also reached Nixon's natal Urania, to which we now proceed.

URANIA (⚚): could be a female Uranus, mythologically the goddess of astrology, and, so far, prominent in the charts of astrologers, including aspects in current patterns when they take up the study. Nixon's natal Urania was within two degrees of his natal Moon in Aquarius in the sixth house, which could suggest a desire for independence, frequent changes in his work, a need for much variety and intellectual stimulation in his job, or sudden, dramatic shifts on occasion. The instinct of Uranus is to resist any limitations, to escape from any ruts, and Urania may be similar or may be somewhat milder in the search for freedom from routine. It seems to indicate intellectual openness at least. It is only when we resist the necessary limits (natural law, cultural regulations, etc.) that we get into real trouble with Letter Eleven.

PSYCHE (✍): was featured in a story by the Roman writer, Apuleius, and we are not sure whether he drew from earlier myths, or created his own fiction in the tale of the romance of Psyche and Cupid. Some students of Jungian psychology have chosen the Psyche story as "the" female myth, considering it symbolic of the effort to bring the unconscious up to consciousness. "The" male myth is the Arthurian story of the quest for the Holy Grail. My personal opinion is that the psychologists who assigned these myths to males and females were (are) male chauvinists.

My first charts with a prominent (strongly aspected) Psyche were mundane charts dealing with world situations, particularly with the conflict in the Near East: Israel's invasion of Lebanon, the Iraq-Iran war, and Russia. Prior to noting the strong Psyche in these charts, I had considered it likely that the asteroid might relate to psychological interests, psychic ability, or romance. The charts of invasions and warring countries hardly seemed to fit such an idea, so I looked up the original story by Apuleius and found it fit very well the situation in the Near East. In the story, Psyche was physically beautiful but had nothing else going for her. She was stupid, deceitful, helpless, dependent, other-directed, had to be talked out of suicide, and really never did a single thing right in the whole story. She seemed the epitome of inadequacy and the self-absorption resulting from it.

I have since seen human charts with progressed Psyche on the seventh cusp when the individual entered a relationship with such a person: one who was basically inadequate, insecure, and self-absorbed so unable to be really aware of the needs of others. I have also seen Psyche in the charts of psychologists who were concerned with understanding others. At this point, though any conclusions must be highly tentative, I see Psyche as either the capacity for being empathic, understanding and caring for others, or the lack of that capacity if the individual is basically insecure and self-absorbed.

TORO (♟): may be another Taurus, associated with a feeling for beauty and comfort, artistic talent and sensual pleasure, with the strong will and some potential for power struggles found with all the fixed letters of our alphabet. Nixon's natal Toro fell between his Vesta and Mars in Sagittarius in the fourth house near their midpoint, closely quincunx Neptune, widely quincunx Saturn and opposition Pluto. At his resignation, progressed Toro was not quite in orb to conjunct Uranus but was trioctile Nixon's natal Ascendant and octile the Descendant, indicating the power struggle with others and major changes just ahead.

The other three asteroids published by Al and Lee all have names somewhat associated with love and relationships, but I have only a limited amount of data on them.

EROS (♊): seems to symbolize romantic love. The happiest marriages I have seen since beginning to observe these new bodies have had harmonious aspects with Eros within the charts and/or with each other's charts. I have also seen interesting cases with Eros in Pisces, where the individuals fantasied a lot about love but managed to avoid really doing anything about it.

SAPPHO (♀): was named for a real person (as was Hidalgo), a poetess in early Greek times on the island of Lesbos. She was devoted to her daughter, taught other young women as a surrogate mother, and may have done more writing about love than real action. So far, I have not found Sappho prominent in the charts of people into heavy sex trips, but have found it associated with poetry and other arts and with nurturing people. The Hollywood sex kittens in Lois Rodden's book on famous women tended to have Lilith in far more prominence than Sappho. But only much more work will support or change these very preliminary impressions.

AMOR (♀): I have so little material on Amor that I hesitate to write anything at this stage. I have seen charts in which it was prominent with individuals who had little sex in the life. It may be a capacity for other kinds of affection, not limited to male-female relationships. One woman that I have known for years has Amor exactly on one angle and Sappho exactly on another angle. She was widowed years ago and only occasionally has sex with a married man who does not threaten her independence. However, her life is totally centered around her mother and her children!

The positions of the four asteroids calculated by our West coast expert, Mark Pottenger, have been published with a humorous discussion of possible meanings written by Batya Stark of Denver. When even the asteroids selected for their amusing names seem to be meaningful in a horoscope, the world looks more and more like a giant mind; maybe a mind that is playing games. I have done even less with three of these four small planets than with the ones described above, but will include a few preliminary ideas.

FRIGGA (♣): is the only one of the four who was named for a mythological figure. Frigga was the wife of Odin, king of the gods in Norse mythology. She was the patron of conjugal love, associated with the ability to foresee the fate of humans. Her son, Thor, is known for his ability to throw thunderbolts, but Frigga seems fairly gentle and domestic. The Norse figures associated with sex and passion were Frey and Freya.

DUDU (♠): has to be one of the most incredible supports for a world of meaning rather than chance if the American slang meaning of this name turns out to be an accurate key to part of the asteroid's meaning. A German astronomer in Heidelberg discovered and named Dudu. In German the word is a personal pronoun used in close relationships.

A well-known song associated with Heidelberg starts Du, du, bist mein. . . Since Dudu has recently been prominent in my own chart, I have had more opportunity to test it than has been possible with some of the other asteroids. It does seem to have Scorpio associations, including the need to clean up emotional relationships, get rid of the garbage of the past, and learn in general how to love and let go. Power struggles and death are an extreme end product of the principle of Letter Eight in our alphabet. Positively handled, we learn to curb excesses, to let go of what we have outgrown, or what is not really ours. In one of the Icarus cases mentioned earlier, the mother and teenaged daughter who shared a career of sex, the mother's natal Dudu was exactly on the daughter's natal Ascendant in Scorpio. Both individuals were involved in a variety of excesses, and the daughter eventually learned some moderation, whether from her own pain or from her mother's negative example. The latter died of complications associated with alcoholism.

PITTSBURGHIA (☐): is the first asteroid we have considered which was named for a city. Pittsburgh's main claim to fame in the past was its smoky air due to heavy steel industry in the area. The air has since been cleaned up and the city is quite cultured and beautiful. It is also noted for its football team, a healthy form of power struggle, while the industry which provides its livelihood represents another form of healthy competition, provided, of course, the competition is "real" and fair. Real competition occurs when we lose sometimes and win sometimes, testing and developing our abilities in the process. If the game is "fixed," such as by cartels or monopolies, so one side always wins, there is no competition. Pittsburghia may symbolize this side of Pluto: developing strength through learning how to compete fairly.

DEMBOWSKA (?): was discovered by an astronomer living in Nice, France. In the last stages of proof reading this book, I was informed by Al H. Morrison of New York that the asteroid was named for a contemporary astronomer in Italy. The glyph chosen by Batya, a question mark, represented our initial total uncertainty over possible meanings for the asteroid. Very preliminary work suggests that Dembowska might be another Saturn. My most dramatic cases so far involve people in public or power positions. Nixon had progressed Dembowska on his natal MC during the Watergate episode. Ronald Reagan had progressed Dembowska on his natal Sun for six years, up to and including his election to the U.S. Presidency. Marcia Moore had progressed Dembowska on her natal Ascendant while she was experimenting with the mind-altering drug prior to her death. In another interesting horoscope of a personal client, natal Dembowska and Moon were closely conjunct in Cancer in the first house. The subject took her mother as a negative role model. Her mother had been very intelligent but had never used her ability, sacrificing herself for her husband and children. The daughter developed her mind, worked in an intellectually stimulating career and remained unmarried but wanted a child and chose to be a single parent, playing both mother and father (Moon-Dembowska).

Other Dembowska people include Indira Gandhi, dictator of India, with a long progressed conjunction of her tenth house Jupiter to Dembowska and Mars trine to both. Hinckley, who shot Reagan, has Dembowska in a lifetime conjunction to his ninth house Saturn. Progressed Dembowska was conjunct the natal Moon in the chart of a woman when her only child died of cancer. Remember that there can be either over-drive or self-blocking with Letter Ten until we learn to use power wisely.

DIANA (☽): in mythology, one side of the Moon. Diana was a virgin (unmarried) mother figure, a protector of animals, but also a hunter at times, with a sense of isolation and self-containment. The client described above consciously disidentified with the Cancer part of her nature but still wanted to have a child and chose to have one without marriage. Her natal Diana was exactly on her fifth house cusp, the house associated with procreation.

Another interesting case comes from a story in the March 1982 *Reader's Digest*. A nurse, who had had a hysterectomy but desperately wanted a child, on two occasions substituted a dead baby for one born alive and took the living baby. The police discovered what had happened when the first kidnapped baby was eight months old, and she was returned to her mother. In the child's horoscope, natal Moon (mother) was conjunct Neptune within minutes in Sagittarius in the fourth house, and Diana was also in the same sign and house but widely conjunct. When progressed Moon reached Diana, the truth came out, the baby was taken from her unmarried foster mother (the kidnapping nurse) and returned to her real mother. Natal Frigga was also in the child's fourth house, exactly square the early Virgo Ascendant. Since the fourth house symbolizes both foster and real mother, Frigga's conflict patterns fit the nurse's struggles with others. Of course, a chart pictures our own character. The others we draw to us are exaggerations of the projected parts of us. The child's chart shows an excessive emphasis on love and relationships connected to idealism. The intense need for emotional attachments drove the foster mother to kidnapping, and it will be a lesson in the life of the subject. The child has been given two mother-figures as examples of the issue in her own chart. She has a chance to learn vicariously what to do and what not to do, but it would be easier if she had a clear conceptual understanding of the issues through her horoscope. The child also has Dembowska conjunct Mars and Pluto in Libra, pointing to potential power struggles in relationships. She might so identify with the need for a partner, that she failed to develop her own potentials. Or, the other side of the coin, she might decide that the only way she could develop her own talents would be by avoiding marriage. The danger is an "all or none" approach. She can manifest either extreme or find a compromise position. For readers who would like to see the whole chart, her data is: September 21,1974, at 4:35 AM in Los Angeles, California.

Phyllis Schlafly

Since Nixon has been mentioned frequently as a good example of how the asteroids amplify and confirm the basic message of a horoscope, his chart has been included for readers though most will already have it. I have chosen the chart of Phyllis Schlafly for a more complete discussion of the new asteroids, and have included her Secondary Progressions for the date when the Equal Rights Amendment (ERA) was not ratified. Schlafly certainly helped to prevent ERA from becoming a law of our land. ERA would have guaranteed equality for everyone, including equal pay for equal work. Despite major efforts in recent years, women are still paid far less than men, and many women are the sole support of families. The so-called "Women's Liberation Movement" has been in the news in recent years, struggling for equal rights for both sexes. Phyllis Schlafly has been a leader on the conservative side, advocating traditional marriage in which women remain in the home and are dependent on and subject to their husbands. In the process of telling other women to stay home, she has flown all over the country, lecturing (preaching) on her convictions, leading the struggle against ERA.

Phyllis Schlafly was reportedly born in St. Louis, Missouri, on August 15, 1924, at 11:25 PM CST. The chart shows considerable emphasis on the mind with Gemini rising and Mercury, its ruler, in Virgo. Jupiter is in its own sign of Sagittarius, and there is a stellium in Pisces including Mars, Moon, Pallas and Uranus. Mercury is exactly opposite Uranus while Jupiter is exactly square Moon, showing a need to work out the mutable dilemma, but a potentially fine mind with which to do it.

The common forms of the mutable dilemma include difficulty in deciding what one wants with a tendency to scatter (not likely here where we find a fixed emphasis and adequate earth, including the strong identification with work with Mercury in Virgo and Mars in the tenth house). A second common form of the mutable dilemma involves a conflict between ideals and the possible. This may well be Schlafly's form of the dilemma with her Jupiter opposite the Ascendant and widely square Mars showing the conflict between what she can do (Mars and Ascendant) and her aspirations (Jupiter). An additional indication of ideals vs. reality is shown by Jupiter square the tenth house and quincunx the Taurus in the twelfth house. Neptune opposing Vesta and the tenth house repeats the theme, and Chiron octile the tenth house Moon says it again. To solve that form of the mutable dilemma, we can either lower our expectations

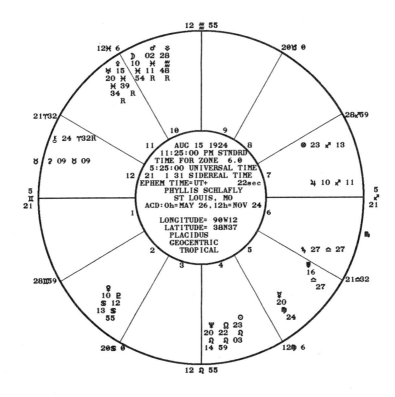

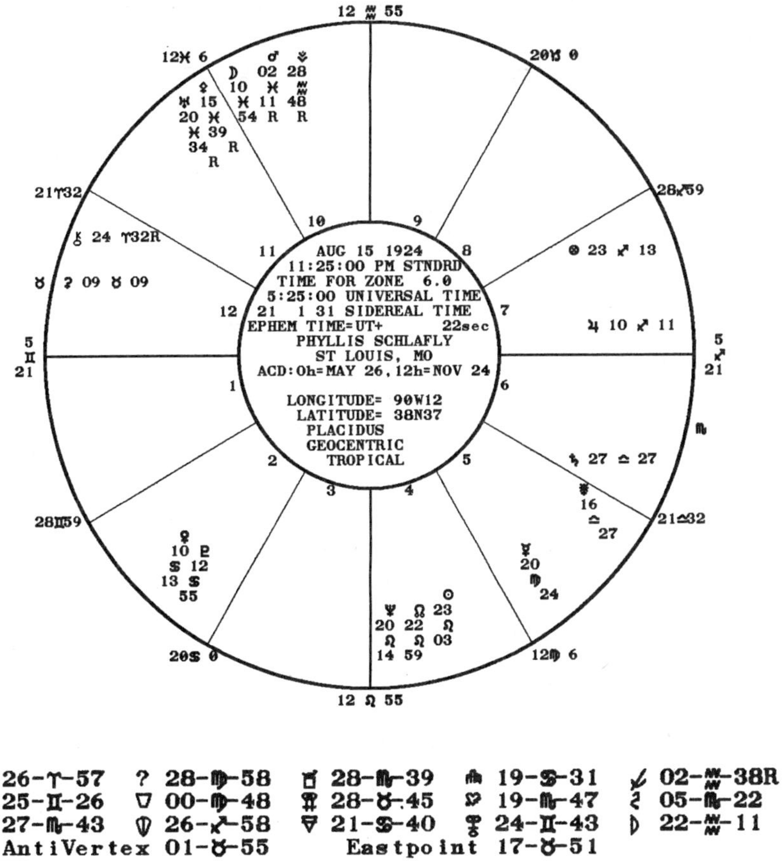

```
                        12 ≈ 55
        12X 6           ♂  ⚸              20♉ 0
           ) 02 28
        ⚴ 10 X  ≈
      ⚵ 15  X 11 48
      20 X  54 R  R
        X 39
        34  R
           R
21♈32                    10      9                      28♐59
         ⚷ 24 ♈32R
                    11    AUG 15 1924    8
♉ ? 09 ♉ 09           11:25:00 PM STNDRD         ⊕ 23 ♐ 13
                       TIME FOR ZONE  6.0
                       5:25:00 UNIVERSAL TIME
                   12  21  1 31 SIDEREAL TIME  7
                     EPHEM TIME=UT+     22sec       ♃ 10 ♐ 11
 5                     PHYLLIS SCHLAFLY                        5
 II                       ST LOUIS, MO                         ♐
 21                   ACD:0h=MAY 26,12h=NOV 24                21
                       LONGITUDE= 90W12
                 1     LATITUDE= 38N37    6
                       PLACIDUS                              ♏
                 2     GEOCENTRIC         5
                       TROPICAL                  ♄ 27 ♎ 27
                      3        4
28♍59                                            ⚸
                                                16
          ♀                                     ♎
          10 ℞                                  27        21♎32
          ♋ 12                           ♀
          13 ♋                           20
          55                             ♍            24
                        ⊙
              ♇ Ω 23
            20 22  Ω
              Ω Ω 03
              14 59
   20♋ 0                          12♍ 6
                        12 Ω 55
```

⚷ 26-♈-57	? 28-♍-58	♂ 28-♏-39	♠ 19-♋-31	⚸ 02-≈-38R
⚸ 25-II-26	▽ 00-♍-48	⚷ 28-♉-45	♡ 19-♏-47	? 05-♏-22
⚼ 27-♏-43	⚸ 26-♐-58	▽ 21-♋-40	⚵ 24-II-43	) 22-≈-11
AntiVertex 01-♉-55			Eastpoint 17-♉-51	

or we can extend our time table and try to enjoy the journey toward our ideals.

Still another form of the mutable dilemma involves a displacement of our faith and ideals onto a fragment of life so that we turn it into an idol and overrate it. That also is possible in this chart. Neptune in Leo in the fourth house could idealize home, love and family. Jupiter in Sagittarius in the seventh house could idealize marriage or other forms of partnership, as could Pallas in Pisces, while Moon in Pisces and Ceres in the Pisces house repeat the theme of idealized motherhood. It is not possible to say with certainty from a chart what form a dilemma will take in the life. It is necessary to observe the life and to talk to the person to see how they are handling their inner conflicts. Often, an individual will express the same dilemma in different ways at different times in the life as they seek to integrate the conflict.

In discussing the emphasis on the mind and ideals, we have brought in another major theme in the Schlafly chart: the importance of personal relationships. There are few stronger indications of the need for marriage than a Venus-Pluto conjunction in any of the signs or houses of relation-ships — Four, Five, Seven, and Eight. Schlafly has them conjunct within three degrees in Cancer in the second house. We note with interest that Icarus and Frigga are closely conjunct each other in Cancer and that they are near enough to form a wide conjunction to Venus-Pluto. If Frigga is a focus on conjugal love and marriage and Icarus, like the Sun, is seeking love, or fame or power and may be a key to overreach, these new asteroids are amplifying the importance of marriage in Schlafly's life. It isn't enough to just do it. She has built a career on promoting it.

We can also note that Eros (romantic love?) closely trines Frigga-Icarus from Scorpio in the sixth house, while Lilith (another Pluto in its "own" sign) is widely conjunct Eros and exactly conjunct Pittsburghia. With Lilith and Pittsburghia in a lifetime progressed trioctile to Pluto, we have three potential forms of Pluto confronting each other, emphasizing something to learn in the area of excesses, equality and cooperation, the handling of power with others. The inclination toward some sort of power struggle in the life is further supported by the Lilith-Pittsburghia exact square to Vesta in Aquarius in the tenth house, with a wider square to the South Node of the Moon which is exactly conjunct Diana. Mythical Diana was partly protective mother and partly hunter and destroyer. Schlafly has made a career (Vesta, tenth house) of protecting motherhood (Diana, Moon's node, Moon all in the tenth house). In the process, she has sacrific-ed equality (Aquarius). Since I interpret the South Node as a lesson area, she should be learning how to have both equality and a career.

I also interpret anything in Scorpio as a desire for a close, intense rela-tionship and sharing at the physical level with a mate of some sort. Anything in Aquarius is a need for space with a tendency to say, "Let's be friends." The combination in Schlafly's chart forms a part of the fixed dilemma, one form of the freedom-closeness struggle. Neptune-North Node of the Moon-Sun grouped in Leo in the fourth house make a fixed t-square with the Scorpio and Aquarius, and Sappho in late Taurus plus the Eastpoint earlier in Taurus, complete the fixed cross, partly in mutable houses and partly in cardinal houses. The Leo in the fourth house, of course, adds to the need to find ego satisfaction through love, home and family. We have already commented on the idealization of that area of life, yet it is clearly in conflict with the strong activity in the sixth and tenth houses which are not satisfied with homemaking alone but want some sort of achievement in the material world beyond the home. We are see-ing a combination of the fixed and cardinal dilemmas: fourth house op-posite tenth house and seventh house square tenth house: home vs. career and mate vs. career, as well as fourth house square sixth house for a repeat of home vs. job. The Libra and Scorpio in the sixth house might suggest making a career out of marriage, but there is no way Saturn, Vesta and Mars can be really satisfied with that. Mars and Saturn need more power, and Saturn and Vesta need more sense of accomplishment. And the power struggle element of a cardinal-fixed mixture has to find some sort of outlet. How to integrate? *Voilá!* One can engage in a career of power struggles to defend the institution of marriage. What a solution to the need for a perfect marriage and a career as professional savior (Pisces in the tenth house). The power drive is satisfied since it is her own show, and she decides how to handle it while she can fight the feminists to the death with her Scorpio squares.

As already mentioned, Pluto maintains a lifetime progressed trioctile to Vesta-Lilith-Pittsburghia and, during the height of the battle over ERA, progressed Mars remains for some years conjunct Vesta, hence square Lilith-Pittsburghia and trioctile Pluto. At the same time, progressed Vesta remains for years in a conjunction with the South Node of the Moon and Diana. Vesta is noted for tunnel vision and the danger of alienating human relationships for the sake of what we see as our job in the world. If other people get in the way of what we feel is our duty, too bad for them. The South Node of the Moon is a lesson while the North Node usually comes more easily. A tenth house South Node is a lesson connected to the Law: natural, human or inner (the conscience). Mars in the tenth may say, "My will is law," but we have to learn it is not. [Progressed positions page 79]

As is normal in a chart, we get the same message repeated over and over. Mythical Diana was associated with the Moon. She protected young animals but was hard on adult people. Both Diana and Moon in the tenth house are saying "professional mother." Yet the Aquarius and Pisces call for a transpersonal involvement. One can be mother to the world, super-mother, using the power of the law to force other mothers to conform to our own ethical standards for the role. Pallas is at the midpoint of Moon and Uranus, all in Pisces: mother, mate and detached friend. Pallas is also quincunx natal Juno and progressed Jupiter has squared it for years. The patterns repeat the tension between personal relationships and a wider scene, social causes to save humanity. If we are fighting to save motherhood and marriage (fifth and seventh houses), we can justify leaving the loved ones to travel, lecture, barnstorm the media, do our own thing to change the world.

Uranus simply wants change. If water and earth houses dominate the chart, we may try to go backward in time rather than forward. "Grandfather knew best." Chiron in Aries can be a missionary: "I have personally found the Truth. Here it is, world." The Washington, D.C. progressed MC remains conjunct her natal and progressed Chiron from spring, 1981 to spring 1985. Progressed Moon joins the conjunction in June and July, 1982. June 30, 1982 was the date of decision. If Chiron is like Jupiter, our ultimate value and goal in life, and Neptune symbolizes our unconscious absolute values, and the MC is the law of the land, and the Moon is home and motherhood, the combination of Moon on Chiron and MC in Washington trine Neptune shows her triumph at the defeat of ERA. At the same time, progressed Eros is conjunct her Washington Descendant, trine natal Neptune and progressed North Node of the Moon, with progressed Sun in the middle in Libra sextile Eros, node, Neptune and trine the Washington Ascendant. For some years, progressed Frigga (potential guardian of marriage) has been conjunct her IC, moving into the fourth house of home and family to reinforce the point.

The power struggle potential in the chart is also shown in other ways. Progressed Pittsburghia has been moving conjunct progressed Jupiter while progressed Lilith has been moving over natal Jupiter. A combination of power and ideals may lead to the use of power to enforce personal ideals on others. For two years, the Sun has been quincunx Uranus and square Icarus. For one year it has been square Frigga and progressed Urania, which is going over Frigga along with the Washington Eastpoint. Eastpoint is like another Ascendant — self-will in action; Frigga, guardian of marriage; Urania, the urge to change whether we go forward or backward; with natal Icarus reminding of the danger of overreach and the square to the Sun as another warning of possible *hubris*.

Then there is that question mark, Dembowska. So far it looks like a danger of overdrive or self-blocking if it is not handled with care. Schlafly has natal Dembowska in the fifth house in Virgo, exactly trioctile the MC and quincunx Vesta in the tenth house. Were her children her career, and now she is making a career of persuading other mothers to imitate her? Progressed Dembowska is conjunct progressed Sun, sharing the quincunx to Uranus and the squares to the Cancer grouping. Anything conjunct the Sun adds emphasis to the issues of love, fame, power, ego. Anything setting off squares between Cancer and Libra shows a need to resolve the parent-child form of relationship with the capacity to be an equal, a peer. Schlafly seeks to turn back the clock to keep marriage a parent-child relationship with the husband as parent and the wife as child. Forget equality. Yet her own progressed Sun in Libra, her natal Saturn in Libra (wherever Saturn falls, we have a major lesson for this lifetime), her powerhouse emphasis on Aquarius and Uranus in its own house, all must be screaming at some level of her being. But she is out in the world, doing her thing!

There is always so much more that could be said. Anything important is said over and over again. The new asteroids just repeat the same message, but they do offer amplification, increased focus and clarity. We haven't mentioned that Schlafly's progressed Sun and Dembowska have been moving in opposition to progressed Dudu. Is the pattern just another equivalent to the Leo-Scorpio squares, or has it a more specific symbolism pointing to a need to do some subconscious cleaning out, to balance personal power against the rights and power of others? Natal Dudu is exactly opposite her natal Saturn, and in a few years, she will have the birthplace progressed Ascendant square Saturn while her Washington progressed MC is opposite Saturn and conjunct Dudu. If she has not learned that lesson about power and equality and respect for the rights of others to guide their lives by their own moral codes, that period is likely to be a time of much learning.

Even with astrology, we can't predict precise details. We can only discuss the principles involved and indicate a range of possibilities. A new ERA might be proposed and might pass at that time in the middle of the decade. Or, her own conscience might wake up to what she has been doing. If the latter proves to be the case, her own relationships might play a role in her awakening. Progressed Venus will square natal Jupiter at the time: a new value placed on equality, or realization that marriage or husband is not God? Progressed Sun will be coming to the octile of Jupiter and trioctile of the Moon, repeating the theme of a confrontation between faith and emotional attachments. Progressed Eastpoint will conjunct Pluto: personal identity facing a potentially equal mate, questioning the handling of personal will and compromise, of personal desire and shared pleasures. Progressed Mercury will reach the square to Icarus and quincunx to Uranus: mental activity in the limelight and possible new ideas on personal love and space. Progressed MC will square Pluto: career vs. mate or shared power and the limits of power. Saturn stays in the trioctile to Uranus for many years — a clear picture of the battle between tradition and innovation, between hiearchichal power and equality. Will her own children repudiate her position? Will she run for public office and be defeated, or win and have to eat her image as devoted wife? Only time will tell. With this chart, we can be sure of one thing. She will be heard. Her attempt to force women back into the role of simple wife and mother is for other women, not for her.

Progressed positions for Phyllis Schlafly, June 30, 1982.

☉ 19-♎-28	☽ 22-♈-24	☿ 10-♎-12	♀ 06-♍-11	♂ 28-♒-05
♃ 16-♐-16	♄ 03-♏-16	♅ 18-♓-23R	♆ 22-♌-05	♇ 13-♋-33
? 06-♉-24R	⚷ 02-♓-54R	⚹ 04-♏-48	⚵ 21-♒-13	⚸ 22-♈-30R
A 24-♋-42	M 09-♈-20	X 09-♊-56	E 07-♋-53	

The Antivertex is represented by an X.

All fifteen asteroids discussed in this chapter can now be included in your charts ordered through Astro Computing Services. Ephemerides are available ($4.00 each) from: Al H. Morrison, P.O. Box 75, Old Chelsea Station, New York, NY 10113.

CHAPTER 7

Aspects

The astrological tools previously discussed have included points in the sky, such as planets, asteroids, Arabic Parts, nodes, and so on, and sections of space such as zodiacal signs, horoscope houses and dwads. Aspects provide a new tool, and a very important one. Astronomically, the term refers to the angular distances between different factors, e.g., between planets, a planet and an angle such as the Ascendant, two angles, a planet and a node. We can visualize an aspect by pointing at one planet with our left arm and another planet with the right arm. The angle between our two outstretched arms will approximate the aspect between the two planets.

Ancient astrology began by noting two planets close together in the sky, the aspect called **conjunction**. By the time of Ptolemy, early in the Christian era, there were four additional aspects in use: **opposition**, when two planets were on opposite sides of the Earth, or 180 degrees apart; **trine**, when two planets were 120 degrees or four signs apart; **square**, when two planets were 90 degrees or three signs apart; and **sextile**, with the planets 60 degrees or two signs apart. As is apparent, the opposition is a division of the circle of 360 degrees by two; the trine divides the circle by three; the square divides the circle by four; the sextile divides it by six.

Ancient astrologers noted, by observing the patterns in the sky and the events on Earth, that the sextile and trine were associated with relative harmony and ease but the square and opposition often were associated with challenges and stress. The conjunction seemed to vary, depending on the planets involved. In more recent years, additional aspects have been added to the Ptolemaic Five. Kepler suggested the **quintile** (a fifth of the circle or 72 degrees) and the **biquintile** (2/5 of the circle or 144 degrees). The **octile** (1½ signs or 45 degrees) and the **trioctile** (4½ signs or 135 degrees) came into general use in the nineteenth century. These names refer to the Latin roots for the numbers, indicating that Kepler's aspect is 1/5 of the circle; the octile is 1/8 of the circle; the trioctile is 3/8 of a circle. The last two aspects are also called the **semi-square** (or half a square) and the **sesqui-square**, but these names are harder to say and the last is not as clear in meaning, so I prefer the other names. Some time before the modern period, the **semi-sextile** (30 degrees or 1/12 of the circle) came into general use, along with 5/12 of the circle, the **quincunx** of 150 degrees. Even more recently, astrologers have suggested using the 1/10 of the circle (the **decile** of 36 degrees); the 1/9 of a circle (the **novile** of 40 degrees); the 1/7 of a circle (the **septile** which gives a fractional result rather than a whole number (51.4286) and the **undecile** or 1/11 of the circle, also a fractional result (32.7273).

Early work with astrology concentrated on the correspondences between the patterns in the sky and overt events on Earth. Since the stress aspects often accompanied traumatic events, while the harmony aspects were often associated with ease in satisfying desires, it was natural for early astrologers to think of some aspects as inherently bad and some as good. With our current understanding of astrology as a psychological model, a symbol system that aids our understanding of human nature and life, we now realize that an aspect is simply one way to understand the relationship between the two parts of our nature represented. A conflict aspect indicates we are in conflict between those two sides of our nature. A harmonious aspect shows that those parts of ourselves are basically complementary, that they reinforce each other and normally blend easily.

But harmonious aspects do not always accompany the achievement of our heart's desire, and conflict aspects do not always indicate serious problems. It is quite common for complementary urges to lead to excess. It is not necessarily true that "if some is good, more will be better." On the other side of the coin, conflict aspects do indicate an inherent conflict between those basic urges in us, but it is quite possible to integrate: to find a way to satisfy both sides of our nature. For example, if we have Mars square Moon (or any other form of Letter One in stress aspect to Letter Four), we need to make peace between our desire to be free to do only what we want and our desire to commit time and energy to a home and family, to being domestic. We integrate two naturally conflicting desires by either taking turns with them, or by finding a compromise position where we can have a little of both, not taking either to its fullest extreme.

The Dilemmas

I am suggesting that the astrological model of human nature includes twelve different ways of being in the world, that all are basically good and necessary to be a whole person, but that it is impossible to do all twelve at once to their fullest extent. Sometimes taking turns works more effectively, and sometimes compromising produces more satisfying results. We have to make the decision. If we understand the conflict, understand what these different sides of our nature are seeking, we can usually find a way to work it out. I call these natural conflicts which are an inherent part of life, the **dilemmas**. Astrology as a conceptual model of life describes the **Cardinal Dilemma**, the **Fixed Dilemma** and the **Mutable Dilemma**. Most people have a little of all three. We are really all working on the same issues; on the challenge of juggling twelve sides of life and trying to do all twelve in harmony with the rest. But it is common for a chart to emphasize one dilemma more than the others, and it is common for one to be more emphasized at one time in our life. We continue to evolve and grow, and so may be dealing with different issues at different times in our lives.

Since all factors in astrology carry their own element and quality, there will be few times when you see a "pure" form of any of the three listed dilemmas. Traditional astrology refers to them as Grand Crosses, but in most cases, there will be mixtures. For example, cardinal planets may be square each other in fixed signs in mutable houses. The important issue is always the repeated theme. If there are conflict aspects involving cardinal planets (Mars-Saturn-Moon) and other planets in conflict aspect in cardinal signs (Aries-Cancer-Libra-Capricorn) and still other planets in conflict aspect in cardinal (angular) houses (1-4-7-10), we have a clear emphasis on the cardinal dilemma. But it is still necessary to consider the whole picture.

My concept of the dilemmas has been presented in two previous books, *The Astrologer's Casebook* and *Finding the Person in the Horoscope*, and has been described in fragments throughout the preceding text, but a brief summary is repeated here. The **four cardinal parts of life** include the desire to simply do what we please, the need for emotional security which is usually satisfied by a home and family, the wish for a mate with whom to share life, and the urge to achieve something bigger in the society, to have a sense of power and accomplishment. Letter One says, "I don't need anyone." Letter Four wants to play baby or mother. Letter Seven wants equality in a shared relationship. Letter Ten wants control, either to avoid the world putting one down, or because of a sense of responsibility which could lead to the conscience feeling guilty if things are not handled well. It is not easy to be independent, dependent, equal and in control at the same time, or to manage time for personal hobbies, family, mate and career. But to be a whole person, we need them all.

The **fixed dilemma** needs to integrate the desire to concentrate on our own pleasures, the urge to do something more exciting, creative, emotionally expressive with others included, the potential for sharing pleasure, passion, power, possessions with a close other, and the inclination to cut loose from all limitations and just take off. With the polarity of Letters Two and Eight, we try to work out self-indulgence vs. self-mastery, or personal pleasure and possessions vs. shared pleasure and possessions (learning to give, or to receive, or to share). With the polarity of Letters Five and Eleven, we confront the issues of a need to feel superior somewhere in our lives vs. recognizing the right of others to equality; the desire for love vs. detachment — "let's be friends," passion vs. intellect. A primary issue found in both the cardinal and the fixed dilemmas involves freedom vs. closeness, or security and stability vs. risk and change.

The **mutable dilemma** lives in the head, trying to know a little about everything and still do something well (Letter Three vs. Letter Six). Usually, a solution is not too difficult. We can't do everything well so we learn to do one or two things with care and thoroughness and to keep the rest for fun, to do lightly. We may have more problems with the two Jupiter letters, Nine and Twelve, where we are looking for an absolute, whether consciously and outwardly, or inwardly and more unconsciously. With conflict between Jupiter and Neptune, Sagittarius and Pisces, or ninth house and twelfth house, we may have conflicts between head values and heart values such as truth vs. kindness; "Say it straight out, but don't hurt anyone." If Nine and/or Twelve are in conflict with Three and/or Six, we are trying to integrate our ideals with the reality of what is possible. There may be uncertainty over beliefs, values, goals. There may be a lack of faith, or too much trust in a small part of life which then becomes an idolatry. In extreme cases, the mutable dilemma leads into a total retreat from the world when we are not able to find ways to bring our ideals into form in the world, or may be waiting until we can do it perfectly.

The solution to wanting too much, too soon or too easily requires either reducing our expectations or extending our time table. It is OK to want perfection if we realize it is a long journey and we enjoy the journey. If the problem is lack of clarity about what we believe, trust, and want in life, we have to work out a clear belief system. If we are in conflict between values, we have to compromise, make room for both. If we are displacing our search for God into a fragment of life, we need to find a bigger God. If we lack faith and are living in anxiety or fear, we need to seek faith. The chart only indicates the issue. We have to take the action, and it is always easier to say than to do. But if we want to move toward integration and inner peace and harmony, we can. We have to know what we want and be willing to keep on trying.

Once we know how to interpret aspects, we have to decide when to count them. The permissible orb of aspects is one of the unsolved problems in astrology. The word **orb** refers to the variance from the exact aspect which may be allowed. If a square is defined as two factors that are ninety degrees apart in the sky, where does the square end? Most astrologers allow a five-degree orb so the square extends from eighty-five to ninety-five degrees, five degrees on each side of the exact aspect. But some astrologers allow an orb as large as ten to twelve degrees, and some systems have a sliding scale depending on the factor. For example, Sun, Moon and planets in angular houses may be given a wider orb. Hindu astrologers form whole sign aspects, e.g., any degree of Aries is square any degree of Cancer. There is no consensus on the subject and no prospect of consensus until we have much additional research in astrology.

In general, astrologers who use a smaller number of factors need to use wider orbs to get the picture. When midpoints, Arabic Parts and new planets are included in the chart, aspect orbs need to be reduced. I consider the one-degree orb supremely important, as a key to the fundamental, central nature of the person. Orbs up to three degrees are still moderately important, but after that they drop off rapidly. However, if a wide orb aspect is repeating a theme shown in other ways in the chart, I note it as a repeated emphasis. If aspects overlap: planet A aspects planet B; planet B aspects planet C; planet C aspects planet D; the whole group or network must be considered interrelated and interacting in the person's nature. In the end, there is some sort of relationship between all parts of us: the questions include what kind of relationship, how intense, how conscious, etc.

Declination

In addition to the aspects in zodiacal longitude discussed above, there is another class of aspect. Astrology and astronomy use a number of coordinate systems to draw their maps of the sky in order to locate planets and other factors. In all of these coordinate systems, measurement occurs around a circle and up and down from the circle. The aspects previously discussed are derived from measurements around the circle of the Earth's path around the Sun, the ecliptic, measurements known as zodiacal longitude. It is also possible to measure up and down from the ecliptic to get zodiacal latitude. Another coordinate system in astronomy and astrology uses the earth's Equator as the basic circle. Measurements around the equator are called Right Ascension. Measurements up and down from the equator are called **declination**. Astrology takes longitude from one coordinate system, and declination from the other system. Astronomers consider this improper, but astrologers use whatever works.

Aspects in declination are called **parallel** if two planets (or angles or other factors), are in the same degree either north or south of the equator. If two factors are in the same degree with one north and one south, the aspect is called a **contraparallel**. The parallel is generally interpreted as similar to a conjunction, with the quality of the relationship depending on the factors involved. Factors that are normally complementary are usually easier to integrate. The contraparallel is interpreted as similar to an opposition in longitude. The aspects are only considered when the aspect is exact within a one-degree orb. If two factors in a chart have both a parallel and a longitudinal aspect, the interaction of those two parts of the nature is much more intense and important.

Parans

Still another form of aspects comes to us from ancient astrology: **paranatellonta**. Robert Hand reintroduced the technique in modern astrology in a publication of the Association for Research in Cosmecology, founded by Charles Jayne of New York. To use the more common nickname, Parans use right ascension rather than longitude, and include only three aspects involving the four major angles of the chart. Two planets can be conjunct on any of the four angles: Ascendant, MC (upper culmination), Descendant, and IC (lower culmination). Planets can also be opposite each other: MC opposite IC or Ascendant opposite Descendant. Or they can be square: Ascendant or Descendant square MC or IC. Standard meanings are used in interpretation, depending on the planet and angle involved. The technique varies from normal aspects in longitude because in addition to parans that were exact at the time of birth (two or more planets within a few degrees of the any of the four angles), any parans that form within 24 hours of the birth are considered to be relevant although not as important as those exact at birth. In my limited work with parans, I have found them sometimes helpful but not enough by themselves. As with many of the new or rediscovered techniques in astrology, they can be added if time and knowledge permit.

John Nelson's Work

As is normally the case when humans make models (simplified representations of the complicated reality of the world), in time, the models are found to be inadequate to do justice to the world, and they are made more and more complicated. The proliferation of asteroids and of aspects in recent years provides a good example of this movement toward increasing complexity. The next step in the expanding number of aspects was taken by John Nelson, a radio engineer with Radio Communications of America. Nelson discovered that he could forecast the state of the ionosphere which affected short wave radio by noting the angular distances between the planets (the aspects of astrology). In developing his technique, he added many more aspects, including all multiples of 7½ (the 48th of a circle), all multiples of 11¼ (the 32nd of a circle) and all multiples of 18 (the 20th of a circle). Two of these series of aspects share the 22½ degree aspect and all multiples of it (the 16th of a circle), and all three series include the conjunction, square and opposition. Nelson's work supported the observations already made by the Uranian school of astrology and by the Cosmobiologists of the importance of the

22½ degree series, including 45 (already mentioned as the octile), 67½, 90 (already noted as the square), 112½, 135 (the trioctile), 157½, and 180 (the opposition). In general, this series of aspects are classed as stressful or challenging. The series including 15, 30, 60, and 120 degrees are normally indicative of more inner ease and harmony.

Nelson and the German schools of astrology also independently discovered midpoints, already mentioned in Chapter 5 with minor forms of the astrological alphabet. The realization that **any** angular distance between factors in a chart could be meaningful really finished off any hope of keeping aspects limited to a few divisions of the circle. In effect, midpoints permit any three factors to be in aspect to each other when one is midway between the other two. There will be a centerpoint between each two factors in the chart on both sides of the chart, opposite each other. For example, if Mars is at 9 degrees of Aries and Saturn is at 29 degrees of Aries, a midpoint exists at 19 degrees of both Aries and Libra. Mars and Saturn are equal distances from both of these points. If a third planet falls at 19 degrees of either Aries or Libra, it is on the midpoint of Mars and Saturn. The combination can be interpreted as similar to a conjunction of all three planets in quality, though not as intense as if the planets had really all been in the same degree of the same sign.

John Addey of England took the next step in the proliferation of aspects. He suggested that logically, one could divide the circle by any whole number and the result would be a meaningful aspect. He carried the process up to a division by 180 which gives an aspect of two degrees. He also took an idea much used in Hindu astrology, the creation of a new chart based on a particular aspect. A variation on the idea had been independently tried in Germany where a new form of chart was called a **dial** of the chosen aspect. The 90 degree dial was most commonly used in Germany, but some students worked with dials of 45 degrees, 30 degrees, 22½ degrees, and even down to 7½ degrees. The most common aspect selected in India was the 40 degrees novile, and the Hindus called the resultant horoscope a **Navamsa** chart. Addey called the new horoscopes **Harmonic** Charts.

To calculate a harmonic chart, the factors in the natal chart (planets, angles, etc.) are first converted to a 360 degrees figure. For example, 9 Aries is 9. A planet at 9 Taurus becomes 39 while one at 9 Leo becomes 129, and so on. The numerical value of the factor is multiplied by the chosen aspect number. To produce a 4th harmonic chart, you multiply all factors by four. The planet at 9 Aries would have a new value of 36 (4 times 9). The planet at 9 Taurus would be 39 times 4 or 156, and so on. When the resultant figures are more than 360, that amount is subtracted, as many times as necessary to produce a figure of less than 360. These final results are then translated back into the zodiac with the original 9 Aries becoming 6 Taurus (36 equaling 30 degrees of Aries and 6 degrees into Taurus). Or, the planets can simply be spaced around a 360 degree circle. Addey and the Hindus used the first method, producing a new chart. It is relatively easy to calculate harmonic charts with a pocket calculator, and very easy to do them on a computer.

The German schools used the latter method, a circle without house divisions. In their 90 degree dial, the 90 degrees are visually displayed on the whole circle of 360 degrees, and there are no individual signs or houses. The dials could be described as a folding of the chart without multiplying. The Ebertins, founders of the school of Cosmobiology, have developed a very quick way to construct their 90 degree dial with minimal mathematical calculations. Planets in cardinal signs (Aries, Cancer, Libra and Capricorn) keep their degrees unchanged. Planets in fixed signs (Taurus, Leo, Scorpio and Aquarius) have 30 degrees added to their degrees. For example, any planet in 5 degrees of a fixed sign would be 35 degrees in the 90 degree dial. Planets in mutable signs (Gemini, Virgo, Sagittarius and Pisces) have 60 degrees added to their degree. All planets at 5 degrees of a mutable sign would become 65 degrees in the dial. The purpose of constructing the dial is to permit the astrologer to see aspects more easily. In the 90 degree dial, for example, all planets that are conjunct, square, or in opposition in the natal chart will be conjunct on the dial. All octiles and trioctiles (45 or 135 degree aspects) will appear as an opposition which is easy to see on the dial. All other multiples of 22½ degrees will appear as squares on the dial, again, easy to spot by visual inspection. Similar formulas are available to easily construct the other dials (45 degrees etc.) which make it possible to see still smaller aspects easily.

The purpose of both the Hindu and English harmonic charts goes farther than the German goal of seeing selected aspects quickly and easily. As indicated above, the harmonic charts are converted back into a horoscope with zodiacal signs though the signs will normally be different than those of the natal chart. To produce houses, both the Hindus and the English normally use equal houses, putting the same degrees on each house cusp that results for the harmonic Ascendant, with the signs placed in the usual order. The Hindu tradition uses the navamsa chart as a key to the goal of the soul, or the spiritual outcome of the life. It is typically done along with the normal natal chart. Addey suggested that each of the different harmonic charts might indicate a basic area of life. He worked especially with the fifth harmonic chart, and felt that it indicated important relationships, and that it was connected in some way with perception and possible problems in that area. Addey also suggested using the harmonic charts as keys to the respective years of the life. For example, the tenth harmonic would be symbolic of the tenth year.

Much more testing will be required before we will know whether these new ideas are dependable. One initial problem in using harmonic charts to symbolize the corresponding year of life is a difference of opinion between Addey and other astrologers who have tested the technique. Addey thought that the natal chart applied to the first two years of life; the second harmonic applied to age two to three; the third harmonic to age three to four, etc. Others who have tried the technique have felt that the second harmonic was related to age one to two, the third harmonic to age two to three, and so on. When there is a disagreement over which chart fits which year, the validity of the whole theory has to be held in question.

Following the exploratory work of the Ebertins, Nelson and Addey, I was eager to try out some of the ideas and to carry them further. By this time, I was convinced of the importance of the repeated themes in a chart, and was easily able to identify them in combinations of planets, signs and houses. For example, when we see Venus, ruling the first house, placed in the tenth house; Moon, ruling the tenth house, placed in the first house; and Saturn, the natural ruler of the tenth house, also placed in the first house, we have repeated the One-Ten combination three times. Such an individual is personally identified with power, though we do not know whether the person will overdrive (try to do more than is possible), or block himself or herself (feel that the world has the power, failure is inevitable so there is no point in trying), or whether the individual will learn to voluntarily live within his or her limits. The chart shows the **issue**, not the details, as has been said repeatedly.

Aspect Themes

While I felt able to see the planet-sign-house themes, I found aspects a much more challenging tool. I wanted a way to get an aspect theme, and the work of the Ebertins, Nelson and Addey opened up some ideas of possible techniques, while the increasing availability of microcomputers opened up the capacity to handle complicated procedures quickly and easily. Our first microcomputer was started with a kit in 1975, and now, eight years later, we have five, one more powerful than the rest. The universe had also provided me with two sons who are computer programmers. All I needed was 24 more hours in each day to test all the ideas.

We are currently working with a variety of formulas, all representing different attempts to obtain an **aspect theme** in a horoscope. In conjunction counting, the computer calculates a chart for each harmonic and then counts the number of conjunctions in the chart. Natal conjunctions will always be included if they are exact enough to be counted. In the second harmonic chart, both conjunctions and oppositions will appear as conjunctions and will be counted. In the fourth harmonic chart (related to the 90 degree dial as described above), conjunctions, squares and oppositions will appear as conjunctions and be counted. The total of conjunctions in a harmonic (which is simply a form of aspect) will include harmonics of all numbers which divide evenly into the higher one, provided they are within the orb being used. If we find that a particular horoscope has a large number of conjunctions in the fifth, the tenth, the twentieth and the twenty-fifth harmonics, we have spotted an aspect theme. The individual has a large number of the aspects involving divisions of the circle by five, ten, twenty and twenty-five. Of course, to count the conjunctions in the different harmonics, we have to decide on an orb. How close must the angular distances be for us to count the aspect? How far from exact is too far to count? Since the work is purely exploratory, we have no answers as yet. We started with two arbitrary orbs, to see if either one produced results that looked significant. Our goal is to run a large number of horoscopes of famous people, and individuals with specific talents or problems or conditions in their lives, to see if the aspect themes offer meaningful information. Due to constant time pressures, the work has barely begun.

A second approach to the same goal, the search for aspect themes, was attempted to determine whether a network of interconnected aspects was more important than the same number of aspects without interconnections. For example, did quintiles become more important if the chart had a grand quintile than if it had five separate quintiles between different pairs of planets? A formula called **vector addition** produced a figure which was higher when the series of a given aspect was interconnected, e.g., a grand cross produced a higher vector addition figure than four separate squares in a chart. Again, the work is still in a very early stage.

In both of the preceding calculations, we ended with a number for each type of aspect (each harmonic), but had no way of knowing which planets in the chart had contributed to the figure (which planets were actually in that aspect to each other). So another formula was fed to the computer to list the planet pairs for each harmonic (aspect). Again, as with conjunction-counting, we had to set an arbitrary orb, and at the suggestion of Rob Hand, who was interested in the problem, we used an orb of 3% of the circle. With this system, as the harmonic increased, the orb dropped. The orb of the second harmonic (the opposition, or half the circle) was half the orb of the conjunction, and so on. In our work with the conjunction-counting and vector addition programs, we have mostly stopped at the 48th harmonic (the aspect of 7½ degrees), though it is possible to go to the 180th harmonic. In the last program, all planetary and angle pairs have normally been listed by the 31st or 32nd harmonic.

All of these programs seek the same goal, the discovery of aspects in a horoscope. No single program can provide all the answers, and each program has its own limitations. The listing of pairs of planets for their appropriate aspect avoids repetition by only mentioning each pair of planets once. The other two programs, in contrast, continue to include the smaller numbered harmonics that divide evenly into the larger harmonics, so long as the orb requirement is met. For example, the twelfth

harmonic in these first two programs will incorporate and count oppositions, trines, squares and sextiles since twelve can be divided by 2, 3, 4
and 6, without a remainder. Limiting the listing of planet pairs to their
first appearance has the effect of inflating the apparent importance of the
prime number harmonics. Numbers that cannot be divided by any number
except themselves and one (11, 13, 17, etc.) will seem more important
than they really are.

In essence, I have just said that there is no single approach to the
search for aspect themes, that a variety of techniques give useful information, and that each of the techniques has its own drawbacks and limitations. Just two months prior to writing this chapter, another possible approach was suggested to us by Austin Levy of Sydney, Australia. He had
developed a formula to calculate what he called **centricity**, or the degree
to which the planets were clustered into major stelliums in the natal chart.
The higher the figure, the closer the chart tended toward what Mark
Edmund Jones had called a "bundle" pattern, with all the planets grouped
into a small section of the zodiac. My son, Mark, immediately added this
program to our collection. Only time will tell whether it provides dependable psychological information. I have not found the Jones patterns dependable. I have seen people with bundle charts who were not at all
focused in their life, who were scattered all over the map when they had
a mutable dilemma and considerable fire and air. In my experience, the
conjunction is the strongest aspect, other things being equal, but I think
the most important variable is number and closeness of aspects rather
than a single type, such as conjunction, as is measured by centricity. Ongoing research by both Austin Levy and Tom Shanks of Astro Computing
Services may soon clarify the potential value of centricity as a concept.
Work with aspect themes is still highly exploratory. We have no final
conclusions.

Synodic Zodiac

Another quite different approach to aspects is possible and is also
still exploratory. Traditional work with aspects considers them as static
facts. A square is a square and a trine is a trine. But it is also possible
to see aspects as part of a dynamic process, as stages in a cycle. Using
the concept of phases, each pair of planets can be conceived as beginning a new cycle with a conjunction. The faster moving of the two planets
then pulls away to form a series of aspects until eventually it catches up
with the slower moving planet to begin a new cycle with a new conjunction. Using this concept, a square when the planets are separating from
the conjunction might be quite different from a square when the planet
is approaching the next conjunction. The same concept can be expressed
as an upper and lower square (or other aspect).

One of the first authors to discuss this idea was Dane Rudhyar in his book on the Lunation Cycle. He wrote of eight phases of the Moon: new Moon, first quarter, full Moon, and last quarter, with each fourth of the cycle subdivided into two parts to make eight sections. Rudhyar named each of these eight phases and described a type of personality he associated with each of them. Marc Robertson added new ideas to Rudhyar's, including work with other planetary pairs, such as Mars-Venus, and with Saturn cycles. But I wondered why we should stop at eight phases when so much of astrology used a division of the circle into twelve parts. Might there be twelve phases that matched the twelve sides of life seen in planets, signs and houses? I also felt that the implication that the slower planet somehow controlled the faster moving planet left Pluto out. A two-way relationship between all pairs of planets seemed more logical to me. Later, of course, I found out that others had thought of the same idea. Rob Hand said he had done some experimentation with what is now being called the Synodic Zodiac.

In principle, the idea is quite simple. Each planet in turn is considered as if it were at zero Aries. If any other planet or angle is within 30 degrees ahead of it in the zodiac, the second planet is in the Aries phase to the first planet. Simultaneously, the first planet is in the Pisces phase to the second one. Two planets within 30 degrees of each other will always be in Aries and Pisces phases to each other. A planet more than 30 but less than 60 degrees ahead of the first planet (we can call it A) will be in the Taurus phase to A while A is in the Aquarius phase to the other planet. Again, these two phases will always pair with each other. Gemini and Capricorn form a similar pair, Cancer and Sagittarius, Leo and Scorpio, and finally Virgo and Libra complete the phase pairs. When calculating the phases by hand, it is easier to do the one for the planet ahead in the zodiac. The other in each interrelated pair need not be calculated since you know the ones that are always matched with each other.

I noted that the pairs always matched a cardinal and mutable sign while the fixed always paired with each other. I also noted that in each pair, one was always earth or water, while the other was always fire or air. Each combination had one planet attending to security issues while the other could concentrate on freer self-expression. The technique is still highly experimental, but there does seem to be some value in the idea. Any new idea is usually tested first on the astrologer's own chart. I have a strong mutable dilemma in my chart, including a Gemini Moon square Virgo and Pisces. Of course, the Virgo indicates the capacity to be organized and productive even though the Gemini and Pisces keep getting over-extended. But I was interested to note that my potentially scattered Gemini Moon was in the Capricorn phase to six of my planets. My Uranus in Pisces also turned up in the Virgo phase to six planets, fitting the career in astrology. Naturally the message was there in many other ways — Uranus rules the MC — but the Synodical Zodiac seemed to say it again.

Synodical Zodiac

Angular Separation	Phase of Planet Ahead	Phase of Planet Behind
0 - 29°59′	♈	♓
30 - 59°59′	♉	♒
60 - 89°59′	♊	♑
90 - 119°59′	♋	♐
120 - 149°59′	♌	♏
150 - 180	♍	♎

I was also fascinated to note that the system seemed to work in progressions as well as in the natal chart. In the five months preceding my only major surgery when I was in my teens, five planets progressed into Mars-ruled signs (either Aries or Scorpio). But most remarkable to me was that my ordination as a minister in 1960 was timed to the month when my progressed Jupiter moved into the Sagittarius phase to my MC. I think my most valuable insight from the new system came with an understanding of the quincunx. I had noted, over and over again, that individuals made major changes in their lives during periods of a progressed quincunx; especially the double quincunx that is generally called a **yod**. If we think of a planet as zero Aries, the two signs which are quincunx Aries are Virgo and Scorpio. I had never been satisfied with calling the quincunx an aspect of adjustment. The word is typical traditional astrology, leaving people feeling like helpless victims who have to adjust to what the world is dumping on them. But thinking of a quincunx as a Virgo or Scorpio action made sense of the separations I saw happening: people leaving jobs, relationships, religions, homes. Or, of course, these others might be leaving them if the results were the consequences of past action or if they were being elicited by unconscious factors.

Once the Virgo-Scorpio theme occurred to me, I started calling the quincunx the closet-cleaning aspect. With Virgo, we are trying to improve our functioning, to handle the job (including any part of our life we have turned into a job) more effectively, to change any method or tool that is not working well. With Scorpio, we are trying to decide whether something is really ours at all; whether it has served its purpose and it is time to discard it as outgrown. At times of a double quincunx, a yod, people do totally alter their lives, or have them altered if they are operating largely unconsciously. Once we realize what we really want (efficiency and to release gracefully anything that is outgrown), we can act with conscious intelligence. Strictly speaking, the Aries-Virgo and Aries-Scorpio relationship is not part of the Synodic Zodiac, but the insight into the quincunx occurred while I was experimenting with it.

I think the idea of the twelve phases, fitting aspects into the Twelve Letter Alphabet, is part of the meaning offered in a horoscope, though less important than other ways of working with aspects. I would not substitute the Synodic Zodiac for classical aspects, but it can be added as another way the chart can give you the same message. For those who want to explore the technique in their own chart or for family members, Astro Computing includes it as one of their services.

CHAPTER 8

Leftovers! House Systems, Retrogrades, Etc.

In discussing any subject, there are usually a variety of small odds and ends that should be included but that do not justify a chapter of their own. The word **retrograde** refers to the apparent backward motion in the zodiac due to a faster planet (closer to the Sun) passing a slower planet. The planets which are outside the orbit of Earth have their retrograde period when they are opposite the Sun (Earth is between them and the Sun). The inner planets, Venus and Mercury, have their retrograde period when they are in their "inferior" conjunction with the Sun. That is the astronomical term for the conjunction formed when Venus and Mercury are between Earth and Sun. Venus and Mercury have their apparently most rapid motion when they appear conjunct the Sun. It may be a note of purely academic interest, but retrogrades are always mutual; that is, if we were on Mars when it appeared retrograde to Earth, Earth would also appear retrograde to our viewpoint on Mars.

The word "apparent" has been emphasized in the preceding statement. Obviously, planets do not really move backward in the sky. Readers who have traveled in moving vehicles, especially trains, will have experienced a similar phenomenon when telephone poles appear to move backward as we pass them. We see the near objects appear to move against the very distant backdrop of the sky. Changes of speed are also apparent. There are very small changes in orbital speed as the planets vary slightly in their distance from the Sun. Most orbits are not quite circular. In fact, some of the asteroids have extremely elongated orbits. But the large changes in speed noted with Venus, and especially with Mercury, are due to Earth's viewpoint.

The Sun is never retrograde since we are circling it, and the Moon is never retrograde since it is circling Earth. All planets and asteroids are retrograde some of the time. Mercury normally has three retrograde periods each year while Pluto is retrograde almost half of each year. As indicated above, we see the apparent retrograde motion when the planet is closest to Earth.

Much negative material has been written about retrogrades, but as with everything in astrology, our life urges can be expressed in positive or in painful ways. The apparent backward motion seems, in my experience, to indicate a tendency to turn the attention and energy of that part of the nature inward before it expresses out. If the individual lacks self-confidence, the drive may be blocked and not allowed out, or permitted minimal expression. But people who trust their inner direction are simply more creative and individualistic. Numbers of very successful and prominent people have had six or seven retrogrades in their natal charts, including Muhammed Ali, the prize fighter who converted to Islam; Angela Davis, the University of California Professor who fought the whole establishment over her right to support Communism; Annie Besant, the leader of the early Theosophy movement; Kahlil Gibran, the mystical writer; a Hollywood song writer who was famous before he was thirty years old. In essence, I think retrogrades indicate the urge to look inside for answers, and it is our choice whether we trust that inner creative potential. Too often, astrology blames the sky for impulsive, or ineffective action instead of taking a moment to listen to the inner guide or to think through a situation.

Intercepted signs, cases in which the same sign falls on two house cusps so that a sign is squeezed inside a house (not found on a cusp), are also often used as scapegoats in astrology. Since the chart is made of two mirror halves, there will, of course, be intercepted signs on both sides of the chart. In horoscopes drawn for the far North, it is possible to have four intercepted signs (two on each side of the chart), and on the Arctic circle at 6 and 18 hours of sidereal time, the zodiac lies on the horizon so the Ascendant is the whole zodiac. As with retrogrades, many astrologers assume negative consequences for intercepted signs. Personally, I have never been able to see any substantial difference in the handling of planets that were in intercepted signs, and I usually ignore the fact. If there is a difference, it seems minor, and the people who emphasize it offer conflicting theories about its nature. Some claim that the planets in intercepted signs are practically wiped out, becoming non-functional. This statement is simply wrong in most cases. Others claim what is virtually the opposite effect, an intensification of the expression of those parts of the person's nature. This latter theory might have some validity, but the difference is usually minor. (I do have one pair of twins where one is normal and one with the Sun in an intercepted sign has serious physical defects.) Generally, I consider interceptions unimportant.

My House or Yours?

However, opening up the issue of the houses of the horoscope has brought up a really important area of conflict for which there are no easy solutions. It is possible to divide the space around Earth in literally thousands of ways, and there is no logical reason to prefer one over another in making a choice among many of them. The long-range solution to the problem must be pragmatic, through extensive testing of different house systems. Since there is no public funding for research in astrology, most astrologers use the system taught them originally, or they find a new one that they think fits their own chart better. Either procedure is quite unscientific, but thorough scientific research requires knowledge, time, money and equipment, which are just not available to practicing astrologers. Despite the subjective risks in choosing a system that seems to fit one's own horoscope, this approach is actually a good one **if** the person really understands his or her own nature. Of course, if people are not self-aware, they should not be practicing astrology, but that is another issue. The reason that this system works well (though as a stopgap until we have more research on the subject) is based on the "world as mirror" concept. We do tend to draw friends, clients who fit our own nature, so the techniques that work well for us may fairly often work well for the others in our lives.

The most commonly used house systems include Placidus, Koch, Campanus and Equal, with others also in the marketplace including Meridian, Morinus, Regiomontanus, Topocentric and Porphyry. Since our concern in this book is with the interpretation rather than the construction of charts, I will simply mention that Placidus and Topocentric are the most mathematically sophisticated systems. They give very similar results, usually house cusps within a few minutes of each other. The Topocentric system was developed in Brazil, and it avoids some of the problems which beset Placidus in the high latitudes, but the Placidus system is much more readily available in tables of houses. My own preference is for either Placidus or Topocentric. In my experience, these systems have given me the most accurate psychological understanding of people. I have also tested them on many twins, and usually found them helpful. As a final note, to counter the suggestion by some astrologers that Placidus is somehow outdated, the couple who have done the only substantial research in astrology, Michel and Francoise Gauquelin of Paris, France use a system that is essentially the same as Placidus. Michel Gauquelin has a Ph.D. in statistics and psychology from the Sorbonne, the famous French university, and he states that the Placidus system gives the best results.

It is important to add that I have also obtained useful information from the Koch and Campanus techniques on occasion. I do not think that there is one "right" system, but that there are many potentially useful techniques. It is quite possible that there are "overlap" zones where different systems would change the house placement, and that the planets in those areas may express a blend of the two possible houses. For this reason, a planet near a house cusp may be considered as incorporating and mixing some of the natures of both houses. For the most part, the differences involve the intermediate house cusps. Most systems use the same angles (the MC beginning the tenth house and the Ascendant beginning the first house). Exceptions include Equal houses which are normally measured from the Ascendant, so all houses have the same degree but successive signs. In this system, the MC is placed in the chart as a sensitive point, wherever it falls. It is also possible to do an Equal House chart from the MC and put in the Ascendant wherever it falls. Both the Morinus and Meridian systems use the Eastpoint as the beginning of the first house and put the Ascendant in wherever it would appear. I put the Eastpoint and the Antivertex in their normal sign placement and consider both of them to be auxiliary Ascendants. In the end, as already stated, until we have much more research, we can only continue to use the system that seems to work best for us in our own experience.

Locality Charts

A relatively new technique in astrology involves the calculation of house cusps for a current place of residence when the individual has moved from the place of birth. The Greenwich time is kept constant so the natal planets are unchanged, but the houses are calculated as if the person had been born in the new location. For example, if the subject has moved from California to New York, three hours are added to the standard clock time of birth, and the normal procedures for chart calculation are followed. If one calculates charts by first obtaining the GMT, instead of then subtracting the interval between the birthplace and Greenwich, the interval between the new location and Greenwich is subtracted. I like to insert the new local house cusps just inside the horoscope circle, surrounded by a box. In this way, it is possible to see planetary aspects to both sets of angles, and to note where the planets would change houses in the new local chart. If the move has crossed a continent, or especially if the person has moved to a new continent, it is helpful to also erect a separate chart for the new residence. The local chart can be very useful, often clarifying issues. As in all areas of astrology, the factors with numerous and close aspects are the important ones. Sometimes the new local angles will be even more important than those from the birthplace. Aspects within one degree are extremely important.

One of the services now available from Jim Lewis and from Astro Computing Services is a map of the world (or a more detailed one of the U.S.) with lines drawn to show where the planets are conjunct the four principle angles: Ascendant-Descendant axis, and MC-IC axis. Such a map is helpful to see where your major planets fall on angles, but if a place of residence is under consideration, I prefer to calculate the whole chart for that location. With such a relocation chart, we can see other aspects to the angles in addition to the conjunction (a trine to the MC or Ascendant might be preferred to a conjunction), and we can include the East-point axis and the Antivertex axis. I also feel strongly that we cannot run away from ourselves. The best local angle aspects we can find will not solve our inner conflicts or give us a free ride. However, if we choose a place with facilitating aspects to the angles, and continue to work on personal self-awareness and growth, we may speed up our progress. Since there is never a "perfect" chart, one without any conflict, we will need to be very clear about our values in selecting a new place. We will want different aspects to different planets depending on whether we are seeking financial security, romance or career advancement. In the end, all of us are juggling the same twelve parts of life, and putting one in high focus might help that one, but at the expense of another important part of our nature. We may find a latitude and longitude that seems highly favorable except that it is in the middle of the Atlantic Ocean. Or, we may be unable to find any location that looks better than right where we are. I know two women who moved to a location that put Saturn on their Ascendant. Both had been relatively dependent in their earlier lives, and in the new residence they discovered their strength and learned to cope with life effectively. There is nothing in astrology that is automatically good or bad. Each of the twelve principles can be painful or pleasant, depending on our own attitudes and actions.

Beware Quick, Easy Answers

Astrology is full of claims and counterclaims, of theories put forth as Gospel, based on experiences with a handful of charts. But astrology is no different than any other area of model building. Economists are at each other's throats. Psychiatrists testify on opposite sides of court cases. Psychology is split into three or four major groups, each with many subgroups. Education changes its collective mind every few years. Physics is looking more and more like metaphysics, and some physicists acknowledge it. We cannot function, make choices, or take action without premises, but we must learn to hold the premises tentatively, as theories to be tested by experience. Experience is real. The theories we invent to explain the experience are always incomplete and sometimes pure fantasy. Astrology is full of quick, easy answers that are not dependable, that are oversimplifications, though sometimes they have a grain of truth. I am often tempted to simply ignore them, and insist that students get a clear understanding of the twelve sides of life and then use logic and look for the repeated themes. But I am continually confronted by students who want to be told whether they can trust one of the simple formulas. Everyone wants an easy answer.

My own conviction after 25 years of experience with astrology is that anything important in the nature will be indicated several times in the chart; that anything only said once is of minor importance. Too often, signs are counted but planets and houses ignored (in weighting elements and qualities). Or, houses are weighted and signs and planets are ignored (looking at left half-right half or top half-lower half). As an example of the latter, a chart may have everything above the horizon but in the signs of personal relationship. Or everything may be below the horizon but in transpersonal signs. All factors are part of the picture and must be considered. I do consider the houses more important than the signs, but both are there. There is a germ of truth in the division of the chart into left and right halves, but it is not clearly explained when the left side is said to be under your control and the right side out of your control. Much of the right side involves the interpersonal area, and to maintain close relationships, we do have to compromise some of our own will to a greater extent than when we are part of an impersonal group or simply meeting our own needs. But the ninth house is our belief system, and we certainly have the option of changing that, and many people do in their lifetimes. On the other side of the coin, some of the most dependent people I have ever met have had most of their planets on the left side of the chart, but they were in water signs and/or houses, and Libra. The top half-bottom half discussions in most books are a similar oversimplification. The lower left quadrant shows personal needs, where we are fairly self-absorbed. In the lower right quadrant, the focus is on family and job. But the third and fifth houses are basically sociable and outgoing. In fact, a fifth house emphasis may lead into the entertainment world and a very public life. Again, considering the other side, the most introverted child I ever knew had all her planets except one above the horizon, but everything was in water and earth signs and houses.

Another of the quick answers suggests that Mercury ahead of the Sun is progressive while Mercury behind the Sun is conservative. Two examples are sufficient to throw out that theory. Ronald Reagan has Mercury ahead of the Sun and Jules Verne had Mercury behind the Sun. Still another theory assigns meaning to a fast or slow Mercury, Moon or Ascendant. It is possible that there is some meaning, but it must be a minor part of the picture. I have never seen any clear associations with the speed of the planets. I have seen a fast mind when the mental planets aspect each other: Mercury, Jupiter, Uranus in any kind of aspect tend to speed up the mind. Fire, and next to fire, air, also speed up the mind and generally the tongue. I'm afraid there are no shortcuts to becoming a good astrologer. After you have a clear understanding of the twelve sides of life in all their forms, and have learned to spot repeated themes in the chart, you have to do charts and ask questions. Do charts on anyone who will give you their data and answer your questions. You learn astrology by looking at charts and personal lives, and noting the correspondences. How does the chart symbolize what you see in the person and in the life? Can you figure out the principle that lies behind the visible varied details? The principles can manifest in many different details. We may guess the details or we may not. But to help people, we need to be able to explain the principles. So they, and we, can choose better details.

CHAPTER 9

Techniques for Current Patterns

Before we plunge into some real horoscopes to illustrate the principles offered so far, it might be helpful to review some of astrology's ways to look at the present and to project into the future. A vast and proliferating number of techniques exist, with transits probably the method in most general use. **Transits** are the actual positions in the sky of the various astrological factors at the time in which you are interested, whether that time is past, present or future. In transits, patterns come and go rapidly, though the slow-moving outer planets may maintain an aspect for some weeks, especially when they are making a station, about to change direction whether the change is to direct motion or to retrograde (apparent backward motion). Retrograde, as already indicated, means that we see the planet against an earlier degree of the zodiac because we are passing it or it is passing us. The most serious deficiency in the use of transits as one's only method for seeing current patterns, is the lack of houses and angles (MC, etc.). The houses turn past all the planets in a single day, and it is pretty impractical, if not impossible, to keep track of them. However, if transit angles are calculated for a major event (hindsight), they are meaningful.

Partly because of the ephemeral nature of the aspects of the faster planets, and partly because of the problem in obtaining current angles, astrologers have sought additional ways to gain insight into current issues and coming potentials. The ancient world developed a system called **Primary Directions**, which equated one degree of Earth's rotation (a movement occurring in approximately four minutes) with a year of life. Since Earth's rotation occurs around our own axis, at right angles to our equator, the movement of the planets and angles was measured around the equator, in right ascension, which is slightly different than zodiacal longitude measured around the ecliptic. As the Earth turned and the sky appeared to move, each degree of movement symbolized a year of life, so if Mars was three degrees from the birth Saturn, an event of the nature of Mars-Saturn would be expected at around the age of three years. Earth would move three degrees in twelve minutes, carrying the birth position of Mars to the birth position of Saturn. At the same time, Saturn would be moved about three degrees farther, but since the placements at birth were considered a basic blueprint of the person, Saturn was somehow thought to have marked its birth position to be permanently there, waiting for Mars. Calculating primary directions requires trigonometry or tedious work with tables, and the technique was largely abandoned when astrologers discovered that the formula of "one degree symbolizes a year" could also be used with zodiacal longitude, the more familiar and simpler figures that were readily available. Larger differences between longitude and right ascension can occur when planets are near zero Aries or Libra. There are minimal differences between the ecliptic and equatorial arcs when planets are near zero Cancer or Capricorn.

A number of minor variations have been used, centering around the "degree for a year" formula. Naibod's measure uses the Sun's average daily motion of about 59 ' to equal a year. Theodore Landscheidt of Germany suggested using 61.' Most astrologers have found that the actual motion of the Sun during the individual's early months gives a more precise and personally tailored result. The Sun is somewhat slower in summer and faster in winter (Landscheidt was born in the winter). To calculate the **solar arc** (distance the Sun has traveled between birth and the period of time being studied), one simply subtracts the natal Sun's longitude from the longitude of the Sun the same number of days after birth as the individual's age at the time of interest. If the astrologer wishes to see the patterns associated with the death of a parent which occurred when the subject was ten years old, the birth position of the Sun is subtracted from the position of the Sun ten days after birth. If the period of current interest is the 50th year of the subject, one looks at the Sun 50 days after birth. The number of degrees which the Sun has moved are then added to every factor in the natal chart. All factors are moved at this constant rate of speed, regardless of their normal speed in the sky. Planets, angles of the chart, nodes, Arabic Parts, etc. — all maintain their birth relationships as the whole chart is turned like a wheel.

In most systems of current patterns, with the exception of transits, the orb of aspects is limited to one degree. In this system of **Solar Arc Directions**, aspects last approximately two years each; one degree applying to the exact aspect, and one degree separating from it. Aspects can only be formed between directed (moving) planets and natal (birth position) planets, since the directed planets maintain their natal relationship. If a one-degree orb aspect exists in the natal chart, it remains a lifetime pattern. There is obviously much artificiality about standard two-year patterns, but the system does usually pick out the times of major changes in the life.

Both of the preceding techniques are called **Directions**, since the sky is turned as a unit at a constant rate of speed (or near constant with Primary Directions since a life of 90 years has been symbolized in the sky within six hours after birth, and only the Moon has moved appreciably in that interval). Other possible speeds have been suggested, including directing (moving) the chart at half the solar arc (the midpoint of the solar arc), at 2½ degrees a year, 5 degrees a year, 7½ degrees a year, 10 degrees a year, etc. One begins to suspect that any systematic treatment of the sky will still give us a clue to life: we still see the same order in a slightly different way.

In addition to the systems of directions, another class of techniques was discovered (or invented?) early in the Christian era. These techniques are called **Progressions**, and three variations are in general use in astrology. The earliest and most popular of these systems has several names: "Day for a Year" spells out what is actually done, but it is also called **Secondary Progressions, Hermetic Progressions**, and **Major Progressions**. Instead of one degree equalling a year, one day is said to symbolize a year in the life. The procedure begins much like Solar Arc Directions; looking in the ephemeris at the date that is as many days after birth as the individual's age at the time of interest. If we are seeking to understand the individual's present situation, and the person is 35 years old, we look at the planetary patterns 35 days after birth. The Sun's position will be the same as in the solar arc technique, but the rest of the chart will be quite different. In Secondary Progressions, each planet has its normal movement. Pluto will rarely move more than a degree or two from its natal position during a lifetime, while the Moon will progress around the chart and return to its natal position about every 28 years (in much the same time as the cycle of transiting Saturn). Secondary aspects can be formed between both progressed and natal positions and between progressed and progressed positions. The duration of aspects can vary from two months (Moon aspects, since it moves about a degree a month in the system) to lifetime aspects, when a slow moving, outer planet remains in a one-degree orb through the first three months of life. When we equate one day with one year, a life of 90 years has been symbolized in the sky during the first three months of babyhood. Often, a progressed aspect lasting several years will clearly symbolize the period in the life, pinpointing the issue, though we never know exactly what the person will do with the opportunity. The long-term progressed aspects are especially important keys to basic, foundation principles in the person's nature.

Where Secondary Progressions equate a day (the period during which the Sun appears to go around the Earth as the Earth rotates) with a year (the time during which the Earth actually goes around the Sun), **Tertiary Progressions** equate a day (Sun apparently going around Earth) with a lunar month (Moon going around Earth). **Minor Progressions** (taught by the Church of Light in California) equate a lunar month (Moon around Earth) with a year (Earth around Sun). Both of these alternate forms of progressions use the Moon's motion, but in different ways.

All three systems of progressions can be diagrammed in two different ways. I prefer the technique of keeping the natal chart always in the center and moving the progressed planets and angles in an outer circle which retains the natal house cusps. In this system, the slow planets normally stay in the same house while the faster planets move forward into different houses. The alternate system sets up a new progressed chart, using the progressed MC and its appropriate houses. Using the latter technique, the faster planets will normally "stay even" with their birthplace houses while the slow planets will be moved backward into different houses. As usual with alternate techniques, each have their enthusiastic supporters, so you can suspect that both work and give part of the picture. In such cases, unless you have time to do an incredible variety of charts, it is most practical to experiment with all the techniques on your own chart. Then decide which gives the clearest picture, and stick to that system. Since life is a mirror, we usually attract people who are like us in many basic ways, and the system that works best for us is likely to work reasonably well for them.

There are also two different techniques for progressing the angles of the chart, each with ardent supporters. My preference involves adding the Solar Arc (the distance the Sun has moved from natal to progressed position) to the MC and then calculating the rest of the angles (Ascendant, Eastpoint, Antivertex) for that MC. The alternate system takes the sidereal time from the ephemeris for the date of the progressions, and calculates all the angles as was done in the natal chart, using the natal time of birth. This method is called the Right Ascension of the mean sun. The two systems will get quite different results, especially for individuals born in the summer or winter when the Sun is slower or faster. As with many other uncertainties in astrology, there are no final answers. Each student either tries the techniques out personally and makes a choice, or accepts what is taught by a teacher or book.

As was indicated in the last chapter, if a person has moved from the place of birth, it is important to also do the houses for the current place of residence. If the new local angles have close aspects, they may be more important than weakly aspected birthplace house cusps. Almost always in astrology, many close aspects are the key to power and prominence of the relevant part of the nature. Aspects show an interaction between one life urge and other urges. The drives or desires may reinforce each other or they may conflict with each other. In either event, they are important. I have seen numerous cases in which both the natal local angles and progressed local angles were highly meaningful and useful as keys to the character and consequent destiny. The Local (or relocation) Chart is calculated as if the person had been born at the current place of residence. The Greenwich time is kept constant so the planets are identical, but the houses change.

In addition to transits, several types of directions and several types of progressions, there are several varieties of **returns**. A return chart is calculated for the exact time that the Sun or Moon or a planet returns to its natal position in transits. The varieties are logically named **Solar Return, Lunar Return, Sol-lunar** (when the transiting Moon conjuncts the natal Sun each month) and **Diurnals**, which are daily charts. The latter may be calculated for the birth time and used for the next 24 hours, or they may be calculated for the beginning of each day. Some astrologers set up a chart for the moment they get out of bed. As you can readily see, it is quite possible to spend so much time doing charts, there is no time left for living. Most of the people I have known who have poured over daily charts or transits have lived afraid of the planets. I don't know whether they developed the fear through their obsessive concentration on astrology, or whether they were simply fearful people, needing to develop some faith in a Higher Power. Either way, the result turned a potentially useful tool for self-knowledge into a destructive prison. Such individuals seem like people squinting into a mirror, moaning over each new wrinkle which they believe the mirror is producing.

For return charts to achieve accurate angles, the calculations must be very precise. The natal Sun must be known to the second. Calculators, computers or a table of diurnal planetary motions can give sufficient accuracy. Logarithms are not accurate. All return charts can be calculated for both the birthplace and the current place of residence. Some astrologers also advise using the chart for your location at the time of the return, even going to spend the birthday at a place where a favorable Solar Return would be produced. Since the planets cannot be altered, they look for a place anywhere on earth that will give harmonious aspects between the planets and the local angles. In one such case, an astrologer had advised a woman client to go to Turkey for her birthday, to be sure of a good year. She went, and the week after her return home, she fell and broke her leg. I would judge that either the technique or the astrologer was not very reliable. Since I believe that character creates destiny, I do not think we can manipulate the world by choosing a favorable place for our birthday. However, our faith is a major power in our lives, so if we truly believe in the technique, it might help some of the time. I think the local chart is highly important **while** we are in that location, and that it ceases to be relevant when we leave it. However, if we have ties to another place, such as a central office of our business or a close relative living there, our house cusps in that area will be useful. We never lose our natal chart (from our birthplace). It accompanies us wherever we go, even if our parents went to a city for our birth and we have never actually lived there.

Still another type of chart for current patterns is the **Kinetic Return**, calculated for the moment the transiting planet (Sun, Moon, etc.) reaches the exact position of the progressed planet. I first heard about kinetic returns at an astrology conference in 1980. They are complicated to calculate since both the progressed and the transiting bodies are moving, though at very different speeds. But my son, Mark, wrote a program to let the computer do the work, and I have found the technique quite interesting. It provided the clearest indication of Reagan's defeat of Carter in the 1980 election of any of the systems that I tried. I have not had time to test it extensively, but have continued to be impressed when I did try it.

In all return charts, the key factor (Sun, Moon, planet) will be identical with its natal position (or its progressed position in kinetic returns), but the rest of the chart will show the transits for the time of the chart. The chart is considered a key to the period until the next return, so a Solar Return lasts for a year; a Lunar Return, for a lunar month (about 28 days); a Mars Return for about two years. Returns for the outer planets cannot give really accurate angles since the slow movement makes it impossible to pinpoint a minute when the return is exact.

It has been mentioned that directions and progressions are normally limited to a one-degree orb on aspects. Transits and returns usually require a wider orb, closer to a natal chart. I consider a one-degree orb always important, while a three-degree orb is still relatively important. As was indicated in the chapter on aspects, there will be cases where planet A is aspecting planet B within one degree; planet B is aspecting planet C within one degree; planet C is aspecting planet D within one degree. Planet A is not within orb of an aspect to planet D, but the whole network must be considered linked together and related through the overlapping aspects. Also, one aspect is not enough. One aspect is certainly part of the picture, but any important message (natally or in current patterns) will be repeated over and over again in the chart. For really big changes in the life, there will always be aspects to the angles, either natal or progressed, birthplace or local. Often, there will be several aspects involving angles. As mentioned above, it is the usual lack of angles that weakens transits as a system. The weakness of Solar Returns is that a year is a long period with changes throughout it, and a static chart once a year is often inadequate. The weakness of Solar Arc Directions is the artificiality of exact two-year periods for all aspects. Tertiaries are complicated to calculate, but tables are provided in my book on *Progressions, Directions and Rectification*.

Out of all these techniques, my personal preferred system is secondary progressions, with Solar Arc Directions my next choice. When we see in our own experience that all the systems work for the big events in our lives, it becomes obvious that the whole thing is a symbol system. We can't say, "Mars is doing it," if in one system we get the message from Mars; in another system it is a planet in Aries; in still another technique a planet in the first house offers the key; and another technique shows it with a planet ruling the first house. The same themes will show, but in different ways in each different technique. The symbolic nature of the system becomes even more inescapable when we note the importance of the angles of the chart which are the intersections of imaginary circles that we have projected against the sky; when the local angles also work; when we can arbitrarily progress these imaginary circles in different ways and they simply give us the message again. When the tiniest little asteroid we can find proves just as meaningful and important as the Sun, the center of the solar system, again we are driven to see that the meaning is there in the cosmos, but those little chunks of rock and ice are not "making it happen." The cosmic order is there. The sky is a visible part of it. Any way we divide it, multiply it, manipulate it, we will still see the same order in a slightly different way. But we are living our lives, creating our character with every decision, every action, and our evolving character is creating our destiny. Our choices today decide our destiny tomorrow. With the help of the mirror in the sky, we can make wiser choices.

CHAPTER 10

Healing: The Power of Mind and Spirit

Whether called mental, psychic or spiritual healing, humans have drawn help from nonmaterial sources as far back as we can trace with writing, even in virtually all primitive groups studied by anthropology. The healers described here have used a variety of approaches. They have lived widely different personal lives. They have held commitments to an assortment of faiths or belief systems. Yet all have been successful as healers. We are forced to suspect that the personal beliefs may be largely myth. Experience is real. Our explanations of the experience are partial at best, and pure fantasy at worst. Yet we cannot do without the beliefs. They guide and shape our lives. If we can keep our beliefs conscious and open-ended, they can help us. If we think that anything coming out of our unconscious is the voice of God, that we have reached final Truth and have nothing left to learn, put up the red flags! Or, as a frequently inebriated acquaintance of my youth used to say, "Get off the train. The track's coming."

Arthur Ford

Three of the healers selected for inclusion are still living. The name and data of one will not be included to protect her privacy, but the other two are still working publicly as far as I know. The first three individuals to be presented have graduated to the next level of life. One of the best known of the latter group is Arthur Ford. Three books have been written about his life. I recommend the first, *Nothing So Strange* by Ford and Bro, if you can find it. Marguerite Bro and Arthur Ford were among the founders of Spiritual Frontiers Fellowship (SFF), an organization devoted to calling attention to the psychic gifts described in the Bible, seeking to restore them to their rightful place in Christian churches. SFF has chapters in many parts of the United States, and they offer a variety of services including regional and national conferences every year. Arthur Ford wanted to see psychic phenomena accepted as a normal part of life, and SFF continues to work toward his dream.

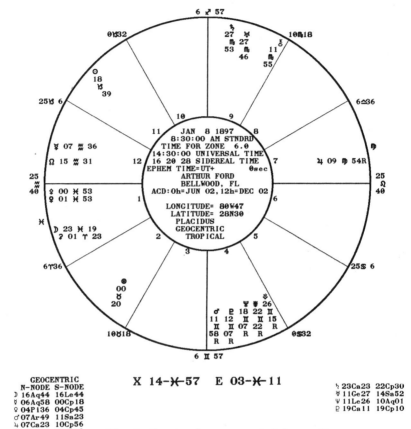

X 14-♓-57   E 03-♓-11

The Antivertex is represented by an X.

I have included Ford with the healers since it was a part of his ministry to humanity, though he is best known as a trance medium. He discovered his psychic gift while still a young man. Some of his disconcerting psychic experiences occurred while he was in military service during World War I. Night after night, Ford would dream of the names of the men who would be reported killed in action, and the next day, his dream list would be posted. After the war, Ford became a minister in the Church of Christ, and began his lifelong effort to bring together his faith and his psychic experiences. He remained a gifted psychic through experiences that would have destroyed a weaker man, including near-death in an accident, drug addiction from the pain-relieving drugs given him during recovery, and alcoholism after he used that "legal" escape to free himself from the drug dependency. He fought alcoholism the rest of his life, and yet he produced incredible quantities of evidential psychic information that helped countless people. For many individuals, his ability to describe their "dead" relatives, the events of their lives, their problems and solutions, including events yet to come, helped them to find a greater faith. People came as total strangers, often as skeptics, to be shaken as this "sleeping" man described intimate details in their lives. In his final years, as his health failed, Ford tried to focus his waning strength on work with materialistic scientists, attempting to prove to them that there was more to life than physical matter spinning in probability orbits.

Ford's birth data was given to me personally. He said that a horoscope had been published as his but that it was for the wrong year. We can note the Aquarius rising with additional power in air from Mercury and the North Node in Aquarius; Pallas conjunct Eastpoint and Ascendant, plus the stellium in Gemini. Since Mars is in Gemini in addition to the rising Aquarius, he is strongly identified with the conscious mind, seeking all his life to learn and to teach. With Uranus and Saturn, co-rulers of the rising Aquarius, both in Scorpio as well as Mars conjunct Pluto, he was also deeply identified with Letter Eight, the urge to probe the unconscious, the search for self-knowledge and self-mastery. The water side of the nature was further supported by Pallas, Venus, Antivertex, Eastpoint and Moon in Pisces, as well as Chiron in Scorpio and activity in the fourth and twelfth houses. Mars could also be considered widely conjunct Neptune, and the first house Moon again repeats the water theme. Charts that emphasize air and water are especially helpful for psychics and psychotherapists. The conscious and unconscious aspects of the mind are emphasized, and if connected by aspects as they are here, there is often an ability to bring out the contents of the unconscious. It is through our own unconscious that we are open to the world beyond physical senses and logic.

Fire is present in the chart mainly through the strong first and ninth houses, though Ceres is in Aries and the South Node is in Leo. Since I consider the South Node a lesson, Ford was learning to handle his emotional needs and vulnerability in relationships with others. The water (signs and planets) in the fire (first and ninth) houses would tend to inhibit the fire, but the spontaneity and creativity and confidence could express easily through the air, i.e., in thought and speech. Since Jupiter is one ruler of the identity (as co-ruler of the first house), its placement in the earth sign Virgo could indicate practicality, although there is always the danger of projection of the part of ourselves in the seventh or eighth houses. His Capricorn Sun in the eleventh house shows a drive to be practical and productive, to climb to the top in a unique career. I see the Sun as more a growth goal than an accomplished reality, and its position in the eleventh house supports practical achievement as a future goal. (We often "grow into'' eleventh house placements). His personal idealism and the importance of religion in his life is suggested by the One/Twelve (Pisces in the first house) and One/Nine (Uranus and Saturn ruling Ascendant in the ninth house; Pluto ruling the ninth conjunct Mars) blends.

The water-air emphasis in a chart is associated with a more passive, receptive form of psychic ability which was the primary feature in Ford's professional work. But he also had the power to go into a self-induced trance which requires the capacity to concentrate or focus, and he did work as a spiritual healer on occasion, a talent I also associate with an ability to focus. Letters Six, Eight, and Ten in our astrological alphabet are the ones most able to concentrate, especially in their planetary form Vesta, Pluto and Saturn. As already noted, Ford's chart is strongly Scorpio with Jupiter in Virgo. He has Vesta closely quincunx Saturn as well as Uranus, the other ruler of the Ascendant. Uranus and Saturn widely conjunct the MC (more Letter Ten). Juno is at the midpoint of Neptune (another ruler of the first house) and Vesta, with Vesta trine Ascendant, all of which strengthens the tie between personal action and Vesta. Pluto is just nine minutes from Mars in a lifetime progressed conjunction. In spite of the relative passivity of the air-water emphasis, these aspects show a natural ability to concentrate, to control the mind.

Unfortunately, we do not yet have positions for the 15 new asteroids for the period before 1900. The planetary nodes may offer a little consolation. The strongest node aspects are the placement of the nodes of Pluto conjunct and opposite Ford's natal Sun, and the North Node of Uranus conjunct while the South Node of Mars opposes Ford's natal Mars-Pluto. He also has the North Node of Mercury exactly on his natal Mercury. All of these aspects have offered themes that repeat the natal chart. The conscious mind is again emphasized (Mercury). The urge to explore the unconscious and to gain self-mastery (Pluto), while the Mars-Uranus mixture echos the restlessness that kept him moving, traveling, searching all his life. He never quite mananged his lessons (relationships and appetite mastery), and that may be why he opposed the idea of reincarnation: he didn't want to face having to do it again. But his life touched and helped the lives of many who wanted more than a book or a guru. They wanted evidence that there was something beyond this world, and they got their evidence from Arthur Ford.

Daddy Bray

While Arthur Ford spent his life trying to restore the psychic gifts to the Christian Church, Daddy Bray spent his life recovering and presenting the ancient faith of his forbears. The religion of Hawaii at the time of its discovery by Europeans was called *Huna*, and its practitioner priests were called *Kahunas*. David Bray did not come from a Kahuna family; normally, the teaching was passed down from parent to child. But he wanted the knowledge, and he was persistent enough to persuade a Kahuna to take him in as an apprentice so that, in time, he became a fully practicing Kahuna. Unlike Ford, Bray married and had a family. In fact, one of his daughters married a close relative of the well-known parapsychology researcher, Dr. Andrija Puharich. Puharich reports a fascinating personal experience while on a visit to Hawaii. While Daddy Bray was performing his normal healing ritual, Puharich suddenly found himself able to see into the body of the woman patient. As an M.D., Puharich was able to understand the internal problem which remained visible while he was in the company of Daddy Bray. In his later years, Bray came to the continental United States several times to lecture on his healing practices and Huna faith. At one of his lectures, I was able to get his birth data from him.

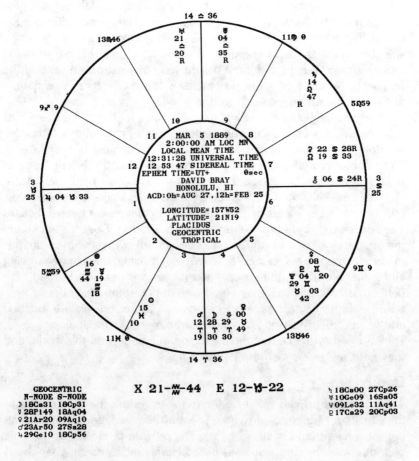

We can see some interesting parallels to the chart of Arthur Ford. Uranus is a ruler of the first house (a few degrees of Aquarius fall in the

first house) and it is in the tenth house. With the strong Capricorn identification, Bray would naturally seek to run his own show and not be subject to anyone else. However, we note that Saturn, ruler of the Ascendant, is in the eighth house, so there is a potential (as there was in Ford's
chart) for feeling vulnerable to others. When any key to Letter One (personal identity) is in Letter Seven or Eight, especially in the houses, but
to a lesser extent in the signs, there are six possible variations we can
choose in our reaction to this feeling. We can give our power to others
and remain dependent and vulnerable. A man with strength in Capricorn,
Aries, Taurus and Leo, signs and houses, is unlikely to do that. We can
try to keep all the power. If a person is truly spiritual, he or she will not
do that. We can retreat from closeness, to protect ourselves from being
hurt. Ford did this, but Bray, with his strong fire-earth combinations, could
stand up to the world. His fire-earth mixtures include Jupiter in Capricorn,
Saturn in Leo and Vesta in Aries, as well as the Capricorn in the first house.
The three positive ways to handle the potential projection of personal
power (first house rulers in Seven or Eight) include sharing the power
through cooperation and compromise, healthy competition, and helping
people. In the latter, we keep the power but use it constructively. Bray
certainly did that. I am not so sure he worked out the capacity to
compromise, which his Saturn in the eighth house suggests was part of
his lesson. But he played a role in bringing his native faith to a wider audience, and his personal healing work assisted many of his own people.

We can see indications of psychic ability in Bray's Neptune-Pluto conjunction and in the water signs and houses, but there is much less of the
passive-receptive and more of the control. Vesta is in a powerful conjunction with Moon and Venus, with its presence in the fourth house as well
as the aspect to the Moon often indicating a problem connected to the
mother. Sometimes the mother is ill. Sometimes the child is alienated for
a variety of reasons. Often there is hard work in the early life when we
have a work sign rising, a ruler in a work house, plus Vesta in the fourth.
I think Bray was born into a poor family and his mastery of Huna let him
achieve the power and security he wanted. The fourth house Venus normally shows affection in the home, and the capacity for an attractive home
which he achieved in time. As with Ford, we lack the new asteroids, but
can check the planetary nodes. Both South Jupiter and South Pluto fall
on Bray's first house South Node of the Moon, suggesting a lesson in personal power. Either overdrive or self-blocking would be possible, but the
general power in the chart makes overdrive the more likely danger. As
readers know, the rising Jupiter has been found in actors, politicians and
Nazi leaders in the Gauquelins' work, but I have also seen it often in
spiritual or intellectual leaders. As a Kahuna priest, Daddy Bray chose the
spiritual path, and for the most part, seems to have used his power well.

Katherine Kuhlman

Our third healer is the well-known Katherine Kuhlman, a Christian evangelist who crisscrossed the country as a preaching revivalist from the age of 16, discovered her healing ability in her thirties, and from then on was a channel for truly miraculous cures. Her primary headquarters was Pittsburgh, but she was a traveling missionary all her life. Her visits to Los Angeles in her later years would fill the largest auditorium in the city, and thousands would still be turned away. I attended her healing services twice, and was a witness to the power that flowed through her. After hymn singing, led by a large choir, and exhortations (real, fundamentalist revival type), Kuhlman would go into a semitrance and point to different parts of the audience announcing cures for various ailments. Soon, people would begin to stream up on stage, to testify that they had been in that area of the auditorium and that they had been cured of the problem Kuhlman had mentioned.

During one of the sessions that I attended, a woman came up to report that she had attended the previous service, two weeks before; she had a chronic back problem diagnosed as the disintegration of the bones in two of her vertebrae of the spinal column. The doctor had put her in a brace, said there was nothing more that could be done, and that she would have pain the rest of her life. In the service, Kuhlman had pointed to the upper balcony where this woman was sitting and had announced that someone up there was being cured of a back problem. At the time she was saying this, the woman felt as if a hot poker was pressing her back in the painful area; then the pain was gone. She felt that she had received a healing, went down to the ladies' room and removed her brace, and still felt fine. But she waited until she had returned to her doctor for a checkup. X rays showed the bones replaced in her spine, and after that, she returned to testify to the healing on Kuhlman's next visit to Los Angeles.

Another of the testimonies during my attendance came from a mother and a teenaged boy. The latter had been born deaf, and had heard for the first time during the service. The mother was practically hysterical with excitement. One of Kuhlman's favorite stunts with individuals who had come in wheelchairs and who found themselves able to walk again, was to have the former patients put the ushers in the wheelchairs and push them across the stage. But the incredible power working through Kuhlman was shown most dramatically when she held her hands up in a blessing, close to the heads of the individuals who came to the stage to testify to a healing. Almost without exception, the people being blessed would stagger as if they had received an electric shock, and most of them actually fainted and fell. The ushers were there, waiting to catch them and lay them gently on the floor. In a few moments, they would regain consciousness and be helped up again. Twice, as too many people filled the stage for Kuhlman to talk to them individually about their healing, she simply walked along the row with her hands in the air saying, "Bless you, bless you," and they went down like a row of dominos. I have only seen one other healer with that kind of energy charge: a young man in Cincinnati named Bill Boshears.

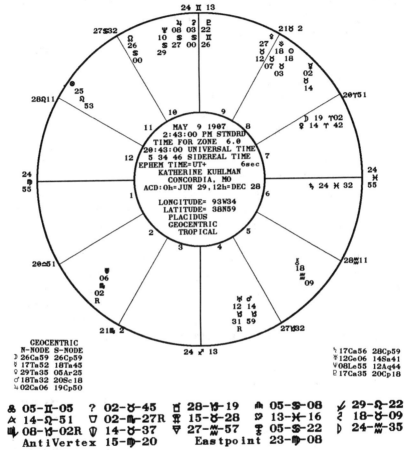

GEOCENTRIC
N-NODE S-NODE
☽ 26Ca59 26Cp59
☿ 17Ta52 18Ta45
♀ 29Ta35 05Ar25
♂ 18Ta32 20Sc18
♃ 02Ca06 19Cp50

♄ 17Ca56 28Cp59
♅ 12Ge06 14Sa41
♆ 08Le55 12Aq44
♇ 17Ca35 20Cp18

☊ 05-Ⅱ-05   ? 02-♉-45   ♇ 28-♑-19   ♏ 05-♋-08   ⚹ 29-♌-22
⚷ 14-♌-51   ℧ 02-♏-27R   ⚵ 15-♉-28   ♋ 13-♓-16   ♄ 18-♉-09
♍ 08-♑-02R   ⚕ 14-♉-37   ♆ 27-♒-57   ♇ 05-♋-22   ☽ 24-♒-35
AntiVertex 15-♍-20   Eastpoint 23-♍-08

Katherine Kuhlman's time of birth is not exact. Her aunt reported that she came to the house at around four PM, to find Katherine's mother nursing a newly born baby. I had very few timed events in her life, so chose this time to let the progressed MC conjunct Jupiter and Neptune in her teens, when she had an intense religious experience, stopped her earlier rebellion against the establishment, left school and started barnstorming across the country. Her strong cardinal dilemma shows the potential of the changes of home, work and relationships as she went from one small church to another as an itinerant preacher. For those who want to explore her life and her beliefs in more depth, Allan Spragett has written a biography about her, and she has written two books about her faith.

Throughout her life, she maintained firmly that Jesus and the Holy Spirit worked through her; she was only a channel. She is an outstanding example for me of the reality of experience in contrast to the dubious nature of the ideas offered to explain the experience. If there is an Infinite, it has to be too big to be limited to one religion. It must be available to some extent through all belief systems. But Kuhlman, like most convinced fundamentalists, could not accept anything outside of a narrow, literal faith in the Christian Bible. Since only men were appointed to be ministers, she allowed no women ministers on stage, though male and female doctors and male ministers were welcome at all times. When someone logically pointed out to her that she was a woman doing religious work, she said that she was only doing it because no men were doing it. As soon as a man came to take her place, she would step down. Since no man appeared to replace her, she continued to enjoy the show and to be a channel for miracles.

If my selected birth time is approximately accurate, Kuhlman has Pluto conjunct her MC and Saturn conjunct her Descendant. Both seem fitting. She certainly worked with the power of the unconscious and had an enormous impact on the lives of thousands of people. She also had serious problems with personal relationships, including one short and disastrous early marriage which she would never discuss. The eighth house Vesta and Saturn remaining on her Descendant most of her life (if the time is right) are both keys to working with people, but require careful handling in personal relationships. The dangers of work themes in relationship areas include displacement of the critical work attitude (a search for flaws and trying to make the situation over) into the personal area. Or, we can pick someone else who is critical of and tries to change us. Or, the work may be so important to us or to the other person that the relationship is neglected. Working together helps to solve the problem.

The tight Vesta-Sun conjunction, which is present regardless of exact birth time, is one of the most important features in Kuhlman's chart. As mentioned in the chapter on asteroids, many healers have a prominent Vesta. It seems to be the capacity to become totally focused into the job; a kind of tunnel vision which can bring great success, but sometimes with alienation of personal relationships. The Neptune-Jupiter conjunction is a key to a deep spiritual drive, however the person expresses it. (The current Pope, John Paul II, has the conjunction in Leo.) Along with Saturn in Pisces and Vesta progressing into the ninth house, the tenth house placement of Neptune and Jupiter shows the potential of an idealistic profession. The Cancer in the tenth house, especially with Ceres there, also indicates a professional mother. She never had children of her own, but nurtured many in her work with the public. With her South Node of the Moon in the fourth house and her Saturn in Pisces, one of her lessons was probably in dependency. The Cancer-Capricorn polarity can indicate a struggle between dependency and dominance, or between home and family vs. career. She chose career and personal achievement. She also has the "identity in the hands of others" as did Ford and Bray, with her Venus and Mercury, rulers of the first house, as well as Aries, all in the seventh and eighth houses: a repeated theme. She chose to help others, but, like Bray, I'm not sure whether she ever worked out the capacity to compromise. Perhaps that total commitment was essential for her to tap the universal power in the way she did. Compromise can lead to mediocrity. Certainly few women have shaken the multitudes as she did.

Since Katherine Kuhlman was born in the twentieth century, we are able to add the fifteen new asteroids to her chart. As mentioned repeatedly, we will mostly note the ones that have close aspects. Hidalgo stands out, in an exact (within one degree) conjunction to Kuhlman's natal Sun-Vesta. Amor and Sappho are also present in Taurus in the eighth house, somewhat more widely conjunct Sun-Vesta-Hidalgo. If Hidalgo is a key to achievement drive, a sort of "little brother" to Saturn, its placement on the Sun indicates high ambition while the contact with Vesta suggests intense potential for focus and concentration. In effect, we may have Virgo (Vesta), Scorpio (eighth house) and Capricorn (Hidalgo) together, the three **obsessive-compulsive** sides of life, with the Sun adding drama, creativity and power. Amor and Sappho close to the Sun add emphasis to the desire for love, but Vesta and Hidalgo choose work. If love needs are not met, sensuality may be substituted in the search for pleasure, especially in view of the Taurus emphasis. At the end of Kuhlman's life, she fought with a long-time manager of her affairs, and he accused her of wasteful spending on luxury and secret drinking. She reacted to the blow to her reputation, her public image, with a heart attack and died of heart failure within a year afterwards. I suspect that even the greatest of our teachers are also still learning something, or they would not return to physical bodies.

Two of the new asteroids, Toro and Frigga, are in Cancer between Kuhlman's Ceres and Jupiter in her tenth house. Frigga supports the desire for emotional warmth, but the house and the rest of the planets in the stellium suggest a career nurturing the public rather than a family of her own. Lilith in Capricorn is exactly opposite Jupiter and more widely conjunct Uranus and Mars in Capricorn in the fourth house, showing again the struggle between home and career. Oppositions across the fourth and tenth houses show conflict between these two parts of life. We can alternate, or try to do some of both at once, or (as Kuhlman did) choose a career which involves emotional warmth with people. Pittsburghia is also in Capricorn and is conjunct the South Node of the Moon, but in the fifth house if her time is accurate. The combination with the South Node shows a lesson connected to power and love and career; basically, the same repeated theme.

With both South Node and Letter Ten (Saturn, tenth house, Capricorn) we have a similar message. Their placement in a chart indicates an area of life where we first have to learn something, and then we have to give something. With Letter Ten, we learn the rules of the game and then are able to establish a career and be productive with our share of the power of the Law. The South Node lessons involve our need for emotional security. For most people, this reassurance is sought through human relationships. When we have found a sense of security, we can share it with others. It is fascinating that Kuhlman's South Node in Capricorn is conjunct Pittsburghia. It was in the Pittsburgh area of the U.S. that Kuhlman discovered her healing power, her gift to the world which became her career, her role in society.

Another interesting pattern involves Dembowska exactly conjunct Kuhlman's Mercury in Taurus in the eighth house with both of them opposite Pandora in Scorpio in the second house. The combination seems to fit her verbal facility but lack of any formal education, as well as the restlessness that kept her traveling much of her life, constantly meeting new people. She demonstrated a very practical mind on financial affairs, but apparently lacked or never developed much capacity for abstract thought. If Dembowska is like Saturn, the conjunction with Mercury in the Scorpio house is another indication of her ability to control and focus her mind. Kuhlman's Eros in Pisces fits a pattern I have seen in others who dreamed of romance but took little or no action, and in some who chose a spiritual life in place of marriage. Urania in Leo in the eleventh house square her five-way conjunction in mid-Taurus and quincunx Eros, suggests the freedom-closeness dilemma, also said by her Aries squares to Cancer and to the fourth house planets. They can also show the potential of power struggles over money or possessions or pleasure. In general, there is immense power in the chart with the fixed and cardinal emphasis. Certainly, the power demonstrated in her healing services was not her personal power, but it took a very strong lady to channel that kind of universal energy. No one can do everything well, and no one in modern times has even approached Katherine Kuhlman's record of dramatic, inexplicable healings.

Miss A: Healer

Two of the healers being presented in this chapter were born in the same year just two and a half months apart, though on different continents. Both gave me their birth data in a personal contact. Both are still living, but the first to be discussed is in semiretirement, so to protect her privacy, I will not give her name. She was one of the psychics who was featured (under a pseudonym) in *Breakthrough to Creativity*, by Shaffica Karagulla, M.D., published by DeVorss. I suspect the book is out of print, but if you can locate a copy, you should find it fascinating. Miss A (for anonymous) was initially trained as a medical technician, and much of her psychic work has been as a diagnostician though she also has worked as a healer. At this point in her life, she works only with M.D.'s who send samples from patients who are difficult to diagnose. Miss A picks up psychic impressions from the item (an article of clothing, a blood sample) and mails her diagnosis to the doctor. Her record is reported to be consistently above 90% accuracy, which is phenomenal for psychic work. Medical diagnostic accuracy, in contrast, is not much better than 50% much of the time. Read Dr. Norman Shealy's book *Psychic Medicine May Save Your Life* for an eye-opener.

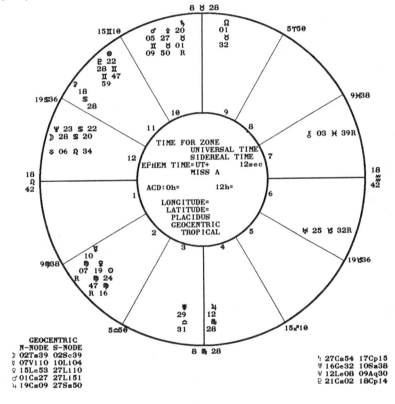

GEOCENTRIC

N-NODE	S-NODE
☽ 02Ta39	02Sc39
☿ 07Vi10	10Li04
♀ 15Le53	27Li10
♂ 01Ca27	27Li51
♃ 19Ca09	27Sa50

♄ 27Ca54	17Cp15
♅ 16Ge32	10Sa38
♆ 12Le08	09Aq30
♇ 21Ca02	18Cp14

& 17-♊-54   ? 19-♏-58R   ♍ 13-♐-37   ♈ 10-♌-06   ⚷ 19-♌-28
⚹ 25-♎-09   ♒ 17-♎-00   ♀ 26-♌-54   ♐ 03-♍-03   ♄ 13-♏-15
♏ 06-♐-00   ♒ 04-♓-02R   ♇ 18-♐-58   ♇ 05-♐-12   ♃ 27-♑-03
AntiVertex 08-♋-39   Eastpoint 03-♌-46

A first impression of Miss A's horoscope shows a major emphasis on earth and water, the combination that can produce the father-mother-savior syndrome. She has a grand trine in earth signs and houses, including Saturn in Taurus in its own house, Venus-Sun conjunct in Virgo in the Taurus house and Uranus in the Virgo house in Capricorn. Mercury, also in Virgo in the second house, trines the Taurus MC and (more widely)

the North node of the Moon in Taurus in the ninth house. The combination indicates not only someone who is able to support herself and work
efficiently, but someone driven to work, likely to feel guilty if she is not
working and likely to be highly uncomfortable with dependency. On the
other hand, the strong water in the chart, including Antivertex, Ceres, Neptune and Moon in Cancer and South Node and Jupiter in Scorpio, with
some of them also in water houses, could manifest as either being dependent or being nurturant and caring for others. Normally, such a combination will be more comfortable caring for others, especially if there is also
some fire. The Leo rising adds warmth and confidence to the picture. Vesta
and the Eastpoint (like another Ascendant) conjunct in Leo repeat the fire
strength and the need to work. Mars in the tenth house again identifies
with career and power and indicates reluctance to be dependent. Planets
in the eleventh house, including Pluto, again show commitment to the
transpersonal area of life and reluctance to be dependent. So you will
not be surprised to learn that Miss A never married. With the rulers of
the seventh house Aquarius, Saturn and Uranus, both in earth signs and
houses, she could only have tolerated a person much committed to work,
and she was successfully handling that part of her life herself, so did not
need the financial support. Juno, the marriage asteroid, is conjunct the
South Node of the Moon, showing marriage to be a lesson area. It is also
quincunx Pallas, the other Libra asteroid, suggesting the potential of a
critical attitude (the south node) and letting go of that part of life (the quincunx). Juno also squares the Moon and Uranus. Since the latter rules the
marriage house and Juno is a "natural" ruler, the square can indicate conflict in that part of life even when there are no planets in that house.

Although Miss A did not want marriage, with all except two of her
keys to instinctive identity (all forms of Letter One) in earth signs and/or
houses, she does have Leo rising and the Antivertex in Cancer, both
associated with home and children. She also has that Cancer Moon, but
in the twelfth house. She wanted children, but chose to adopt them, one
of the possible ways of expressing the Letter Twelve idealism when the
Moon is associated with the transpersonal part of life. In her time, it was
almost unheard of for a single woman to be permitted to adopt a child,
but Miss A knows what she wants and has the capacity to go after it —
not with theatricals, despite the Leo Ascendant, but with quiet earth persistence and practicality. She adopted two boys who needed a home and
mother, so was able to enjoy the mother role in person as well as in helping and healing others in her work. We can note that Jupiter rules her
fifth house (the capacity for procreation), which again connects idealism
to home and family, as did the Moon conjunct Neptune in Cancer in the
twelfth house. Ceres (as another key to mothering) in Cancer right at the
cusp of the twelfth house repeats the theme again. When we note that
Neptune is the midpoint of Ceres and Moon, what initially seems a wide

aspect with an orb of five degrees becomes the equivalent of Ceres and Moon exactly conjunct Neptune, a very strong bond between idealism and mothering.

As already indicated, water symbolizes the unconscious part of the mind which is open to, connected to, the rest of the cosmos. The Cancer grouping just mentioned includes two water planets in a water sign and house, with Neptune strengthened by being in its own house and Moon strengthened by being in its own sign. Putting together two different forms of one letter in our astrological alphabet is one of the simplest ways to repeat a theme, and any repetition is an indication of the increased importance of that part of the nature. The Moon is also very closely semi-sextile Pluto, the third water planet, repeating the water emphasis in the nature. With Pluto in an air sign and house, we have the potential of bringing the contents of the unconscious up into consciousness. Next to water factors in a chart (planets, houses and signs), Uranus is often a key to developing psychic ability. Letter Eleven symbolizes the urge to go beyond all earlier limits, and the capacity to take in the whole perspective almost in one gulp. The Uranus opposition to Moon-Neptune and its quincunx to Pluto, connects it to all the truly psychic planets, and adds to the potential for interest in the area and possible skill there. Mercury is trioctile Uranus and octile Neptune-Moon, bringing the other major air planet of conscious intellect into the pattern. The combination indicates the capacity for both an excellent, practical and thorough mind, but also the openness to the psychic. It is common for people with an earth emphasis in their natures to be skeptical of psychic impressions; to want tangible proof before they can trust anything. But once they have satisfied themselves that the psychic ability is dependable and useful, they will use it, commonly turning it into a profession as was done by Miss A.

When the new asteroids are added to the horoscope, we see many repetitions of the themes already discussed. Hidalgo closely conjunct Jupiter in Scorpio in the fourth house adds to the potential power, seeks an idealistic career or highly values the career, may make a career of mothering people with depth understanding and psychic openness. Also, she has conducted her psychic work in her own home for years. Lilith and Toro conjunct each other in Sagittarius in the fourth house, opposite Mars, and trine Eastpoint-Vesta, add to the strength of will and the fire self-confidence, along with the Sagittarius faith in a Higher Power. Mars-Toro-Lilith also form a grand cross with two of the asteroids associated with personal love, Eros and Amor, repeating the difficulty in the marriage area. Dembowska in the seventh house may be similar to Saturn there; some caution and possible avoidance if we fear that others may put unacceptable limits on us. I have often found Dembowska associated with overdrive or blocking, so it may eventually be another Letter Ten which is prone to those extremes when not handled with care. We would normally expect a first house Sappho to indicate some interest in affectionate relationships, but it is quincunx Uranus, a primary ruler of the seventh house, repeating the tug of war between relationships and work. Clearly, work won. Psyche very closely conjunct the Ascendant may be another indication of psychic ability or of interest in the workings of the mind. Frigga, potentially another key to the desire for marriage, is in Leo in the twelfth house with Vesta, the midpoint of Eastpoint and Frigga, repeating the theme of work vs. marriage. Icarus, if it is another little Sun or Sun-seeker, is in its own house in Sagittarius repeating the idealization of love and/or children. Pandora and Urania in an air sign and house and both by their own nature potentially associated with the quest for knowledge, support the good mind. If Dudu and Pittsburghia are additional Scorpio keys, the Dudu opposition to Pittsburghia and Icarus, like the South Node of the Moon in Scorpio, indicates a challenge from Letter Eight. The Scorpio lesson may be learning to give, to receive or to share. Miss A gave much throughout her life, but the capacity to be dependent and to receive may have remained a difficult issue. As with the rest of these talented individuals, a major investment of time and energy in one area means neglecting another part of life. We cannot do everything well. So we make our choices. I am sure that the thousands of people who have been helped by Miss A are thankful for her choice.

Yolanda Betegh

Yolanda Betegh was born in Roumania just two and a half months after Miss A's birth in the U.S. I was able to attend a healing demonstration in New York, in which Betegh was featured, and had a chance to talk to her afterwards. She discovered her healing talent when still a young woman, and used it for family and friends initially. After coming to the United States, she worked intensively with an M.D. who was interested in psychic research. She demonstrated other psychic abilities under test conditions, including telepathy. She stated that she had experienced levitation, but it had not occurred during the controlled experimentation. Mrs. Betegh was married and had children and grandchildren. When I saw her, she was surrounded by a group of talkative and happy relatives. She is a very large woman, the only one of our subjects to fit the old stereotype associating mediumship with fluid retention and overweight.

In Betegh's chart we note grand trines in fire and earth, (the early degrees of earth plus Mercury in late Sagittarius.) The Sun-Moon-Ceres trine in fire signs and earth houses is an indication of strong natural enthusiasm, drama and achievement drive: all much in evidence when I saw her. The Sun at the Midheaven and exactly sextile the Ascendant emphasizes her dramatic flair. The Pisces Antivertex (as another Ascendant) plus the Eastpoint (auxiliary Ascendant) conjunct Chiron in Pisces in the first house and trine Pluto but square Jupiter show the idealism that drew

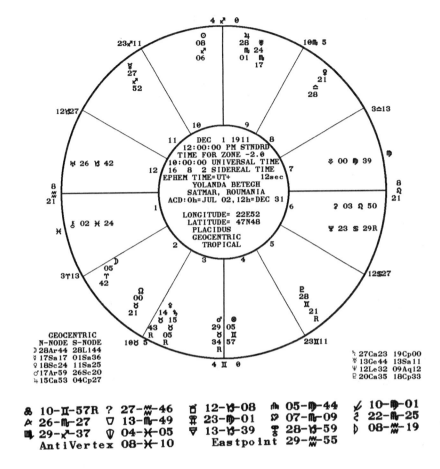

♋ 10-♊-57R   ? 27-♒-46   ⚷ 12-♑-08   ⯛ 05-♍-44   ⚸ 10-♍-01
⚴ 26-♏-27   ▽ 13-♏-49   ⚵ 23-♍-01   ⚶ 07-♏-09   ⚷ 22-♏-25
⯔ 29-♐-37   ⯐ 04-♓-05   ⯑ 13-♑-39   ⚳ 28-♒-59   ☽ 08-♒-19
AntiVertex 08-♓-10   Eastpoint 29-♒-55

her to healing and the psychic openness that played a major role in her life. Mars trine Uranus in earth signs and air and water houses shows the helpful combination of practicality and logic, supported by additional activity in earth and air houses. The potential importance of relatives (as well as the mind) is suggested by the loaded third house. Betegh's idealization of marriage and the mate relationship is shown by the connections of Letters Seven and Eight with Nine and Twelve. Sun (ruling the seventh house) is in Sagittarius. Mercury (also ruling the seventh house) is in Sagittarius. Juno (asteroid of marriage) is in the ninth house and conjunct Jupiter. The nodes across the second and eighth houses point to sensual, sexual issues (potential self-indulgence versus self-control conflicts) and a need for depth sharing. Venus in a partnership sign (Libra) and house (eighth) plus Juno in Scorpio adds to the emphasis on close, personal relationships. Yolanda Betegh shares Miss A's high value placed on children and adds it to grandchildren. With a ruler of the fifth house (Mercury) in the ninth sign and a ruler of the ninth (Pluto) in the fifth house, we have the potential of grandchildren being raised as if they were our children: a close continuing bond. With the Moon ruling the Cancer in her fifth house and placed in Aries, she is identified with fifth house matters. In some cases, this placement indicates a child who is very close, or much like one, and who becomes a role model; a way to see ourselves reflected back. If a chart does not support the desire for home and family, then Moon in Letter One may be reluctant to be tied down by children and may have only one or none.

In Betegh's case, a water planet (Pluto) in the fifth house further supports the importance of home and family, and Pluto's rulership of the ninth house again connects children to ultimate ideals and grandchildren to personal family. Since Letter Nine represents our search for the Absolute and the willingness to go wherever we must to find it, Jupiter, Sagittarius and the ninth house are associated with long distance travel and foreign countries. A ruler of the fourth house (Mercury) in the ninth house or sign (Sagittarius) can therefore indicate the possibility of a home in a foreign country, as is the case here. A wide variety of details can occur with any astrological principle, and often several will manifest. They are not mutually exclusive. So Betegh is making her home in a country other than her birth. She highly values home and family. She is close to her grandchildren, as if they were part of her own immediate family. Her separation from her homeland and frequent travels (at the time I met her, she was commuting between Miami and New York) are further suggested by the Mars opposite Jupiter and quincunx Mercury in the Jupiter sign, Sagittarius, with Mars in the Mercury house. These patterns link letters Three and Nine repeatedly in different ways.

As usual, the new asteroids reinforce many of the same themes already seen with the traditional planets. Three of the asteroids associated with love and/or marriage are in the seventh house: Frigga, Sappho and Psyche. Eros joined Venus in the eighth house. The need for marriage could not be said more emphatically, and Amor on the Eastpoint hammers at it yet again. Chiron, conjunct the Eastpoint in the first house, repeats the idealism and potential for travel in search of answers. Urania conjunct Jupiter in the ninth house adds to the willingness to go beyond traditional answers in the search for Truth. Three asteroids in Capricorn emphasize the practicality and the desire to be in charge of her own life, to move into a power position. She demonstrates her power in her healings and in other forms of "mind over matter" phenomena. She seems to be using her power constructively. With South Node in the eighth house and Saturn in Taurus and conjunct Pallas (an asteroid of partnership), her lessons seem connected to handling the world of money, possessions or sensuality including joint resources and pleasures. Perhaps the primary challenge is in appetite control. My personal contact with her was too brief to acquire any in-depth knowledge of her life, but it appears that Yolanda Betegh has handled her potentials well and is making a real contribution to life without losing out on the interpersonal area of family.

Psychic Surgeons

Our last featured healer is Feliciano Omiles, a psychic surgeon born in the Philippine Islands. Most readers will be familiar with the remarkable development of a unique form of spiritual healing in the general area between Manila and Baguio. Amazing stories and films have circulated for years, with some witnesses convinced that they have seen miracles while others are equally sure that the whole performance is fraud. I was able to visit the Philippines in the fall of 1978, and saw both genuine psychic phenomena and sleight of hand trickery, though not in the same person. A woman healer named Josephine Sisson was genuine and effective. She was totally uneducated, sincere, and dedicated to her service to humanity. There was no charge though a donation was welcome. I took my mother to see her, and Mother was helped in many ways. Cataracts had stopped Mother from reading, but she was able to read after seeing Josephine: and was still reading in 1982, four years later. Mother was also on a very restricted diet because of gallstones, and since seeing Josephine had been able to eat anything she wanted without any problem. Other problems remained or returned after a brief improvement, but in general, there was a major gain in well-being after the visit to Josephine.

Although I did get Josephine's birth date from her, I was not able to understand her place of birth and her time was only approximate, so I do not have a dependable horoscope for her. I was fascinated to find that she had a close Vesta-Sun conjunction, like Katherine Kuhlman. She also had her Moon and Mars conjunct in Aries and told me that she had been ill and had many surgeries herself before she became a healer. She has been very healthy since beginning her spiritual work. During the earlier period, the water Moon could have held in the fire Mars and Aries, especially since they were probably in the tenth house for further danger of inhibition and since, as a woman, the cultural pressures would have pushed in the same direction. Now that she is letting her energy out in the healing, she is healthy. As a child, Josephine saw healers and wanted to become one. She became an apprentice to an established healer and continued to work with him until she developed her own ability. She is also married and has two small children, so has been able to integrate a family with her transpersonal work. That accomplishment is no small feat!

Feliciano Omiles

I have never met Feliciano Omiles, but was given his chart by a friend and decided that it would be a helpful addition to the group of healers since he comes from a very different cultural background than the other healers. Unlike Josephine Sisson, Omiles was born into a family of healers, with both parents and grandparents manifesting the talent. Unfortunately, I do not have any information on his current personal life. I understand that he has worked in the United States and in Mexico on occasion. The U.S. is not friendly to psychic surgeons, and some have been jailed or denied visas which are necessary to enter the country. The official position of the American Medical Association is that they are all frauds and a threat to the public. My own experience included both genuine psychic phenomena as well as sleight of hand, but even the man using trickery was helping people. I talked to several of his patients, and their problems had improved. My impression even with Josephine was that most of the cure came from the faith of the patient. I think that she gave them a charge of psychic (spiritual?) energy which offered temporary help, but unless the person was able to change the emotional tensions which had caused the original problem, it was likely to remain or to return after a time. For many people, the experience of seeing someone actually put her hand inside the body, seeing blood come out, and then seeing the skin closed and normal afterwards, was enough to stimulate intense faith. Medical work in this country with placebos (pills thought to be drugs but actually made of inert substances) has shown that around 50% of the public is given as much help by their faith in the supposed medicine as they would be by an actual drug. And faith has far fewer side effects. Much of the illness in Western countries is now acknowledged to be iatrogenic, that is, caused by the doctor. One drug helps one problem but causes another; another drug is given for the drug-caused problem and it produces a different problem, in endless regress. Among people who are less educated into skepticism, the faith comes more easily and the number who can be helped is correspondingly higher. The healers of the Philippines work in a context of Catholicism, convinced that the power of the Holy Spirit is working through them. As with Katherine Kuhlman, miracles can happen in such a climate of faith.

In Omiles' horoscope, we can see the potential for spiritual or religious parents with Neptune in the tenth house and Pisces in the fourth house; the two houses of parents. The seventh and first houses are the fourth and tenth counting from the fourth and tenth, so are keys to grandparents, parents of parents, just as the ninth house is the fifth from the fifth and therefore potentially children of children. With Sagittarius rising, the first house grandparent is also connected to the search for Something Higher. Ascendant-Saturn-Pluto form a tight grand trine that is mixed fire and water, the emotional elements, while the Cancer Moon conjunct Pluto in the eighth house adds more water for psychic potential. With Saturn in the fourth house, we probably have a fourth house father and a tenth house mother. Mars in Capricorn, as well as conjunct Jupiter, co-ruler of the fourth house Pisces, shows father as major role model. Antivertex conjunct

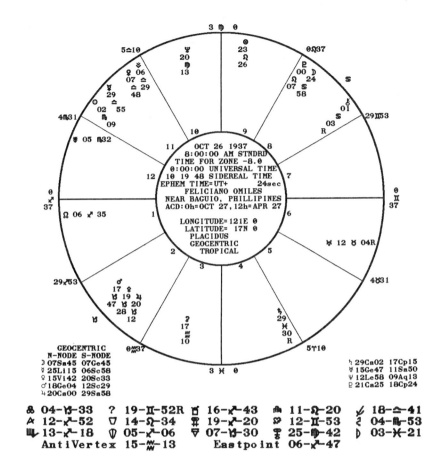

Ceres suggests the mother was also an important role model, while the third house placement may point to a sibling role model. These people around us in our early lives are important since we have a chance to see a part of ourselves reflected back, and we can see what to do or what not to do.

The theme of the new asteroids is clearly an emphasis on the mind, ideals and people. Five of the little planets were in Sagittarius when Omiles was born and two more in the ninth (Sagittarius) house. Two more fall in Gemini, one in Pisces and one in the Pisces house, one in Virgo and one in an air sign and house (Libra in the eleventh house). Only Dudu and Icarus fail to support that mental emphasis. Since I have little information on Omiles' personal or current life, there is little point in speculating on the new asteroids other than to note the unanimity of their support for a life lived largely in the mind. With the South Node of the Moon in the seventh house and Saturn in the fourth house, some of

Omiles' lessons presumably are being learned through personal relationships as well as through integrating his faith and the limits of the possible in a material world. With his Scorpio Sun square Pluto in Leo, his Mars-Jupiter conjunction in Capricorn in the second house, and his Ascendant-Saturn-Pluto grand trine, there is ample power in the chart, and he seems to be using it constructively to help others.

CHAPTER 11

Psychokinesis: Mind Over Matter

The healers discussed in the last chapter could also have been placed in this one. All of them demonstrated some ability to directly influence the material world with their minds, but they used this power primarily for healing. The individuals to be considered here are primarily using the psychokinetic power to affect physical objects rather than people. Five charts are of relatively young people producing what is sometimes called the **Geller effect**. Following the public demonstrations of Uri Geller, surprising numbers of mostly young adults or children discovered that they could do some of the things that Geller did. Sometimes under careful scientific control, and more often in their own homes, they found that metal objects bent while they concentrated intently on the objects. Again, following Geller's lead, kitchen utensils and keys were the most common targets. In the course of my travels, I have met three individuals who also had a broken watch begin to work while they held it in their hands. In all cases, they were watching Geller perform the feat on TV, and the watches only ran a day or two before they stopped functioning again.

The five charts presented here are all of young people who have repeatedly been able to produce bending in metal objects through mental concentration. Since they are not public figures, names and birth location are omitted to protect their privacy.

Looking first at the young lady born on December 31, 1953, we can note the intense emphasis on power in the chart. A major theme is the desire to be in control of herself and her life, with the Mars-Saturn-MC-Moon conjunction in Scorpio and the Mercury- Venus-Ascendant-Sun conjunction in Capricorn. Pluto in its own eighth house, along with three asteroids, repeats the Scorpio theme. With Letter Eight, we can learn to control ourselves, and we must learn not to control others. With Uranus,

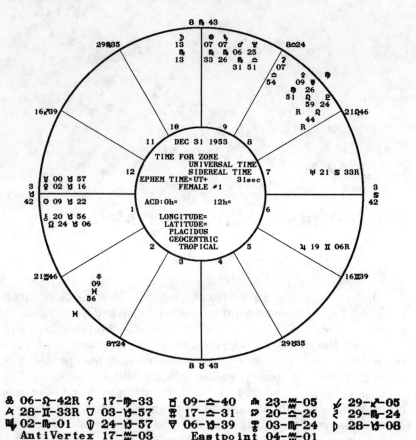

♆ 06-♌-42R	? 17-♍-33	⚷ 09-♎-40	♠ 23-♏-05	⚸ 29-♐-05
⚵ 28-♊-33R	▽ 03-♑-57	⚘ 17-♎-31	♼ 20-♎-26	⚶ 29-♏-24
♇ 02-♏-01	⚕ 24-♑-57	▽ 06-♑-39	♇ 03-♏-24	▷ 28-♑-08
	AntiVertex 17-♒-03		Eastpoint 04-♒-01	

ruler of the first house Aquarius, in the seventh house, she could feel that her power was in the hands of others and could try to keep it all to herself for security. Theoretically, she could also give the power away, but there is too much strength here for that outcome to be likely. If she engaged in serious self-blocking, she could also retreat from others or become ill. Apparently she is using her immense potential for power in the psychokinetic feats which are basically constructive. The two primary dangers of such an emphasis on control would be trying to control other people, or blocking the power and becoming ill. Spoon-bending seems less idealistic than healing others, but it has its role in assisting in the decline of materialism as a viable philosophy.

Since I have virtually no information about these individuals other than their unusual talent, I will simply point out the ways in which each chart shows a similar potential for concentrated will and/or desire for control. Two of my subjects were born in 1962.

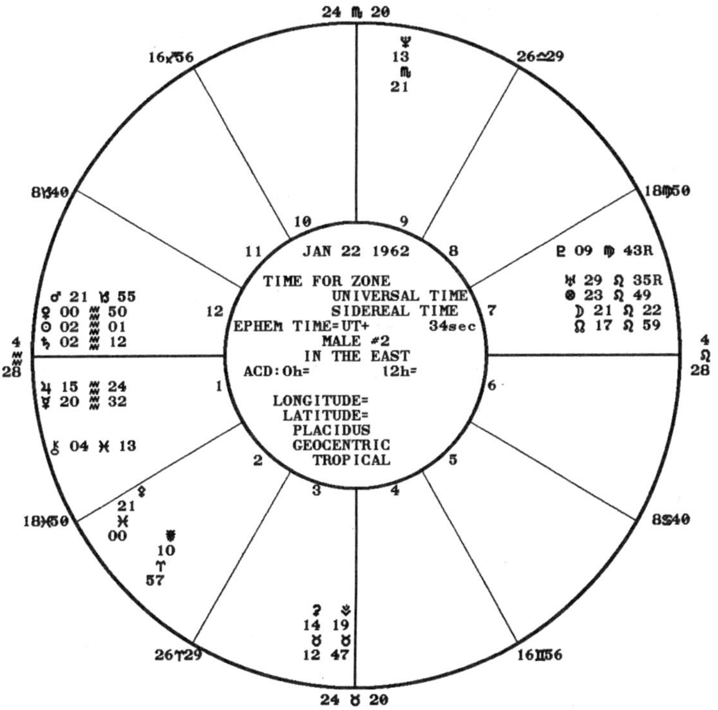

24-♉-08	? 15-♓-26	00-♌-40R	21-♑-06	15-♍-00R
10-♎-39	07-♏-24	07-♑-50	19-♒-23	06-♓-47
11-♍-26R	08-♒-51	24-♑-27	12-♏-23	15-♑-15
AntiVertex	03-♓-46	Eastpoint	19-♒-32	

The young man born on January 22 has Saturn rising conjunct Sun and Venus in Aquarius. Mars in Capricorn repeats the One-Ten mixture which may express as "my will is law." The Moon's node, Moon and Uranus in Leo add more potential for strong will, and their position in the seventh house shows a desire for attention from others. His psychokinetic skill may be bringing him the limelight he would like. I have found Vesta prominent in most of my charts of metal benders, usually conjunct an angle or aspecting the Ascendant, MC, Sun or Moon. In this case, Vesta is conjunct the IC. Vesta symbolizes the Virgo capacity for tunnel vision: total focus. The new asteroids which may be additional keys to the Scorpio principle are also prominent in this chart. Dudu is exactly on the IC. Lilith is conjunct Pluto. Pittsburghia is on the Descendant. As with the first chart in this collection, this young man might have felt threatened by others with his Ascendant ruler, Uranus, in the seventh house, though Uranus is far less vulnerable than fire or water planets. Using

his power on material objects is a healthy way to gain approval while he
sharpens his capacity to focus without any damage to others.

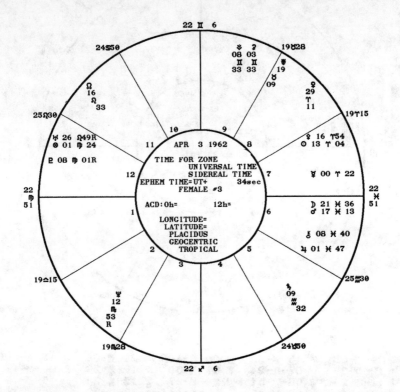

The young lady born on April 3, 1962, has an Aries grouping in the
seventh and eighth houses pointing out the same issue as in the others:
personal power (Letter One) potentially in the hands of others. With such
One-Seven or One-Eight mixtures, we can give in, fight, run, or learn to
compromise and cooperate, to engage in healthy, game-playing competition, and to help people. By developing her psychokinetic skills, she gains
attention (desired by the Sun in the seventh) without alienating others.
Normally, Aries is a sign of intense but very short bursts of concentrated
attention. In this chart, the capacity for sustained attention shows in the
trine between Saturn and Vesta, with Pluto aspecting both of them and
closely conjunct the Antivertex. The planets are more important than the
signs, so the link of these three obsessive-compulsives to each other shows
the enduring will that is otherwise less obvious in a chart with most of

the emphasis in air and fire along with Mars and Moon in Pisces. The Moon on an angle (Descendant) suggests potential psychic talent. Pisces is noted for psychic receptiveness but not for the willpower that we find in the charts of individuals specializing in psychokinesis. But the placement of Mars and Moon in the Virgo house (along with Chiron and Jupiter) helps to explain the capacity for focus.

Three of the new asteroids are connected to the Vesta-Saturn-Pluto combination, adding to its importance. Dudu is conjunct Vesta; Diana is conjunct Saturn; Pandora at eight degrees of Scorpio is widely conjunct Neptune, for curiosity about the inner or higher worlds, and closely square Saturn, sextile Pluto and quincunx Vesta. The conjunction of Pandora to Neptune brings the second water planet into the pattern with the obsessives, and the Moon, our third water planet, is octile Saturn and trioctile Pandora. Mercury's close conjunction to Hidalgo, another potential Saturn, suggests more persistence and control than is normally expected from Mercury in Aries. Lilith on Uranus repeats the theme: a key to a restless, changeable mind connected to a key to sustained effort. Toro in Scorpio in the Taurus house in a close trine to Mars is still another repetition of impulse to change steadied by enduring will. If Dembowska has Saturn overtones, its conjunction with Pallas and Sun is saying it again. The restless, changeable, inquisitive mind is still clearly present in the chart, but the series of aspects just noted show the capacity for sustained focus and effort that are shown in more familiar ways through signs or houses in some of the other charts offered in this section.

In the chart of the young man born June 24, 1963, mutables dominate the scene. Ascendant and Eastpoint are in Sagittarius, and a stellium in Virgo falls in the Sagittarius house with Vesta, the super Virgo asteroid, just over the line in the tenth house. He also has Mercury and Venus conjunct in Gemini, and Chiron is in Pisces in the Gemini house. He clearly lives in the head a large part of the time, but with the earth emphasis, wants tangible results out of his mental efforts. Although not associated with strong will as are Capricorn and Scorpio, Virgo is one of the three letters of our alphabet that indicates the capacity for narrow focus and sustained effort. Unlike the three charts already discussed, this subject does not have a ruler of the first in the seventh or eighth houses, but he does have the Sun in the seventh and Leo in the eighth with Moon on the cusp, so he needs the limelight and gets it with his unusual talent. He was about sixteen years old when I saw him demonstrate his psychokinetic abilities at an astrology conference.

To add emphasis to the strength of will and potential for power, almost all of the new asteroids fall in the fixed houses. The exceptions are Lilith in Scorpio, a fixed sign that I think symbolizes the same principle as Lilith, and we have three of the asteroids in mutable signs with two also in mutable houses to repeat the importance of the mind. Of course, the

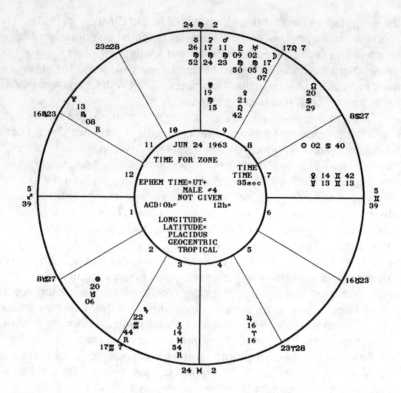

& 07-♌-48   ? 18-♋-53   ♅ 00-♏-06   ⚳ 05-♊-59   ⚸ 08-♏-35R
⚘ 23-♑-49R   ⚴ 10-♒-54R   ♇ 07-♋-43   ⚵ 28-♑-10R   ⚶ 07-♌-17
⚷ 17-♏-21R   ⚹ 04-♊-32   ⚺ 08-♓-36   ⚻ 13-♌-12   ☽ 25-♈-26
    AntiVertex 19-♑-18   Eastpoint 24-♐-58

capacity for a strong will and concern with power was already present
in the chart with the traditional planets. Jupiter, ruling the Ascendant, is
in Aries, and Mars and Pluto are closely conjunct with Uranus widely connected. The new asteroids just make it clearer and more emphatic with
such combinations as Dudu and Hidalgo (potential Pluto and Saturn) exactly conjunct in Leo in the Scorpio house, and with Toro also in Leo conjunct the Moon. Psyche, at the midpoint of two more potential Plutos (Pittsburghia and Lilith), creates the equivalent of a close conjunction between
them. The more we add to the chart, the more it says the same thing again.

    The young lady born on May 14, 1966 shared the limelight with the
subject just discussed, at the same astrology conference. She was only
thirteen at the time, but was demonstrating psychokinetic ability with a
number of other young people. The group was being trained by a young
married woman who was deeply involved in parapsychology. The two-
year-old son of the woman leader was already showing psychic talent.

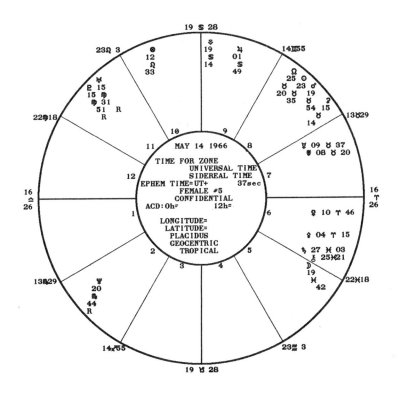

 ♋ 26-♉-13   ? 24-♒-10   ♉ 12-♋-00   ♠ 02-♒-46   ↙ 03-♋-42
♈ 06-♏-02R   ▽ 15-♍-42   ⚷ 05-♉-29   ♌ 19-♋-52   ? 09-♏-49R
⚺ 02-♌-18   ⚳ 07-♊-03   ▽ 19-♒-13R   ⚴ 19-♉-07   ♭ 01-♒-10
   AntiVertex 10-♏-34   Eastpoint 22-♎-47

This chart, like the preceding one, has Vesta conjunct the MC, which also aspects much of the chart: the Ascendant, the Uranus-Pluto conjunction in Virgo in the eleventh house, the Taurus stellium in the eighth house, with Mars exactly in aspect within a few minutes of arc. Vesta-MC also form a grand water trine to Neptune and Moon. The chart is dominated by the earth and water trines and sextiles, and has considerable emphasis in the fixed houses as well as the fixed signs Taurus and Scorpio. Ample strength and persistence of will are indicated in these patterns.

The new asteroids add Toro and Dudu to the Taurus stellium for repeated Taurus and Scorpio fixity. Lilith is in Leo in the tenth house, another indication of a powerful will and capacity for control. Hidalgo closely conjunct the Antivertex in Scorpio repeats the same theme as does Dembowska (like Saturn) square the Sun. Pandora conjunct Uranus and Pluto suggests the curiosity about non-traditional matters, and Virgo wants to do something tangible with them. In general, the chart suggests a person who takes herself and life rather seriously, and may need to work out power issues in her relationships to others. Controlling physical objects is a better way to gain a sense of power than trying to control other people. With Aries in the seventh house and Venus, ruler of the Ascendant moving into the seventh in her early life, she does need to reassure herself about her power and to use it in healthy ways. Mars in the eighth house repeats the theme, while the eighth house Sun is similar to most of the subjects discussed here. Somewhere, somehow, that Letter Five has to shine and be admired. The psychokinetic feats are a good way to satisfy those needs.

Uri Geller

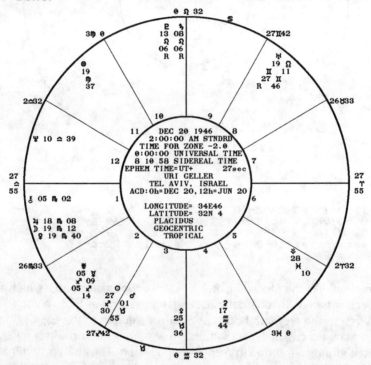

After this brief survey of five individuals who have developed a capacity to produce the Geller effect, the next logical step is to look at the source of this phenomena, Uri Geller himself. The power theme is immediately obvious in his chart. Saturn conjuncts Pluto in Leo in the tenth house; a combination of king (Leo), executive (Saturn, tenth house) and self-mastery (Pluto). Eastpoint, Jupiter, Moon and Venus in Scorpio in the first house (instinctive action) add to the potential for inner exploration and a need to control his life. Uranus and North Node of the Moon in the eighth (Scorpio) house further accentuate the high focus on Letter Eight. Mars in Capricorn repeats the emphasis on the One-Ten combination offered by Pluto (ruler of the first house Scorpio) in the tenth house, and Mars' conjunction with the Sun repeats the tenth house-Leo blend (a planet in Capricorn conjunct the Sun as key to Leo). The added fire of Sagittarius and two fire planets conjunct indicates high drive, self-confidence, creativity. Activity in the fixed houses reiterates the potential for a strong will and an involvement with sensuality and the material world.

Vesta, our key to tunnel vision, is also in high focus in the fifth house with several aspects within one-degree orb including a square to the Sun, a quincunx to the Ascendant and a trioctile to Pluto. Vesta's trine to the MC is just over a two-degree orb. If Ascendant and Pluto (first house ruler) are keys to what Geller was able to do instinctively from the beginning of life, and if the Sun and anything in the fifth house symbolize areas of life that we hope to expand and develop further, he has certainly been living up to his potential. The Sagittarius-Pisces square shows a conflict between beliefs or values based on beliefs. There are always many details that might manifest with such a pattern. Vesta's own earth nature, Pluto in an earth house and Mars (in a wider square to Vesta) in an earth sign, suggest the common struggle between ideals and aspirations vs. the earth limits of what is possible. Geller has certainly pushed the limits, doing things considered impossible before his meteoric rise to prominence.

Enormous controversy has swirled around Geller from the beginning of his public career in the U.S. He was a professional magician in Israel, trained in sleight of hand tricks to entertain an audience. He was "discovered" and brought to the attention of the Western world by Puharich, the psychic researcher already mentioned in the discussion of Daddy Bray. Geller claimed that many of his feats were not contrived tricks but were psychic phenomena, and that he could not always control when and how they would happen. Sometimes in his TV appearances, he would be unable to produce a result, and then as attention turned away, an unexpected phenomena would occur. Similar things happened in the scientific laboratories which tested Geller repeatedly. Delicate instruments went haywire in his vicinity. Metal rods enclosed inside sealed containers bent or broke in his presence, even when he could not touch them. Seen under a high-powered microscope, the metal had been changed in ways the scientists could not duplicate. Geller's telepathic or clairvoyant feats were remarkable also, demonstrated under tightly controlled scientific conditions at the Stanford Research Institute in Palo Alto. But it was the physical phenomena that blew the minds of the materialists. Nothing quite like Geller's metal-bending had been seen in the annals of parapsychology.

The storm that broke around Geller's head has abated, mainly because he is no longer center stage. There are still large numbers of individuals who are convinced that everything he did was accomplished by trickery; some unusually creative magic tricks that no one has been able to duplicate, but still tricks. Naturally, the materialists choose this explanation. One's basic belief system dies hard. John Taylor of England is a shining example of how hard it is for "true believers" to change their views, even when confronted by seemingly incontrovertible evidence. Taylor experimented with more than a dozen individuals who could produce some of the Geller effects, with tight scientific control against fraud, working with kids as young as seven, with no access to elaborate magic paraphernalia. Taylor got results, over and over again, that could not be explained by the premises of materialistic science, and he finally wrote a book trying to explain the results through the electric power of the brain. But his beliefs were too strong. He later repudiated his own experience and returned to his faith in materialistic theories. We do live in the world of our own theories, and it is not easy to deal with experiences that contradict our theories.

William James, who is usually considered the greatest of the early American psychologists, ran into the same issue and was able to maintain his objectivity. He was trained in the scientific tradition and was a leader in the effort to turn psychology into a science. But he was also fascinated by psychic phenomena and continued to investigate it throughout his life. His description of one experience and its aftermath is a classic example of the struggle between beliefs and experience. James had maintained for years that all he needed was one incontrovertible personal experience to really accept the power of the mind to directly influence the material world. He finally had such an experience. He saw a material object moving without being touched by any of the people in a spiritualistic circle. The light was good. There were no hidden wires or magnets. James wrote that at the time of the experience he accepted it as his long-sought proof of mind power, and yet, so strong was the power of long-held beliefs, that within a few weeks he was doubting his own experience. "Maybe it could be explained in another way." Gardiner Murphy, a more recent leading American psychologist who was also interested in psychic research, commented that unless a person was exposed to the idea of the psychic in his early life, he was likely to have difficulty in accepting it, no matter how strong the evidence for it. Murphy's parents were interested in psychic phenomena in his childhood so he grew up considering it a possibility in the world, and the materialistic training of science was not able to brainwash away his early experience.

Presumably a person with more mutability in the nature could and would be more likely to change world views sometime in the life. I would love to see John Taylor's horoscope, including the current patterns when he was wrestling with his faith. We have the birth date of William James but no time of birth. His mixture of Capricorn and Aquarius fits his effort to blend pragmatic scientific methods with openness to nontraditional ideas. Of course, awareness of the reality beyond the material world is only nontraditional to materialistic science. Prior to the advent of modern science, almost everyone took for granted the reality and the importance of the nonmaterial. It is obviously easier to trade one faith for another than to abandon the power, prestige and security of a system thought to be free of faith, one supposedly founded purely on fact. The unconscious beliefs are the ones that rule our lives. To the extent that science denies that it has beliefs, to that extent it guarantees that they will remain unconscious and in control.

It's time to return to Uri Geller after our philosophical detour. I saw him once: charming, dramatic, magnetic and a master showman. He demonstrated telepathy (interesting but inconclusive), starting broken watches and clocks (the skeptics could claim they were "plants" by confederates), moving the hands of a clock and bending a spoon. The last two were the most interesting. Coming up to that part of the program, he kept complaining that there were no children in the audience and that he needed a child. A thirteen-year-old girl was finally produced, and Geller tried to make the hands of a large pocket watch move without his touching it. He pointed at it while the girl held it and said, "Move," very loudly several times. The watch hands did not move. Geller sent the girl back to her seat and looking around in frustration, he spotted a baby being held by its father. He asked the father if the baby was able to hold on to an object, and the father said it was. The baby was carried on stage and held by the father while it held the watch. This time, when Geller pointed to the watch and said, "Move," the minute hand jumped twenty minutes.

Essentially the same performance was repeated later with the spoon-bending. First the thirteen-year-old girl was brought on stage and Geller had her hold the large spoon while he stroked it with his forefinger. Nothing happened. Then the baby was carried up by his father. With the baby holding the spoon, and Geller's slight touch on the top of the spoon, it bent up in the opposite direction that would have occurred if Geller had actually been putting pressure on it. Geller explained that he could have produced the effect alone but it might take him twenty minutes or more. With a baby or small child's energy added to his own, Geller said it could happen very quickly. A very young child was needed because "they don't know yet that it is impossible." Our beliefs determine what we see as possible and as desirable. For me, one of the most fascinating parts of the Geller phenomena was the discovery of literally hundreds of people who could bend metal with their minds once they saw Geller do it and realized it was possible. By itself, bending a metal object is pointless or even destructive, as some people have discovered when their bent keys would no longer open the door. The only value of the Geller phenomena was that it widened human consciousness. How many people made a lasting change in their beliefs about human power and human limits, we will never know. Hopefully, we will be able to obtain more horoscopes of the individuals who discovered they had the talent. I hope that readers who have birth data on such individuals will share them with me.

Let's take one more quick look at Geller's horoscope, since we do have information on his life from a biography and an autobiography. His parents fought and separated; we note the Ceres in the fourth house for the mother opposite the tenth house Pluto and Saturn for father. He stayed most of the time with his mother, but for some periods with his father. Both parents are clearly role models: Moon in the first house and Pluto ruling the first in the tenth as well as conjunct Saturn. He waited a long time to marry and have a child: searching for an ideal (Pisces in the fifth house, Juno in Sagittarius and Venus conjunct Jupiter). He wanted money, fame, sensual pleasures, and he got them: fixed signs and houses connected to letters One and Ten. If you trust the competence and the integrity of the scientists who worked with him, he is a highly gifted psychic: water factors, Pluto, Neptune, nodes of the Moon, in close aspects with each other and with the air planet, Mercury, showing the contact between conscious and unconscious aspects of the mind. He also has the first house triple conjunction in a water sign, including the water Moon, all closely aspecting Uranus, the other planet of consciousness, in the water eighth house. The nodes across Gemini-Sagittarius are the mark of the perpetual student, teacher, writer and/or traveller. He has done them all.

The new asteroids repeat the same themes. Sappho and Eros in the twelfth house and Amor in Pisces symbolize the search for a romantic, ideal love and partner. Chiron exactly on the Eastpoint suggests the intellectual versatility, writing, traveling. Pandora and Urania in the tenth house point to a career of learning, teaching, communicating, or work with the media. Psyche in Virgo in the eleventh house again ties work to the mind and expanded knowledge. The "power" asteroids cluster in Capricorn and early Aquarius, in the third house and on the cusp of the fourth house. Toro, Dudu, Pittsburghia form a midpoint cluster in Capricorn, suggesting the focus on mind control: using the mind to control the physical world. Icarus and Hidalgo are widely conjunct. If Dudu and Pittsburghia are like Pluto; Icarus like the Sun; Hidalgo like Saturn; we have just repeated the tenth house mixture of Pluto and Saturn in Leo. If Dembowska is another Saturn, its position on the fifth house cusp repeats the Leo-Capricorn mixture again: a blend of king and executive, a career on stage, power over the material world, personal will testing the limits of universal Law. We can manifest the principles in many different ways, but they all spell power, whether we overdrive with it, or block it and become ill, or learn to live voluntarily within the limits. As with the young people already discussed, directing the power against the material world is certainly more constructive than using it to control other people. I don't know how much of Geller's performance is magic tricks, but I'm glad he came along to stretch the beliefs of humanity.

Komar: Firewalker

I have selected Komar as the last subject in this section on psychokinetic power. Komar has demonstrated some remarkable talents, including walking on fire. Natives of the South seas might not consider fire walking unusual. It used to be a standard part of religious ceremonies, and is still done routinely in some remote areas. But modern science has no explanation for it, and prefers to ignore it. When experience collides with beliefs, which do you choose? I saw Komar walk on a bed of mesquite logs that had been burning for hours and were so hot, the observers maintained a healthy distance. A doctor who was present in case of emergency said that any normal person taking one step into that trench of fire would have been crippled for life. Komar walked slowly, deliberately, barefoot, twenty feet on that bed of coals. At the end, he did not even have a blister on his feet.

Among his other demonstrations, many conducted under scientifically controlled conditions in laboratories, Komar can climb a ladder of swords in his bare feet, lie on a bed of nails and let men jump on his stomach, and put metal skewers through his body without bleeding or becoming infected. He says he controls the pain of such experiences with a kind of self-hypnosis. Despite such seemingly superhuman powers, Komar is a loving and lovely human being. There is no sign of the power or ego trip so common in individuals with exceptional abilities. He claims that everyone could do what he does.

The power theme is clearly present in Komar's horoscope. He has a stellium in Capricorn in the fourth house including Sun, Moon, Mars and Saturn. Pluto is opposite them in Cancer in the tenth house. The planets of the four supreme power letters of our alphabet are present in that combination: One, Five, Eight, and Ten, with Ten repeated by sign and house as well as by planetary ruler. Normally, such a focus on Cancer and Capricorn might express as anxiety and self-blocking. When we identify with the baby side of Cancer, the world side of Capricorn has the power. Only when we have used the power ourselves do we know we have it, and stop projecting it into the world. The Virgo Ascendant with the South Node of the Moon conjunct it are also frequently associated with self-criticism and hence self-doubts and self-blocking. To counter this very

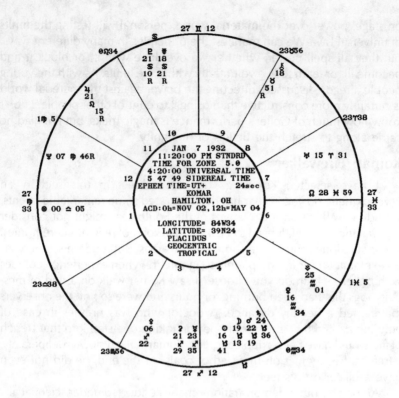

real potential in the chart, we have some strong fire. Mercury, ruling the Ascendant, falls in Sagittarius, and Venus, ruling the Libra in the first house, is in the Leo house. Jupiter in Leo closely trines Mercury, and Uranus in Aries is widely trine them, to add to the fire potential for self-confidence and faith in a Higher Power. But the Aries in the seventh house is also the danger of projecting some of the personal power, and I have seen many people with Leo in the eleventh who needed approval from everyone they met rather than from a few close loved ones, the "easier to manage" Leo desire.

How is the average astrologer likely to handle such a mixture in a chart? One of the exercises presented to many of my classes has been a sheet of six charts: three individuals with psychokinetic power of mind over matter, and three individuals who lacked the power to control their own mind and body — three epileptics. Almost all students have chosen Komar's chart as one of the individuals with the problem. In contrast, Uri

Geller's chart was usually selected as one of the people who had power. I consider the guesses quite reasonable. Komar's chart is a difficult one by most standards in astrology. But his life is a triumph in almost every way. Such guessing games are a helpful part of astrology. We need to know the limits of our knowledge. As has been said repeatedly, the chart shows the principles, the issue. The person determines the details. Komar's chart could easily have indicated a self-blocking and ill person. His life has manifested the other end of the pendulum of power; overdrive, sometimes taking incredible risks. But he seems to be handling the overdrive successfully. He risks his own safety, not that of others. He puts himself through tortures, not others. He works often with scientists, seeking to disprove the limiting theories of materialism, demonstrating his phenomenal mental control over the material world.

A brief look at the new asteroids seems to support the tentative meanings being assigned to them. Three of the power asteroids fall in the first house or conjunct the Ascendant: Dudu, Lilith and Pittsburghia. These are the three I see as variations on Pluto, and that certainly fits Komar's life devoted to self-mastery. Hidalgo and Icarus, our potential new Saturn and Sun, join the Capricorn stellium: power again, with two Suns and two Saturns combined with Mars. Dembowska, the other possible Saturn asteroid, is exactly conjunct Pandora to repeat the mind control, mind over matter theme. Frigga and Eros are in the fifth house supporting love and possible children. Komar worked with children before he discovered his talents, and he did marry and have a family, though he can't spend much time with them in view of his constant travels for his work. The other four new asteroids fall in the third, ninth and twelfth houses, supporting the emphasis on the mind and travel. Komar's many earth trines do fit his power over the material world, while his mutable cross (including the MC to complete it) is common in people with too many talents who live constantly overextended trying to do it all. I have watched him battle faith vs. fear, another common form of the mutable dilemma, and so far his faith in himself and in a Higher Power has triumphed. May it ever be so.

CHAPTER 12

Other Roads to Power

In Chapter 5 we gave you the horoscope of Richard Nixon. There are some interesting parallels with the chart of Komar which was just discussed. Virgo is rising with a first house South Node (though it is not conjunct the Ascendant for Nixon), so we have the need to do something well and the danger of self-criticism and self-doubt, overdrive or self-blocking. Keys to the identity are again in Sagittarius, in Capricorn and in the fourth house. In this case, Mars is in Sagittarius and Mercury in Capricorn; the reverse of Komar. Jupiter conjunct both Mars and Mercury repeats the identification with the Absolute, whether this expresses as "I ought to be perfect and always do the right thing," or as "I have the right to play God and do anything I want." Pluto in the tenth house reiterates the concern with control, however we direct that power. Saturn in the ninth house is like Jupiter in Capricorn, executive power as an absolute value and goal in life. Initially, father may be God, but when he lets us down, we have to find a bigger God. Assuming the role ourselves or giving up the search for Something Higher are both dangers. Nixon's chart repeats the power theme with his Capricorn Sun in the fifth (Leo) house, the nodes of Pluto conjunct and opposite his Sun, while the nodes of Saturn fall conjunct and opposite Neptune. Komar had the nodes of Pluto conjunct and opposite his Moon and the nodes of Saturn on his Mars-Saturn midpoint. Both charts also have Aries in the seventh house, the potential of feeling the need to defend themselves against the power of others. Faith can counteract defensiveness and insecurity.

Nelson Rockefeller

Since Nixon's chart was used to illustrate the planetary nodes, Arabic Parts and new asteroids, perhaps we can move on to another power seeker.

Nixon gained and then lost the presidency of the United States. Nelson Rockefeller wanted it and never made it. As most readers already know, he was born into one of the richest families in the world. When you have more money than you could ever spend, you need a different challenge. Rockefeller found that challenge in politics, working in various appointed posts in the federal government and finally being elected governor of New York. He left that position to travel the country on a commission investigating the political feelings and attitudes of the public. Most observers felt that this undertaking provided an opportunity to barnstorm the country, meeting people and impressing them, as a prelude to running for president. But he could not get the Republican nomination. He was too liberal for most Republicans. He came close with his appointment as vice president after Nixon's resignation, but the door closed after that and he passed on with a heart attack: the signal of frustrated ambition.

Rockefeller's horoscope shows a blend of concern with power and

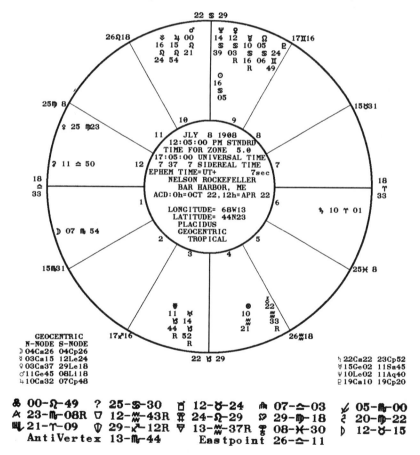

security in combination with a search for the Absolute. The stellium in the ninth house includes Venus, ruler of the Ascendant, Sun as key to the desire to do more and be recognized for it, with Neptune symbolizing the emotional Absolute. A Venus-Neptune aspect is often a sign of artistic talent or love of the aesthetic. Rockefeller was an art collector, and his last activity after giving up on politics was an art business. The mixture of Cancer in the ninth house can express in many ways, including a home in other countries; a high value placed on home and family, or homeland if the vision is broad; humanitarian activity for the public; mental activity that affects the public.

The Cancer stellium is part of a cardinal grand cross in mutable houses, and Rockefeller's first house Moon in Scorpio squares the midpoint of his Mars-Jupiter in Leo in the tenth house, giving a mixture of fixed and cardinal conflict. Most individuals with a fixed and cardinal emphasis expect life to be a power struggle. As long as the struggle is game-playing, it is fun for all. We win some and lose some and everyone increases both skills and confidence. The drive for personal power is especially indicated by Mars in Leo in the tenth house and Saturn in Aries, both combinations of Letter One and Ten. Leo in the Tenth and Sun conjunct the MC are Five-Ten combinations: the king and executive, as noted in Nixon's chart. Jupiter in the tenth is also similar to Nixon's Jupiter in Capricorn. Father could be idealized or a source of disillusionment. Power, or status, or achievement could be worshipped. Vesta closely connected to Jupiter shows the potential for the work being an ultimate value and goal. The Sun ruling the Leo in the tenth house and placed in the ninth house repeats the theme of ultimate value connected to power and career. The Moon ruling the tenth house and placed in the first house is another identification with executive power. "My will is Law," or "If I don't take charge and do it right, I'll be guilty." Uranus ruling the fifth house and in Capricorn is another Five-Ten combination; king and executive, yet Uranus and the third house have equalitarian instincts. There is air in the chart, but the idealism and power drive are stronger themes. The South Node and Saturn in Mercury ruled houses (natural Gemini and Virgo), but strong-willed signs, suggest that learning to be an equal, learning detachment or learning to be practical were among his lessons.

Making peace between one's ideals and the limits of the physical world is a common form of the mutable dilemma, and was probably part of Rockefeller's challenge with his grand cross in mutable houses. Conflicts between values are also common with ninth house-twelfth house squares: head goals vs. heart goals. Sometimes the mutable conflict manifests as learning disabilities in the early life, and I have seen Pallas involved with this problem at times. It seems to be a difficulty in seeing patterns, in perspective. We are so focused on what we want, we literally can't see the larger picture: part of the air lesson is learning personal detachment.

Rockefeller was considered dyslexic as a child, having problems with reading. The fire, water and Capricorn mixture can be pretty intense, and when one feels that everything should be done perfectly (two rulers of the first house in the ninth house), trying too hard can be self-defeating.

Adding some of the new factors in astrology produces the usual repeated message. The nodes of Saturn fall across Rockefeller's MC axis while Vesta's nodes conjunct Neptune and oppose Venus. The North Node of Jupiter is conjunct his Venus. The new asteroids confirm the power focus. Dembowska (another Saturn?) is conjunct the MC in the tenth house. Dudu (another Pluto?) is exactly conjunct Mars. Lilith (another Pluto?) is close to the Descendant. Pittsburghia (one more Pluto?) and Diana (a warrior goddess?) conjunct the Vertex, so oppose the Antivertex. Icarus (another Sun?) conjunct Pandora (another Mercury?) forms squares to Pittsburghia and Diana, and more widely opposes Jupiter and Vesta. Though the first house Moon is a bit wide, we have filled in a grand cross in fixed signs in cardinal houses: the classic statement of a power struggle life. Hidalgo (another Saturn?) is sextile the MC and semisextile the Ascendant, plus forming a yod (double quincunx) to Lilith and Chiron. The latter symbolizes the common dilemma of a pull between career and the transpersonal part of life versus the commitment to home and mate. Life should be big enough for it all, but we can't do it all perfectly. The overdrive people have to learn to live one day at a time and to enjoy the journey.

Ida Rolf

I've chosen one more overdrive person to conclude this look at different varieties of power. Ida Rolf founded the form of physiotherapy which bears her name: Rolfing. Her birth date in 1896 deprives us of the new asteroids, but the traditional planets give us a clear picture of a very strong lady. If her birth data is accurate (there is always that question with famous people), she has the last degree of Leo rising, and her Sun is in the last degree of Taurus, square the Ascendant from the tenth house. Mercury also rules the first house and is placed in the Tenth house, so we have the One-Ten combination twice, while the Sun in the tenth is a Five-Ten and Pluto in the tenth is an Eight-Ten. Personal will is certainly identified with the Law, indicating a danger of overdrive (more likely), self-blocking (possible, especially in the early life until she discovered her strength), or learning to live voluntarily within the limits. With all the fixed signs occupied, Mars in the fixed (eighth) house, in addition to the One-Ten emphasis, a power struggle life is highly likely. The eighth house Mars is especially in danger of feeling that others may have our power and that we have to get it back. We can give in, fight or run. Or we can learn to share the power and compromise; to compete in healthy, game-playing ways; and to help people.

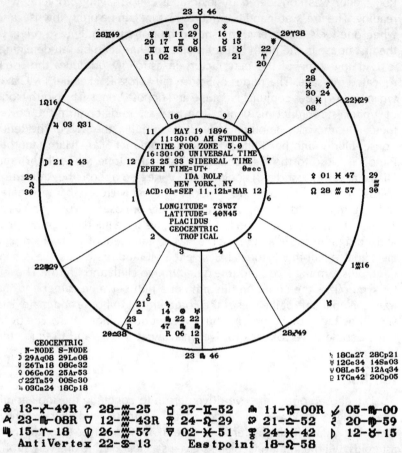

GEOCENTRIC
N-NODE S-NODE
☽ 29Aq08 29Le08
☿ 26Ta18 08Ge32
♀ 06Ge02 25Ar53
♂ 22Ta59 00Sc30
♃ 03Ca24 18Cp18

♄ 18Ca27 28Cp21
♅ 12Ge34 14Sa03
♆ 08Le54 12Aq34
♇ 17Ca42 20Cp05

☍ 13-♐-49R ? 28-♒-25 ♅ 27-♊-52 ⚴ 11-♑-00R ⚸ 05-♏-00
⚷ 23-♏-08R ♒ 12-♒-43R ⚳ 24-♌-29 ⚵ 21-♎-52 ? 20-♍-59
⚶ 15-♈-18 ⚿ 26-♒-57 ⚵ 02-♓-51 ⚶ 24-♓-42 ☽ 12-♉-15
AntiVertex 22-♋-13   Eastpoint 18-♌-58

As with both Nixon and Rockefeller, Ida Rolf was also identified with
the Absolute. Both Mars in Pisces and Mercury, ruling the first house and
conjunct Neptune, repeat the same message. The general importance of
ideals is shown by the active ninth and twelfth houses, with a lesson in
the area since the Venus-Vesta conjunction squares the Eastpoint and
Moon. Clearly, she had to discover her own Truth (Aries in the ninth house
says it again), and was eager to share it with the world (Mercury and Neptune in Gemini in the career house). The South Node in Leo on the Ascendant and Saturn in Scorpio indicate a lesson in handling power, while
the twelfth house position of the node connects the lesson to ideals. The
mutable sign and house emphasis in the chart shows an active mind and
tongue with the powerhouse Uranus on the IC and trine the Antivertex,
indicating a highly original mind and (supported by the rest of the water
in the chart) probably considerable psychic ability. The North Node of
Uranus is conjunct Rolf's Pluto, and the North Node of Mars is conjunct

her MC, reinforcing both the original intellect and the need to be on top and in front. If we interpret the Part of Fortune as a key to character brought from past lives, as suggested in Chapter 5, Rolf's Part of Fortune exactly conjunct Uranus once again gives the message of an original mind.

For those not familiar with Rolfing, the techniques use extreme physical force to break loose the body rigidities that exist in most people. Elbows, knees, knuckles are forced into the patient's joints to loosen the muscles, cartilage and bones. The treatment is normally very painful, but people often claim an emotional "high" after it is over. Those who have not gone through the treatment sometimes suggest that the relief felt afterward is like the relief when one stops punching a wall. However, some who have gone through it claim enormously increased flexibility, vitality and energy. I have not been through it, so only report the statements of others. Rolf's chart fits both the idealism that can choose a healing career, the verbal ability and drive to teach her unique creation, and the power to change bodies by brute force. She showed her Leo too, not only in always being in the limelight and running her own show, but in her sense of self-worth and love of family. Long after many hundreds of Rolfers had been trained and had established careers using the techniques, when asked for a list of competent professional Rolfers, Ida Rolf replied, "Myself and my son."

CHAPTER 13

Power, Faith and the Capacity to Care

All of the charts discussed so far have been concerned with the issue of power or control, of self or of the material world. Faith and a search for Something Higher, has also been an important theme in many. The basic principles have been repeated often enough. It is time for readers to try their hands at the game. Six charts will be considered in this chapter, but they are presented ahead of the discussion and identification to let readers make their own judgments first. A range of ages is represented. The sex is given for each chart: one female and five males. The new asteroids are placed at the bottom of the charts to try to minimize the information overload. Ignore them if you like. After you have analyzed the six charts yourself, read the analyses presented in this chapter and see how it compares with your own impressions. Then look up the names and life stories of the individuals. Of course, if you recognize any of the charts, you can skip that one.

Chart 1 — male

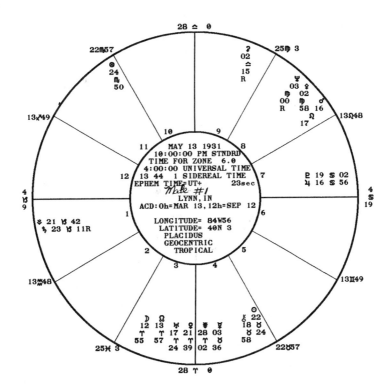

   ☊ 22-♋-18   ? 25-♒-25   ⚷ 03-♋-21   ⚸ 22-♑-16   ⚵ 01-♋-23
   ⚴ 11-♈-31   ▽ 18-♒-36   ⚳ 13-♈-12   ⚶ 23-♍-24   ⚵ 19-♑-33R
   ⚹ 14-♋-12   ⚿ 15-♉-47   ▽ 10-♉-45   ⚘ 06-♋-54   ♄ 08-♎-45
      AntiVertex 14-♒-15   Eastpoint 24-♑-07

Chart 2 — male

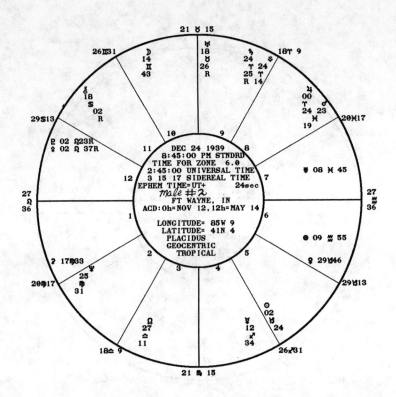

  ♋ 18-♋-07R ? 14-♏-05   ♃ 13-♋-49R ♏ 29-♐-02   ♌ 24-♒-05
A 21-♍-12 ▽ 17-♐-23   ♀ 10-♎-14   ♌ 01-♏-04   ♌ 28-♏-16
♅ 10-♌-37R ♆ 24-♌-32   ▽ 24-♑-33   ♇ 28-♏-33   ♭ 21-♏-42
     AntiVertex 19-♋-33   Eastpoint 16-♌-22

Chart 3 — male

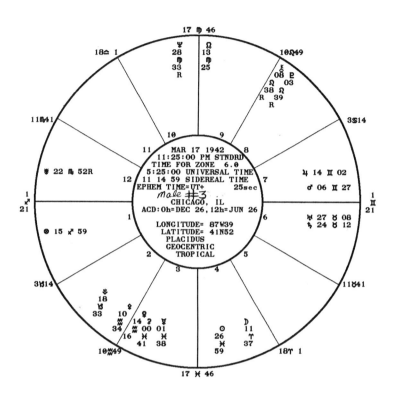

& 02-♏-07   ? 08-♈-34   ♅ 26-♑-07   ⚭ 26-♊-22   ⚸ 04-♏-00R
⚹ 18-♓-35   ▽ 16-♊-47   ♇ 05-♉-20   ♌ 25-♑-31   ⚷ 18-♐-14
♏ 16-♑-02   ⚳ 09-♉-44   ▽ 23-♒-55   ⚴ 08-♓-03   ☽ 29-♓-37
       AntiVertex 15-♑-07   Eastpoint 19-♐-39

Chart 4 — male

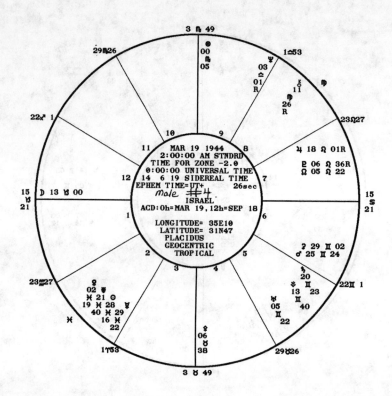

MAR 19 1944
2:00:00 AM STNDRD
TIME FOR ZONE −2.0
0:00:00 UNIVERSAL TIME
14 6 19 SIDEREAL TIME
EPHEM TIME=UT+   26sec
male #4
ISRAEL
ACD:0h=MAR 19,12h=SEP 18

LONGITUDE= 35E10
LATITUDE= 31N47
PLACIDUS
GEOCENTRIC
TROPICAL

☊ 12-Ⅱ-25   ? 07-♍-18R   ♉ 10-Ⅱ-10   ♏ 08-♑-44   ⚸ 26-♑-58
⚷ 28-♎-16R   ▽ 06-♐-36   ♅ 05-♐-32   ♙ 18-♒-23   ? 07-♑-00
♒ 17-Ⅱ-00   ♈ 09-♈-26   ▽ 14-♒-25   ♇ 04-♋-54   ☽ 25-♏-56
AntiVertex 22-♒-48   Eastpoint 29-♑-25

Chart 5 — male

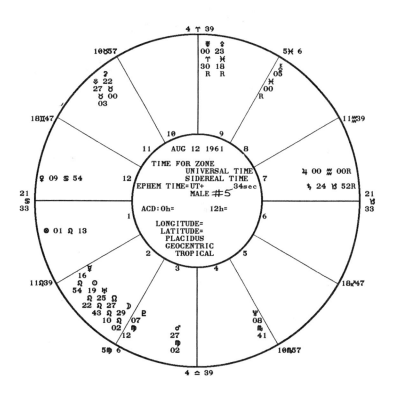

AUG 12 1961

TIME FOR ZONE
UNIVERSAL TIME
SIDEREAL TIME
EPHEM TIME=UT+   34sec
MALE #5

ACD:0h=   12h=

LONGITUDE=
LATITUDE=
PLACIDUS
GEOCENTRIC
TROPICAL

& 04-♊-40   ? 24-♒-40R   ♉ 11-♋-13   ♠ 28-♏-02   ↙ 07-♌-55
♈ 12-♌-15   ▽ 14-♍-47   ♈ 24-♎-03   ♋ 22-♏-09   ♄ 03-♓-19R
♏ 23-♋-55   ♍ 24-♍-16   ▽ 12-♌-12   ♈ 19-♋-29   ♭ 20-♏-03
     AntiVertex 07-♊-15   Eastpoint 03-♋-55

Chart 6 — female

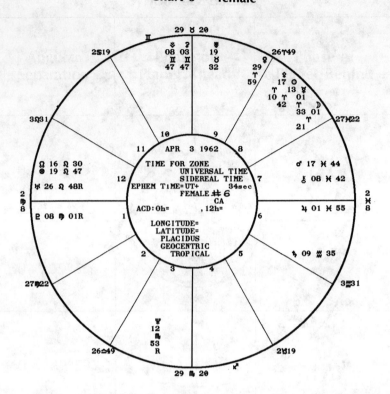

& 06-Ⅱ-14   ? 15-♈-59   ♉ 24-♋-53   ♏ 18-♏-30   ⚡ 02-♍-40R
A 00-♎-44R   ▽ 08-♏-40R   ♇ 15-♒-33   ♉ 04-♈-56   ⚶ 29-♓-57
♇ 28-♌-12R   ⚶ 14-♓-54   ▽ 24-♒-26   ♇ 16-♏-32R   ☽ 08-♒-21
      AntiVertex 15-♋-34   Eastpoint 24-♌-51

The **first chart** in this set of six shows a clear cardinal dilemma with part of the fixed dilemma as well. A father figure was probably an important role model, whether positive or negative, with Saturn in Capricorn in the first house. Saturn is between Vesta and the Eastpoint, closely conjunct both. Vesta connected to either parent can indicate high effectiveness or a lack of ability to handle the world. An ill parent is one possibility. The Aries Moon suggests mother is also a role model, and the Moon closely conjunct its own node increases the importance of the mother or mother-figure. Sometimes Aries in the third house symbolizes a sibling as role model, and sometimes it is found with an only child. Aries can indicate a loner. Personal relationships are important when there is strong activity in the fourth, fifth, seventh and eighth houses. Juno right on the fourth cusp suggests an intense need for a mate, Cancer in the seventh house shows mother as role model for mate; he could be consciously or unconsciously looking for someone like or unlike his mother figure. Remember the chart shows the issue. There are always a variety of ways it can be expressed, and often people vary their expression as they grow and learn to understand themselves.

Besides the mother, we could also say that God is a role model for his mate. He has Jupiter in the seventh house and conjunct Pluto, one key to mate, and Neptune in the eighth house as well as conjunct Pallas. Mother is also connected to his faith and ideals. Ceres is in the ninth house; Jupiter is in Cancer; Chiron is in the fourth house; all showing the association. Faith, as well as equalitarian relationships, are also lessons with the South Node of the Moon in Libra in the ninth house. Saturn in the first house points to personal action as another lesson. Since the cardinal signs fall partly in mutable houses, we have to include the mutable dilemma as part of the picture. He might want more than is possible. He might lack faith, or put it in a small part of life which is then overrated.

He might try to do it all. The atlas syndrome is common in individuals with a cardinal dilemma and strong fire and earth. If they play parent to the world, they can keep the power, take freedom when they want, have closeness as the nurturer, and permit equality if they choose. They only have to give up dependency, the baby side of Cancer. It sounds like a reasonable solution, but we cannot ignore any part of ourselves without inviting trouble. The neglected part will be repressed to create illness, projected so that others overdo it for us, or displaced and be manifested in the wrong place or time. Mars in the eighth house is a special warning of the danger of trying to keep all the power. Remember the options are: give in, fight, run, or cooperate, compete fairly and help people. With his identification with the parent or power role, and his fear of others having power over him, with a lesson in being an equal, we can suspect that he went through some uncomfortable relationships. Yet his grand trine in earth shows that he is quite capable of handling the material world successfully. The problems will be with people, and yet with the strong fire and water he can be emotionally moving. With his Mercury and Neptune in the grand trine to the Ascendant, he could be eloquent. With the Moon on its own node, there is often much magnetism, and Mars in Leo plus Sun on the cusp of its own house support the potential charisma. The talent is there to be a winner if he can learn to cooperate with others and to trust a Higher Power.

The new asteroids offer the same message. Hidalgo, potentially a new Saturn, is on the Vesta-Saturn-Eastpoint combination in the first house, identifying with career, father, power. Frigga is also there, identifying with marriage. The three potential Plutos, Pittsburghia, Lilith and Dudu, are all in the seventh house or conjunct the Descendant. We can care deeply for others and share with them, or we can fight them and try to protect ourselves with a heavy emphasis on letters Seven and Eight. Toro and Psyche are also conjunct the Descendant, putting still more emphasis on interpersonal relationships. He might enjoy them or study them, or try to understand them if he worked out the power issues. I'm not sure what to do with Diana in the ninth house between Ceres and the Moon's node. Mythologically, Diana was sometimes a protector, so in this position, it might symbolize valuing and protecting children. However, Diana was also sometimes a killer. Sappho and Urania in the third house, both in Aries, indicate again the quick mind and tongue and ability to sway people. Pandora on the Antivertex says it again. Dembowska in the second house may want control over money as well as over the mind in Aquarius. If sheer willpower can swing it, he should make it to the top.

Chart number two in this section has a fifth house Sun and the South Node of the Moon in the ninth house again. With Leo rising and the Sun in Capricorn, we have a One-Five-Ten combination: personal will, king, executive. Saturn in Aries repeats the mixture of personal will and executive law, and brings in the Absolute in the ninth house. Mercury ruling the first house Virgo, placed in Sagittarius, connects the identity to God again. Mars, always natural ruler of the first house, in Pisces, again identifies with the Absolute. Jupiter in Aries and Aries in the ninth house offer two more One-Nine combinations. Chiron conjunct the Antivertex adds the statement once more, and the Eastpoint in the twelfth house offers it one more time. With such combinations, we may say, "I ought to be perfect. Since I'm not, I'm no good." Or, we may say, "I am absolute. I have the right to do anything I want." The solution to both dangers is to accept being human on the way to becoming God, to do our best to move toward perfection but to enjoy the journey.

There are additional interesting parallels to the first chart. Sun ruling the first house and in Capricorn shows an identification with work and with a father figure. Saturn in Aries and conjunct Vesta says it again. Ceres in Virgo in the first identifies with work again, but with a mother-figure.

We don't know whether the relationship with parents was positive or negative. Mercury opposite Moon in the tenth house could indicate parents who were emotionally estranged or physically separated. Sometimes the latter has occurred because one parent traveled, so was gone some of the time. The ninth house Saturn can suggest that, and it ties the father to faith. South Node and Vesta on Saturn emphasize a lesson with father or other forms of authority and limits. He needed to learn something from his father about self-will, self-confidence and faith in a Higher Power. If father handled power and responsibility well, did his share and let God do His, then this man got a good example. If father copped out through illness, incompetence, selfishness, harshness or whatever, the subject of the chart had a chance to learn what not to do.

If the fourth house is father, which seems likely with Moon in the tenth house, the issue of faith is again tied to father since Sagittarius is in the fourth and Pluto ruling the cusp is in the twelfth house. Letter Nine is our more conscious beliefs and values and goals; Letter Twelve tends to be partly unconscious, but all the more important because of that. Pluto has many aspects, including a trine to Jupiter, a quincunx to Sun, an opposition to Venus and wide squares to the nodes and Saturn-Vesta. The combination could suggest power struggles or conflict over faith and values. As was the case with our first subject, Mars in the eighth house needs to learn to cooperate, compete fairly, and help people to avoid the "give in-fight-run" syndrome. The Mars opposition to Neptune is part of the mutable dilemma by sign and the fixed dilemma by house. As with the last chart, he may want more than is possible, or he may overvalue a small part of life. Some of the potential for power struggle might manifest in handling money, possessions or appetites. The fifth house square to the eighth house is like Leo square Scorpio, again a common theme in both the charts considered in this section.

To help him work out the challenges, he should have a bright, quick mind with the Gemini-Sagittarius polarity by both sign and house. But he may only express easily with people he trusts, with the signs in the fourth and tenth houses and with South Node and Saturn in the ninth house. He should have considerable artistic talent with Neptune in the Venus house and aspecting Mars in Neptune's sign. I have often found Venus in Capricorn in the charts of professional artists. He should have a competitive outlet for the power struggle potential in the chart, and it is imperative that he find some kind of faith in a Power higher than himself.

The new asteroids offer interesting confirmation of the power theme. The three potentially like Pluto are all connected to identity. Dudu, and Pittsburghia more widely, are conjunct the Antivertex, while Lilith is widely conjunct the Eastpoint. The two potentially like Saturn are both in Scorpio with the IC at their midpoint. Since this position puts them opposite The MC, which is still another form of Saturn, the issue of Letters Eight and Ten are really important in the nature. Letter Eight is learning self-knowledge and self-mastery, what is ours and what belongs to others, to respect the rights of others, to share the world for mutual pleasure. Letter Ten is learning the rules of the game, the outer laws and the inner conscience, to live voluntarily within the law. Icarus, potentially like the Sun, is in the Sun's house, restating the importance of the ego, the desire to be admired, to put out creative energy and feel a sense of power. Capricorn should gain this admiration and sense of power through the career. As with the first subject in this section, the chart shows a potential steamroller. We hope he uses the power constructively.

At first glance, **our third chart** looks very different from the first two. It is mostly mutables, both signs and houses, showing a major part of the life in the head. However, there is a wide grand trine in earth, or a series of earth trines for those who object to wide orbs, with Saturn and Vesta, two earth planets, included, so he should be able to cope with the material world. Verbal fluency shows with the Sagittarius rising and both Jupiter and Mars in Gemini in the seventh house. The Pisces stellium suggests a sensitive, empathic nature, backed up by the Moon in its own house. Venus in the third house in Aquarius might enjoy a wide range of friends and neighbors, and Ceres there might play a nurturing role. He could be rather psychic, with Mercury in Pisces aspecting Pluto in the eighth house, and the close Uranus-Neptune trine plus Moon octile Uranus linking the water planets with air. Uranus is square Mercury, but conflict aspects between these two air planets often just show a more original mind. He could have considerable artistic talent with the Pisces and Taurus; in fact, he might have chosen an artistic career if it offered sufficient financial security. His Pluto, Ascendant and Sun form a grand trine that is partly water and partly fire. The combination shows a deeply emotional nature.

On the challenge side, the mutable cross could indicate a lack of faith (anxiety) or conflict between different beliefs and values, or overvaluing part of life, probably home and mate with Pisces in the fourth house, Jupiter in the seventh house and Chiron in the eighth house. Or, he might have trouble deciding what he really trusted and wanted in life. Neptune in the tenth house could also value the career and be pulled between it and home or family. The placement of two rulers of the first house in the seventh gives us our familiar reminder to learn to cooperate, compete fairly, and help people. If we neglect any of the positive solutions for the One-Seven mixture, we may have corresponding problems. If we can only help people, only deal with weak people, we eventually wonder why no one does anything for us. Life is interdependent. If we have no place for healthy competition, the aggressive side of the nature may be repressed and create illness; it may be projected, and others use our power against us; or it may be displaced so that relationships that should be harmonious turn into power struggles. With the strong mutable emphasis in this chart, especially the Pisces and especially in the Cancer house, finding a way to express the aggression may be a problem. Sports or games should be a good solution, and with Saturn in the sixth house, he might have a competitive business. Certainly, the Saturn and Uranus in the sixth house show the desire to control his own work. He can run his own business, manage a department in a larger business, or be a professional with his own office. Neither Saturn nor Uranus will work under anyone if they can avoid it.

I usually look for a common theme for Saturn and the South Node, as a clue to the basic lessons in the life. Air and mutability are shared with South Node in a mutable sign and house and the house naturally air; Saturn is in a mutable house and conjunct an air planet. The air lesson is equality with other people, detachment and objectivity, learning to take things lightly and not to try to change people — just to accept them. The mutable dilemma has been discussed. The Pisces lesson is the development of faith in a Higher Power once we have done the best we can. So our subject is learning how much trust to put in himself, how much to expect of others (if we idealize others, we may be disappointed or we may feel inferior if we keep them on a pedestal), and how much faith to give to God.

The new asteroids hit the grand cross in mutable signs and cardinal houses, making the orbs tighter. Hidalgo (Saturn?) is in Sagittarius conjunct the Eastpoint, wanting personal power to do what he wants, and Sagittarius wants it all immediately. Urania is on the IC, suggesting ambivalence about the rooted home the Moon wants, with the potential for being uprooted periodically. Pandora fills in the fourth corner, close to Jupiter in Gemini in the seventh house, inquisitive, wanting communication. Lilith conjunct Vesta and the Antivertex suggests ambivalence between work and mate, with work likely to win in view of the dominance of earth and the close trine to the MC. Dembowska on the Moon repeats work versus home/family. Diana conjuncts the Sun in the fourth, and I'm still uncertain about what to do with Diana. If she is another Moon or mother figure, we have a really strong desire to mother or be mothered. If she is a warrior or hunter, we have ambivalence: protection of children and the nest or destruction? Sappho and Psyche form another trine in earth, so at least there seems to be no question about his ability to cope with the material world: work and earning a living. As usual, relationships are probably the challenge: Saturn opposes Juno, the marriage asteroid. But the issue of faith is also central.

Our fourth subject in this section is another male with a Pisces Sun, Capricorn in the first house, and a very mutable chart concentrated in Pisces and Gemini, but in fixed houses. Both parents may have been role models with Capricorn in the first house pointing to father or grandfather, supported by Mars conjunct Saturn, while Moon conjunct Ascendant as well as Mars conjunct Ceres point to mother. A strong identification with work is shown by both the One-Ten mixtures already mentioned, but also by Vesta at the midpoint of two first house rulers, Saturn and Uranus, while Mars is in the Virgo house. The Saturn and Uranus placement in the fifth house also shows a dramatic instinct which is supported by the planets in Leo in the seventh house. A Leo emphasis in a chart can manifest in many ways. A need for love or for admiration and attention, and a sense of personal power can be satisfied through working with children, through selling and promotion or through the dramatic arts, etc. The artistic potential seems important with Pisces in the second house, Venus in its own house in the Neptune sign, while Neptune is in a Venus sign and there is a close aspect between them. Generally, a chart that features Pisces and Leo indicates a person with a vivid, creative imagination and a strong sense of showmanship. If they choose the martyr route, they make really dramatic martyrs. However, with the Capricorn-Virgo identification, there may be too much inhibition to allow expression of the dramatic instincts except in the mind. He certainly might be a writer or work in some other field of communication.

His challenges seem to be mostly in the mutable dilemma by sign, and the fixed dilemma by house, though he does have Pallas square Pluto and the nodes in fixed signs and cardinal houses. The mutable lesson, as you know by now, involves the need for clear and reasonable goals. The Pisces-Gemini squares may be manifested as difficulty in deciding among many talents and interests, but the strong Capricorn and Virgo makes this alternative less likely. Individuals with an identification with productive accomplishment are more likely to experience a conflict between ideals and reality. They want to do more than is possible, and may never feel satisfied. The second house emphasis and the stellium in Gemini may help to solve the problem. Letters Two and Three are usually able to enjoy the journey, to avoid the extremes of perfectionism. But it will be important for him to feel a sense of major accomplishment, and to get some recognition for it.

Both of our lesson factors, Saturn and South Node of the Moon, are in air signs and fire houses but also connected by conjunctions to earth factors, so their lessons could be in many areas. Learning to be an equal, to detach, to let others be themselves without trying to change them, to let them handle their share of things: any of these might be air lessons. It is always puzzling when a chart has so much in an element and yet it is indicated as a lesson. Sometimes, the challenge is that we are overdoing the element, or doing it in the wrong time or place. The fire lessons usually involve overreach or self-blocking, too much self-will and impulsiveness, or too little. Of course Letters One and Five are more connected to will than is Letter Nine. The earth lessons center around practicality and the so-called "Puritan" virtues when Virgo and/or Capricorn are involved as they are here. South Node is conjunct the Capricorn East-point and Saturn is conjunct Vesta and Mars in the Virgo house, so they are part of the picture. He might not want to do what he should do and want to do the impossible. He might dream great dreams of fame and pleasures but not do much and get sick. But he should have a versatile, creative mind and plenty of capacity for success if he can be satisfied with "bite-sized" goals, small steps toward his dreams.

The new asteroids provide some interesting themes. All except two (Diana and Psyche) are in air or mutable signs or houses, reinforcing the mental emphasis in the chart. Especially Urania (like Uranus?) in the Sagittarian house, trine Mars and Ceres and quincunx Sun and Mercury, plus Pandora (like Mercury?) in Sagittarius in the Aquarian house, Psyche on the Eastpoint, and two more of the little planets in the first house in Aquarius keep hammering at the desire to go beyond present knowledge, to discover something more. Another fascinating group is the clustering of the three asteroids that seem similar to Pluto, all three conjunct Vesta and close to the first house rulers, Saturn and Uranus. That is a power package though it might express purely in the mind. The two asteroids that seem like Saturn, Hidalgo and Dembowska, form a grand trine to Pallas in earth signs and water houses. Again we have the urgent need to accomplish something, but water may remain dependent and feel vulnerable and miserable. Eros and Icarus in Aquarius in the first house, trine the Gemini grouping, suggest energy to carry out the ideas, at least verbally. A first house Icarus, like a first house Sun, adds to the showmanship and the high aspirations. The general picture suggests a man with a very creative mind who wants to do something great and dramatic with his life. If he can integrate his ideals and the limits of the material world, he might offer a mental gift to the world. If he finds the ideal love he wants (Venus and Juno in Pisces, Jupiter in the seventh house, Neptune in Libra in the ninth house), he might be content without the plaudits of the world.

Our fifth subject in this chapter is just coming of age this year, as this book is being written. Born on August 12, 1961, his chart features a Leo stellium in the Taurus house, wanting a pleasant, easy and loving life. Cancer rising, and the Moon on its own node, show an important tie to a mother-figure. With Ceres square the Leo Sun, one of the rulers of the first house, there might be friction in the relationship with the mother. Vesta, widely conjunct Ceres, and Ceres in the eleventh house suggest the possibility that mother is busy working or involved in transpersonal activity so our subject may not get the full attention and love that he would like. Vesta connected to a parent sometimes means that either the child or the parent is critical of the other (or there can be a mutual criticism society), but this is less likely with Taurus and Letter Eleven involved. Both tend to be more accepting.

Saturn shows mixed patterns for father. Its opposition to the Ascendant

can indicate estrangement from the parent, sometimes physical separation and a grandparent replacing the father. Saturn also is quincunx the
Moon, an aspect often found when the parents separate emotionally or
physically. But Saturn also is in a grand trine to Mars and Ceres, so our
subject and mother and father may have worked things out. Mars in the
third house can also indicate a sibling as role model. If we like the part
of ourselves reflected back from the sibling, we may have a good relationship. Otherwise, there may be sibling rivalry. With Mars in Virgo, there
may be self-criticism and/or the subject and the sibling may be critical
of each other.

Since both the tenth and fourth houses are ruled by Mars and Venus,
it is possible that the parents are similar or that one parent is playing both
roles. Idealism is connected to one or both parents, with Neptune in the
fourth house and Venus, ruling both parent houses, in the twelfth house.
He will also want an ideal mate, with Neptune in Scorpio (one of the
partnership signs), Jupiter in the seventh house, and Juno and Pallas in
the ninth house, as well as Pallas in Pisces. When we connect the search
for the Absolute to human relationships, there are several dangers. We
may expect them to give us a perfect life and be disappointed. We may
put them on a pedestal and put ourselves down. We may look forever
for the ideal and never make a commitment, or keep changing because
everyone turns out to have feet of clay. We may choose to play God
ourselves and pick out victims that we can save. With Saturn also in the
seventh in this case, the subject might prefer weak people to avoid the
risk of being dominated or controlled in any way. He clearly wants the
power in his own hands for his own pleasure with the first house rulers
in Leo in the second house. Both South Node and Saturn in the partnership houses point to that as the basic lesson area: to be able to compromise and cooperate, to fully respect the rights of others.

Again, the new asteroids offer intriguing patterns. Both the potential
Saturns, Dembowska and Hidalgo, fall in the eighth house, hammering
home the lesson of sharing power, possessions or pleasure with others;
of mastering ourselves but not trying to control anyone else. Three more
asteroids are in Scorpio in the fifth house, all potentially connected to
love or relationships: Diana, Eros and Frigga. An intense need for love
and closeness is suggested, but a danger of power struggles with the
squares to the other fixed signs and houses. These Scorpio asteroids filled
in the last corner of a grand cross, and Dembowska also tightened it. Two
of the asteroids associated with will are on the Ascendant and another
is on Venus. With two potential keys to Scorpio (Pittsburghia and Lilith),
combined with one that may be Taurus (Toro), connected to Venus (ruler
of Taurus) and Ascendant (instinctive action like Mars), we have a Two-Eight
action potential to reiterate the fixed dilemma. As if we needed any more,
Icarus and Urania (like Leo and Aquarius) are in Leo in the second house:

more and more fixity. The other possible Pluto asteroid, Dudu, is in the eleventh house (fixed again), but in early Gemini. Its conjunction with the Antivertex is a repetition of the Lilith conjunct Ascendant, giving the same message as Pluto conjunct the Ascendant. His major life issue lies somewhere in the fixed dilemma. Is he controlling the world or himself?

Our last subject in this section is the female born April 3, 1962. Our first glance at the chart shows another Letter Eight theme. Pluto is rising, and Mercury, ruler of the first house, is in the eighth house. With Mars in the seventh house and a stellium in Aries in the eighth house, there could be a very intense feeling that others have our power and might use it against us. With Jupiter on the Descendant and Pisces in the seventh house, there is also the association of others with ideals, whether we over-rate them, choose weak people to save, or any of the other variations. The chart is strongly water and fire, showing an emotional, volatile person. Jupiter, Chiron and Mars, all fire planets, are in a water sign. The fire Sun, and the water Moon are in a fire sign in a water house. Water Pluto is in a fire house. Leo is in the Pisces house. If the fire-water mixtures are not handled, they may manifest as the emotional yoyo (strong mood swings), or as the pressure cooker (holding back and then blowing). She needs to recognize her emotionality and learn to channel it. With the strong competitive instincts, competitive sports or game-playing would be very helpful.

Mother is a major role model with Moon in Aries and conjunct the ruler of the Ascendant, Mercury. Another way that personal identity can be connected to a parent is a shared rulership, i.e., when the same planet rules both the first house and the house symbolizing the parent. In this case, Mercury rules both the Ascendant and the sign in the tenth house. We tentatively assume a tenth house mother since Ceres is in the tenth. Since Vesta is conjunct Ceres and they are square the first house Pluto, and the Moon is quincunx the Ascendant, there might be conflict with mother, or a separation from her. But the chart also suggests lessons from father with the South Node on Saturn, even though widely, and with Jupiter opposite the Ascendant. Pluto, ruling the fourth house and in the first house, brings in father as role model. Aspects suggesting possible separation (quincunx and opposition) may mean emotional distance, or temporary trips, or differing ideas. We can never assume details. The chart shows the issue, and we can learn to handle it in constructive ways as we mature. Usually, a tenth house mother will be a working mother, but even that is not certain. Father is tied to work with Saturn in the sixth house, but also to intellect with Aquarius, maybe to openness and acceptance. Air is the element of conscious mind and people, good for communication and detachment. If we want emotional closeness to the parent, air might be less desired. To a child, it might feel like coolness and indifference. But she has a chance to learn from both parents how to detach and how to work, how to relate comfortably with other people in an open, accepting way.

Our subject's assets include a quick, sharp mind and tongue though Mercury's water house, plus an earth sign and a water planet rising, might inhibit the speech. The fire emphasis shows much creativity, a pioneering spirit, but in the eighth house, a need to work out issues in relationships. The will should be very strong, and also the sense of the dramatic, with both Leo and Pisces present, especially Leo-Pisces or fire-Pisces mixtures. Her third house Neptune adds to the creative imagination and probable love of fantasy. She could have high energy and much magnetism if she is not blocking the fire. Saturn trine Ceres and Vesta shows a good potential for success in the work world. But because both Saturn and South Node are in the same sign and house, there is also a lesson there, in earth or in air. The Virgo lesson is often to be content with small accomplishments, to accept authority and not have to run the show, to be practical. Since she has Virgo rising, she came in able to do at least some of the Virgo part of life. Part of her lesson may involve self-criticism and a need to prove herself to the world. If she can know when to be logical and practical without losing her emotional warmth, she will work it out.

The new asteroids, as with the last chart, accentuate the issue of power. Dudu (one possible Pluto) is on the Vesta-Ceres-MC grouping and Lilith (another possible Pluto) is rising. With eleven more asteroids in either fixed signs or fixed houses, the power theme is pretty strong. Psyche is one exception, exactly on the Ascendant in Virgo, suggesting that much of the life might be lived in the mind, or that mental work should be chosen (said already by the air signs in the work houses). Or she might initially express the inadequacy, self-absorption potential of Psyche in view of the strong danger of projecting her power into others. The other exception to the fixed emphasis is Amor in Pisces in the seventh house, conjunct Mars and repeating the desire for an ideal love and the ambivalence over freedom versus closeness. Hidalgo and Dembowska, our two potential Saturns, also highlight the power issue. Hidalgo joins the Mercury-Moon conjunction; Dembowska midpoints Pallas-Sun in the eighth house. The combination indicates a need to handle power wisely, joining self-will and the limits of self-will with the need to share power and pleasures with others. We may hold the power in and retreat from others and usually end up ill. We may use our power against others, which can be fine in game-playing competition but less fun if one person wins all the time. We may help others; again, fine if we can also accept help from others some of the time. The One-Eight mixture (Aries in the eighth house, Pluto in the first house, and Mercury, ruler of the first house, in the eighth house) will be reinforced once more in her teens when Mars moves into the eighth house by progression. Self-will versus self-mastery; our rights versus our ability to share with others. The issue is clear. Her handling of it is up to her.

If you are following the suggested procedure, and have not yet looked ahead to discover the identity of these six people, having now read an astrological interpretation of their charts, you might study the horoscopes once more and draw your own conclusions on how they handled their challenges and assets. Then it will be time to discover who they are and what they actually did in their lives. Have you noticed that all six individuals have Jupiter in the seventh or eighth house (or on the Descendant)?

*   *   *   *   *

The **six individuals** discussed in this chapter **are all murderers**. Our **first subject** is **James Warren Jones**. He was an only child, very close to his mother and rejecting of his father who was a veteran, injured in the war, and never able to do much. The family could not survive on the small pension, so Jones's mother worked to supplement their income. Jones despised his father, who joined the Ku Klux Klan to be able to bolster his deflated ego by putting someone down. Jones chose to befriend blacks, and after becoming a minister, he courted them as members of his church. He married at 18 and his wife was devoted and loyal to him to her death, in spite of his outrageous behavior in his later years. He dropped out of college to become a minister, and worked at a number of selling and promoting jobs to survive financially. He had one son, but he and his wife adopted a number of children.

Over the years, Jones became more and more paranoid. When his progressed Mars was conjunct Neptune, he began the fake healings in which his church members had to pretend to be ill and pretend to be healed at public services. Jones apparently lost whatever faith he had before and told his church members that they did not need to read the Bible or believe in God. They just had to listen to and trust him. Some of his followers dropped away as they saw him change, but the love and loyalty of the group held many. As a group, they moved from Indiana to Northern California, then to San Francisco, and finally they started a settlement in the jungles of Guiana. The church members were largely lower class blacks and middle-class whites with a strong sense of mission to heal the schism between the races.

In addition to his growing paranoia, Jones had also grown increasingly violent, physically and mentally attacking anyone who displeased him. He had also become sensually excessive, indulging in sexual acts with both males and females in the group, while claiming that it was for their benefit rather than his own pleasure. He was also apparently taking drugs, both for increasing health problems and for "kicks." In his need for money to maintain his establishment, he pressured people to give all they had to the church, including selling their homes. There was even a suspicion that he might be involved in the murder of someone who resisted his control. Jones had put local officials in his debt by being able and willing to turn out his church members for demonstrations or for a vote, but finally a California magazine printed an article accusing him of destructive and illegal activities. Jones had seen the attack coming, and he and most of his flock fled to the settlement in Guiana. When a congressman followed to investigate some of the charges, he and his party were attacked, several killed, and then the whole church was persuaded or forced to drink poison in a mass suicide.

Jones himself died from a gunshot, and no one knows who killed him. In the analysis of his chart, the tie between his mother and his religious beliefs was mentioned. His mother had a vision before his birth and told him that he was destined to be a great religious savior. A tape recording was running during the mass suicide, and Jones's last words on the tape were, "Mother, Mother, I tried, I tried." The cardinal and fixed conflict in his chart showed the potential for power struggles. Mars in the eighth house showed the potential for the projected power that became paranoia. But it was the mutable dilemma that undid him, the loss of faith in a Higher Power and the attempt to play God himself. From the days of the fake healings with Mars on Neptune, it was downhill all the way. The tragedy was the number of people he took with him, the people who trusted him too much, too long. He was charismatic, and many of the people had been together a long time, shared love and suffering and a dream of a better world. They clung to their faith and ignored the visible reality of Jones deteriorating into madness, or they believed him when he said the rest of the world was against them and only he could protect them. In the world created by our beliefs, we live and we die.

Our **second subject** is **Dean Corll**, the Houston, Texas murderer. I have very little information on his early life but believe that he was raised by his mother. He did not marry, but engaged in sexual acts and torture with a series of young men. Two men who participated in some of the activity finally killed Corll in the summer of 1974. They were sentenced to jail for some of the crimes.

Our **third subject** is **John Wayne Gacey**, a Chicago plumber who also murdered a series of young men after having sex with them. He had been married and divorced twice, and was known in his neighborhood as the one to call when anyone needed help. His neighbors could not believe it at first when the bodies were dug out from under his house. He said that he killed to protect himself, to keep his victims from reporting his sexual acts. He strangled most of his victims. Note that his Saturn is conjunct Algol, the star associated with death by the throat. In 1979, he was sentenced for some of the murders.

Our **fourth subject** is **Sirhan Sirhan**, sentenced to jail for shooting Bobby Kennedy in Los Angeles. He had been a very introverted person who read and fantasied a lot on the problems of the world and what should be done about them. He left a confused diary about the struggle over Israel and his wish to force the authorities of the world to solve the problem.

Our **fifth subject was a teenager when he killed**. He adored his mother and bitterly resented his younger sister. One day, he says, he blacked out, and when he came to, he had killed three little girls who were friends of his sister and about her age of 8. Though he was only 17 at the time, the murders were so vicious, he was tried and sentenced to jail as an adult.

Our **sixth subject** was also a **teenager when she killed**. Her parents were divorced and she was essentially a total loner, reading and daydreaming about guns. Her father had a rifle in the house, and one morning, she took it and shot her high school principal and custodian. She also was sent to jail for it.

I do not think that astrology can say that a person will be a murderer or a victim. These charts have had patterns similar to some of the healers and psychokinetic practitioners presented here. We don't have final answers on why some people use power to help others, some limit their power to control over objects or over themselves, some attack others. It does seem that faith in oneself, capacity to care for others and faith in a Higher Power are the foundation for a constructive life. Fear and/or anger against ourselves or others lead to destruction. The same power can light and warm a city or can destroy it. Astrology points out the issues. Each individual chooses, consciously or unconsciously, his or her manifestation of the principles. If we believe in reincarnation, we have faith that there will be another opportunity to learn and to grow.

CHAPTER 14

A Case for Locality Charts

A horoscope is a map of the sky drawn for the date, time and place of an event, such as a person's birth. The individual may move to new places, but the original map continues to provide useful information on the developing life. It is also possible to draw a map (calculate a horoscope) with the positions of planets as they were at this individual's birth, but placed as they would have been seen from the new residence. In the locality chart, the calculations are carried out as if the person had been born in the new place of residence, keeping the birth date and Greenwich time identical to the birth chart. The planets do not change, but the house cusps change. If the new location is in a different time zone than the one at birth, most or all planets will appear in different houses. In my experience, the locality chart has been very important and valuable on numerous occasions. The case presented here is an extreme example of the way that local angles can highlight issues in a life.

Dramatic events should correspond with a dramatic horoscope, and Azaria's chart is an impressive example. She was born in Australia to a family which included a minister father, a mother and two older brothers. When she was only two months old, the family visited Ayer's Rock, a tourist mecca in the outback of central Australia. While having a picnic at the huge rock that is in the midst of fairly wild desert country, the parents reported that a wild dog (the Australian dingo) seized the baby and carried her off. She is assumed to be dead. Blood was found in the family car, and on a pair of scissors, and the authorities have charged the mother with the murder of the baby. The father is accused as an accessory after the fact, as covering up the actual events to protect his wife. They were due to come to trial in April 1982, but the hearing was postponed for some months. The case was headlined in the newspapers of Australia during my visit there in January 1982.

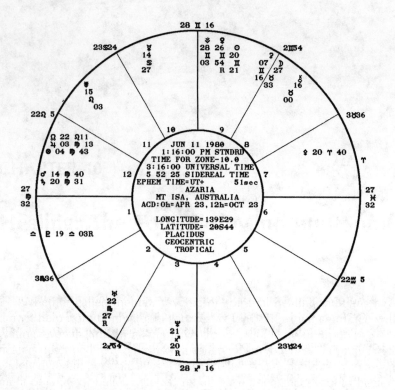

JUN 11 1980
1:16:00 PM STNDRD
TIME FOR ZONE-10.0
3:16:00 UNIVERSAL TIME
5 52 25 SIDEREAL TIME
EPHEM TIME=UT+ 51sec
AZARIA
MT ISA, AUSTRALIA
ACD:0h=APR 23,12h=OCT 23

LONGITUDE= 139E29
LATITUDE= 20S44
PLACIDUS
GEOCENTRIC
TROPICAL

⚷ 18-♊-10   ? 17-♏-33R   ⚶ 20-♍-07   ⚳ 25-♈-00   ⚸ 13-♉-38
� 12-♍-52   ♦ 03-♎-43   ⚴ 29-♉-47   ⚵ 29-♋-43   ⚷ 05-♏-58R
♆ 19-♎-49   ♇ 22-♑-29R   ⚵ 09-♈-21   ⚿ 17-♒-05   ☽ 22-♈-31
AntiVertex 29-♍-02   Eastpoint 27-♍-56

Azaria's horoscope shows a heavy conflict pattern which includes the Sun-Venus-Vesta-MC opposite Neptune (across the third-ninth houses), and all of them square the Virgo in the twelfth and first houses. Jupiter is too early in Virgo to be included except in a square to Ceres, but Mars is widely, and Saturn exactly, square Sun-Neptune, while the Ascendant-Eastpoint-Antivertex square the Venus-Vesta-MC grouping. The Moon in the eighth house is widely opposite Uranus and octile Mercury in the tenth house, and the nodes of the Moon turn the opposition into a grand cross in fixed signs and partly in fixed houses. Pluto in the first house is widely square Mercury, which rules the Ascendant and the MC. The fixed cross shows possible power struggles with relationships that could affect health (South Node in the sixth house), and that can end in death if not resolved. The mutable t-square shows a conflict over faith (truth) vs. reality, which also could involve relationships since the aspects include Ceres (mother), Saturn (father), Jupiter (third house ruler, so siblings) and Neptune in the third house.

The heavy Virgo emphasis includes the planets and angles in the sign, the South Node in the house of Virgo, and Vesta exactly on the MC and square the Ascendant. Virgo represents the capacity to function efficiently in a job and in our body (to be healthy). To do a good job, we have to look for flaws and correct them, and we have to limit the energy and time devoted to emotional relationships and recreation. Too heavy an emphasis on Letter Six can lead to a variety of problems, including illness (if we hate our work and want to get out of it); displacement of the critical attitude into the wrong areas of life (people) and consequent destructive relationships; or neglect of other parts of life in order to accomplish more in the work. Such theories seem irrelevant in the chart of a baby, but if we are to use astrology to understand people, we must be clear about the principles regardless of the age. If we accept reincarnation, there is no problem with age. The character formed in past lives is present from the beginning of this life, and produces the destiny that fits that character. In babyhood, the destiny is clearly beyond our control, affecting us through the actions of others. But the only way we can learn to take control in time is to understand what in our nature is permitting that destiny. When life is cut off early, we have to hope that learning will take place on the next level, and that the next return will provide a chance to do more.

Since Azaria was not ill, the work-avoidance issue of Virgo is not relevant in this case. Another possible reason for early illness is neglect of the body in past lives, perhaps due to religious ideas that spirituality required abuse of the physical body. But in Azaria's case, we have to look to the other potential Virgo problem of strained human relationships, quite possibly past life relationships, since the problem existed right at the beginning of life this time. Astrology alone cannot make a definitive statement about details to determine whether a wild dog took Azaria, or whether her mother, her father, her sibling(s) or a stranger was guilty of her presumed death. We can make an educated guess from the chart, and watch as the jury tries to decide a very difficult issue.

Traditional astrology assigns domestic animals to the sixth house and wild (or large) animals to the ninth or twelfth houses. I suspect that this assignment applied to domestic animals that were contributing workers: guard, herd, or retriever dogs, cats that caught rodents. Nowadays, pets may well come more into the fourth house where they are often a substitute for children. But wild animals may still correlate with Letter Nine. We have enough conflict from both ninth house and Sagittarius placements square twelfth house planets, including Ascendant (the life force) so that we could not rule out an animal. But the relationship area is so implicated, that we have to consider a possible human agent. We also cannot rule out a stranger with both rulers of the eleventh house (Moon and Sun) in stress aspect to the natural ruler, Uranus. But the aspects are not exact, so it seems less likely, and if the dog story is untrue, the mother would hardly have fabricated it to protect a stranger.

So the finger points to the family. All of them are certainly emotionally involved, their lives disrupted by the court proceedings even if the verdict is "Not guilty." So there have to be conflict patterns to all members of the family. Saturn (father) is certainly central in the conflict aspects. The two rulers of the tenth house (mother in this case) are Moon and Mercury, and the progressed Moon, just two months after Azaria's birth, was twenty-nine Taurus, exactly octile Mercury, showing mother in a state of inner conflict as well as confronting the power of the Law. Ceres (mother) also squares Jupiter (both father as ruler of the fourth house and siblings as ruler of the third house), showing the stress involving the whole family. But the Ceres aspect is not exact, and the natal Moon is trine the natal Ascendant while the progressed Moon is trine the Antivertex (an auxiliary Ascendant). The aspects suggest that the mother's relationship with the baby was basically positive. We cannot rule out the mother as killer, but we can certainly consider it a less likely possibility with those aspects.

What about the brothers? They are young, around seven or eight years old, and one is reported to be not quite mentally normal. Children can be highly resentful of a new baby that pushes them out of center stage in the family. A mother might lie to protect a child, hoping the wild dog would be accepted as villain so that a living child would not carry such a stigma the rest of his life. One of the Arabic Parts that can sometimes provide information is called the Part of Death: Ascendant plus eighth cusp minus Moon. In Azaria's chart, it falls on three Virgo, exactly conjunct Jupiter, ruler of the siblings and the father. But the fourth house is also considered a death house, as much as the eighth: the end of life, so the link of houses three and four (the same planet ruling both) could link the brothers to the death. Mercury is also a natural ruler of siblings, and as already indicated, the progressed Moon was octile it at the death. Neptune, certainly a major key to the event with its exact aspects, is in the house of the brothers. If I were on the jury, I would certainly want to check out the brothers, perhaps with a psychological examination.

A primary reason for including this case is the dramatic picture presented by the locality chart. At Ayer's Rock, Azaria's MC became twenty Gemini, putting her Sun on the Midheaven, Neptune on the IC and Saturn exactly square the angles. The local Ascendant became fifteen Virgo, just over one degree from natal Mars. The local Part of Death is at the midpoint of the natal Ascendant-MC-Vesta, octile all of them. The locality chart presents a stark picture of the situation. With her Sun on the MC, she was headlined in newspapers all over Australia. With Neptune on the IC, her end was, and still is, a total mystery. With Saturn square its own house from the first house, her "will in action" met the limits of her will in a permanent form. When we do not or cannot use our own aggression (Mars), it may be used against us. Mars conjunct the local Ascendant shows the capacity for aggression. However, Virgo in the Pisces house can inhibit the self-assertion. Obviously, a baby lacks the capacity for self-defense, so we have to think about unconscious, ingrained character from past lives. We wonder about the relationships in past lives with this family to which she came for so short a time, but there is no way to know the details.

Extreme cases such as this one offer us a chance to test many of the minor factors of astrology. In Chapter 5, a standard type of Arabic Part was suggested as potentially another form of the twelve sides of life: Ascendant plus planet minus Sun, as an alternate key to the planet. Azaria's Part of Saturn falls conjunct her natal IC and square her Ascendant axis. Her Part of Neptune falls on her Descendant and square her MC axis. Her Part of Mars falls on her Neptune and local fourth cusp, opposite Sun and square Saturn. Her Part of Pluto is quincunx Venus. Her Part of Uranus is quincunx Antivertex, square progressed Moon and trioctile Mercury. These are all aspects within a one-degree orb. When we turn to other classes of minor factors, we get the same message. Azaria's heliocentric Saturn is on her natal Ascendant square Venus. Heliocentric Mercury conjuncts heliocentric Pluto at twenty degrees of Libra in the first house.

There are also numerous close aspects involving planetary nodes. The nodes of Ceres fall across the Sun-Neptune opposition square Saturn. South Jupiter is opposite Mercury. North Pluto squares Pluto with North Saturn and South Pluto tied to it in overlapping orbs. South Neptune is trioctile Ascendant and MC-Vesta. South Mars is trioctile natal Moon. North Uranus squares natal Mars. Remember, these are one degree orb aspects repeating the same messages: tension and potential disruption of the life associated with power outside of Azaria's control, possibly involving relationships.

The new asteroids hammer at the themes again. The three potential Plutos are all important. Dudu is on the Sun and Pittsburghia on Saturn, intensifying the mutable t-square. Lilith is on Pluto. The two potential Saturns are both in Scorpio, Hidalgo octile and trioctile the mutable t-square and Dembowska quincunx the Sun-Dudu. Dembowska also forms a fixed grand square with other asteroids: Juno, Chiron and Toro. Urania conjuncts Mars. Icarus in Aries in the seventh house is octile-trioctile the grand cross of Moon-nodes-Uranus. A whole series of yods are formed with the asteroids, including three with Uranus as one corner of the pattern. The yod or double quincunx is typically an indication of major changes in a life, moving in new directions, leaving the past behind.

As has been said frequently, astrology is repetitive. There are many tools and techniques that repeat the basic message, give the basic meaning of the chart. If we can understand our nature, we can choose more effective ways to move toward our desires. When a life is ended so soon, as was Azaria's, it is important to focus on the principles and not limit our attention to the drastic details. Until we understand how the principles can permit or produce the details, we are doomed to play victim and grow through suffering. When we understand, we can change our expression of the principles and produce happier details.

CHAPTER 15

Making Friends With the Twelfth House

As indicated in the chapter discussing the basic astrological alphabet, Letter Twelve (Neptune, Pisces and the twelfth house) represents our search for the emotional Absolute, for infinite love and beauty, for oneness with the Whole. The three primary forms of manifestation of Letter Twelve (each with many possible details) include becoming an artist, a savior or a victim. Unfortunately, many astrology texts assume the victim outcome, and neglect the other two options. Many astrologers are still unaware of the research of Michel and Francoise Gauquelin who calculated the horoscopes of thousands of famous individuals. The Gauquelins found that the planets placed in the ten degrees below the horizon (the first ten degrees of the first house of the chart) and in the whole twelfth house were keys to both the vocation and basic personality of the individual. A similar **zone of power** extended through the first ten degrees of the tenth house and the whole ninth house of the chart. For example, Mars was in the twelfth house of the chart more often than in any other part of the charts of the famous athletes, military men and surgeons. The statistical odds against the Gauquelin results occurring by chance were as high as a million to one. In other words, if the Gauquelins duplicated these experiments one million times, these results might occur once by coincidence. The study of sports champions has now been repeated five times with different groups of athletes from different countries, achieving the same results for all sports except basketball players. The latter must be very tall to be successful, and Mars is not associated with height, but with a wiry strength. With five repetitions of the same study using different subjects, the odds against the results being chance or coincidence have gone up to astronomical figures.

The Gauquelin results fit well into the theories presented in this book.

Letters Nine and Twelve (planets, houses, and signs, in that order of importance) are different sides of our search for the absolute, with Letter Twelve more unconscious and potentially, therefore, more powerful. The nature of the planet in these two houses will then be highly emphasized in the person. If the person trusts the desire symbolized by the planet, he or she will express it vigorously, often excessively. Those who lack faith in themselves and their desires, or who are in conflict between those desires and other parts of their nature, are likely to block the urges. Self-blocking or sustained conflict can lead to many varieties of victim: repression, producing illness; projection, attracting others who overdo what is being blocked in the subject; displacement, an expression of the urges in the wrong place or time or way. It is also possible to simply stay frustrated because the warring desires block each other so the individual does neither. Michel and Francoise Gauquelin have studied only highly successful individuals who are expressing the nature of their twelfth house planet, often to an extreme degree. Many astrologers deal with clients who lack faith, are in conflict within themselves, or want their dreams provided in an easy way, so the astrologers see the negative form of Letter Twelve. Since life is a mirror, the more an astrologer or other counselor is personally in conflict over faith or personally committed to the savior role, the more he or she will attract victims.

Teilhard de Chardin

The individuals presented in this chapter are or were primarily two of the three basic choices, since I have been more involved in the savior-victim polarity, with minimal contacts with professional artists. Our first subject was actually a bit of an artist but he was also a scientist. He is best known for his writings, and his primary vocation was a Catholic priest. Teilhard de Chardin entered Jesuit boarding school at the age of ten and became a novitiate of the Order at the age of eighteen. He specialized in studies of paleontology and geology in addition to his philosophical and religious training. His work in the scientific studies of evolution ranged through several continents, and included participation in the discovery of the famous Peking man in China. Partly out of his experiences tracing the development of Earth and human beings, de Chardin conceived his theory that humans are evolving mentally and socially toward a final spiritual unity. The official Catholic position questioned his ideas; his books were published after his death on Easter Sunday, April 10, 1955. His fame came after death, as his blend of science and religion appealed to many who sought a synthesis of the two seeming opposites.

Since de Chardin was born before 1900, we lack the new asteroids, but do have the first four to be discovered and Chiron. The chart is clearly marked by the Letter Twelve emphasis. Nine of our nineteen factors are in the twelfth house, Mars is in Pisces, and Jupiter progressed to the

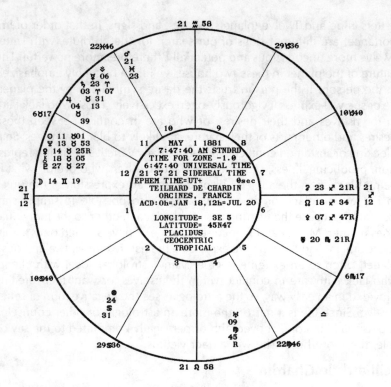

X 18-♉-51   E 06-Ⅱ-05

CEOCENTRIC
N-NODE S-NODE
☽ 20Sa14 20Ge14
⚷ 12Ta25 06Ta14
♀ 25Ta21 25P153
♂ 15Ta33 02Sa21
♃ 01Ca07 20Cp15

♄ 17Ca24 28Cp57
♅ 11Ge34 14Sa47
♆ 08Le39 12Aq29
♇ 17Ca15 20Cp08

twelfth house cusp around the time he entered his religious studies as a child. He was personally identified with the Absolute (Mars, natural key to the identity in Pisces; Moon, actual ruler of the first house in the twelfth house, along with the Antivertex and Eastpoint, our auxiliary Ascendants). With the Sun also there, de Chardin wished to expand that part of his life and find a sense of self-worth there, through one of the Letter Twelve forms of expression. Mercury, the other key to instinctive identity, as ruler of the first house, shows the importance of the mind in his life. Mercury in Aries in the eleventh house shows an original and pioneering mind, determined to go beyond prior limits. Mercury's trioctile to Uranus repeats the theme of mental ability and need to go beyond previous mental limits. Aries in the eleventh house repeats the identification with the mind, and Vesta in Aries shows an identification with work.

My normal method of chart interpretation is to look first for themes: combinations that repeat the same basic message. When I do not see an immediate theme, then I often start as I have here, with an analysis of all forms of Letter One in the chart. We could easily have begun with a theme here, the concentration of planets in personal signs in transpersonal houses. The neglected third of life is obviously the interpersonal area. He has only Uranus (a transpersonal planet in a work sign), in the fourth house (home and family) and Ceres (which can express as either protective mother or in work) in a transpersonal sign in the partnership house, and Juno, the marriage asteroid, in Scorpio (potential sign of a mate) in the work house. We have as clear an emphasis as possible on the likelihood of a life with a strong sense of personal needs but absorbed in transpersonal issues: the search for Truth and concern for society as a whole. It is true we also have the Sun conjunct the Antivertex and Venus, but with Neptune and Chiron also there, and the stellium in the Neptune house, the scales tip back toward the Absolute. Moon conjunct one of its own nodes could also want emotional ties, but the South Node is a lesson. He gave up the home and family side of the Moon and its nodes, but found his emotional security in thinking, speaking and writing about God. Juno's opposition to the whole Taurus stellium in the twelfth house, more or less at the midpoint of the Taurus group, is a further statement of his separation from marriage. With Juno in the sixth house, he was married to his work, and with Sagittarius in the seventh house, he was married to God and the Church. His South Node of Juno conjunct natal Vesta repeats his choice of work rather than marriage, and combined with Virgo in the fifth house, is one of the keys to potential celibacy. Even the parallels give the same message. Juno is parallel Vesta, while his Sun is parallel both Chiron and Neptune, two of the keys to the quest for spiritual Truth.

The possibility of a spiritual career is said by Sagittarius in the sixth house and Pisces in the tenth house, as well as by the Jupiter-Saturn conjunction, with both planets moving into the twelfth house in progression. De Chardin walked a tightrope all his life between his scientific knowledge and his traditional faith, seeking to integrate the physical evidence accumulated by science partly through his own work and his deep mystical experiences. One of the ancient traditions predicts the birth of world teachers at twenty-year intervals, when Jupiter and Saturn conjoin to begin a new cycle. With Jupiter a key to religion-philosophy-science, our theories about the Absolute, and with Saturn symbolizing the **law**, the actual nature of the world about which we are theorizing with Jupiter, a meeting of the two could indicate the birth of individuals who arrived in possession of innate knowledge of the Law, and who came to share it with the world. De Chardin's life would fit that ancient idea. Obviously, not everyone born with a Jupiter-Saturn conjunction achieves that potential. Some struggle unsuccessfully to integrate faith and doubt or fear. Some swing between excessive overconfidence, leading to overreach, followed by holding back or being told by circumstances that they were out-of-bounds. Some manifest one side and end with problems from the other side of the nature. De Chardin's struggle shows in many ways, including his Mars exactly square his Ascendant. He could have fought the establishment, the Catholic hierarchy. He could have blocked his nontraditional theories and become ill. He took a discrete path and wrote out his ideas, but they were published only after his death, when the hierarchy could no longer threaten him. Although the official Church position is still cautious, increasing numbers are seeing his vision as a healing hope to mend the schism between science and religion.

De Chardin's Taurus in the Pisces house, Venus in its own sign and Neptune in its own house, conjunct each other, could have indicated a highly talented artist. He expressed the ability primarily through his writing, with his nodes in mutable signs and houses, marking the perpetual student, teacher, writer, and traveller. The nodes of Mercury repeated the mental emphasis in the chart with South Mercury on the twelfth cusp (where Jupiter conjoined it for years in progressions) and North Mercury at the midpoint of Sun-Antivertex with Neptune. Mercury was also parallel Pluto, pointing to depth and persistence of mind, in addition to the quick bright capacity suggested by Mercury in Aries in the eleventh house aspecting Uranus. Solar arc Mercury was on his Jupiter-Saturn conjunction when he entered the Jesuit school at age ten and on his Sun-Antivertex when he joined the Order as an adult at eighteen. Though he never married, he lived a full and stimulating life, and both his words and his deeds continue to be an inspiration to many.

Frank Buchman

There are interesting parallels between de Chardin's chart and that of Frank Buchman, our second subject, with nearly half the chart in the twelfth house. Again, nine factors fall in the twelfth, mostly in Taurus but with Gemini rising. Venus is closely conjunct the Antivertex and widely conjunct Neptune, both indicating potential artistic talent or love of beauty. Chiron conjuncts Neptune again to indicate the high focus on the Absolute. Jupiter is conjunct the MC instead of Saturn, but the meaning is the same though the pattern may be less intense. The eleventh house Saturn chooses to work with humanity or knowledge, often beyond previous limits. The nodes are in the other teaching polarity, this time Leo-Aquarius. Uranus is again in the fourth house for many moves or many trips: inner tension between the stable rooted nest and the transpersonal interests and need to go beyond all limits. The rising Vesta is similar to Vesta in Aries, identification with one's work, and the desire to work in one's own individual way: a potential entrepreneur. Even twins do not have identical charts, but the basic similarities between the horoscopes of these two men born three years apart are quite striking.

Certainly, there are also differences. The rising Sun is in the first house

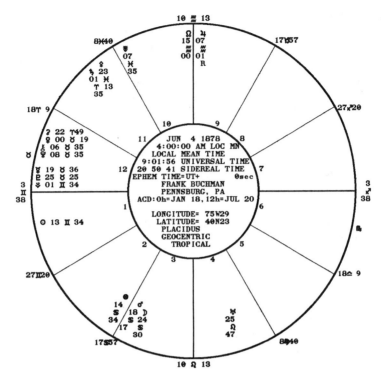

X 00-♉-41   E 15-♉-08

GEOCENTRIC
N-NODE S-NODE
☽ 16Aq28 16Le28
☿ 07Ge21 01Ca58
♀ 14Ge24 08Ge31
♂ 28Ta45 14Li21
♃ 05Ca18 15Cp28

♄ 19Ca18 27Cp07
♅ 13Ge10 13Sa08
♆ 08Le56 12Aq11
♇ 17Ca54 19Cp42

in Gemini, just inside the Gauquelins' power zone that extends ten degrees below the horizon. With its trine to the MC and North Node in the tenth house, there is a strong probability of success and prominence through the mind and communication. The nodes of Uranus fall conjunct and opposite the Sun, strongly supporting some type of new mental frontier. North Venus is also conjunct the Sun, suggesting charm and magnetism. Additional planetary node aspects in Buchman's chart include North Pluto and North Saturn conjunct Mars. I find the Saturn and/or Pluto nodes prominent in the charts of many people who seek or wield power in the world.

A more major difference between the two charts is suggested by the increased focus on Letter Four in this chart. The Mars-Moon conjunction in Cancer in the third house suggests strong ties to his original family of orientation, and a possible investment in a later family of procreation. But I have also seen many cases with Cancer or Moon in the third house who felt they had enough family experience while growing up and were not interested in becoming a parent. Placement of the fifth house rulers, Mercury and Venus, in the twelfth house can mean commitment to transpersonal issues, saving the world rather than becoming absorbed in one's own family. However, if the person chooses to become a parent, the savior role might lead to adopting or producing children who need help. To repeat the basic premise of this book once more: the chart shows the **issue**. The details can seem absolute opposites yet stem from the same psychological dynamics. Whether we are so ego-involved in children that we have a large family as our ultimate value, or whether we adopt and help the children of others, or whether we choose a profession to create love or beauty in the world and never deal with children; all are possible along with many other variations with a Five-twelve mixture. The major emphasis in the horoscope as a whole is on the personal and transpersonal parts of life, as was the case with Teilhard de Chardin. But there is enough Cancer and fourth house activity here to include a parental role though there would be conflict between that interpersonal side of life and the transpersonal commitment with the squares from the twelfth house to the Cancer sign and house, the node opposition across the tenth and fourth houses, and the Pallas quincunx Uranus from the eleventh to the fourth house.

Frank Buchman's life was centered in the transpersonal area. He began as a Lutheran pastor, with social work and teaching included in his professional activities. In 1922 he began an evangelistic campaign based on his concepts of God's guidance and moral absolutes: absolute purity, unselfishness, honesty and love. In 1938, the movement was renamed **Moral Rearmament**. Its worldwide members were committed to working for peace and brotherhood among all peoples of earth. Buchman met and sought to influence many top political leaders in countries all over the world, and he was honored in many countries. People who believed in his goals were encouraged to give the Foundation all of their physical possessions, and the Foundation would then give them something for subsistence. Buchman traveled widely through much of his life, lecturing and trying to elevate the moral consciousness of humanity, devoting special effort to individuals with wealth or power, hoping that they would speed the process of moving the world toward his spiritual ideals. He had a sanctuary on Mackinac Island in Michigan to which he could retreat for personal restoration and where he could see special guests that he hoped would aid his cause. The Foundation had another sanctuary in Switzerland, and one in Japan. Buchman lived a long and healthy life (he died in 1961) in a single minded effort to establish his personal morality as a universally accepted way of life. He wanted it enforced by governments as a quicker way to materialize it in the world. It will be interesting to see the final outcome of his and de Chardin's efforts, to see whether his concentration on individuals who could wield economic and political pressure will have as lasting or widespread effects as de Chardin's philosophical theorizing. In the history of humanity, most organizations that have concentrated on economic or political power, or were dependent on individuals, have disintegrated soon after the death of the founder. The power of spiritual ideas has often shaped individual humans and nations long after the death of the visionary who spoke or wrote of his or her inspiration.

Miss X

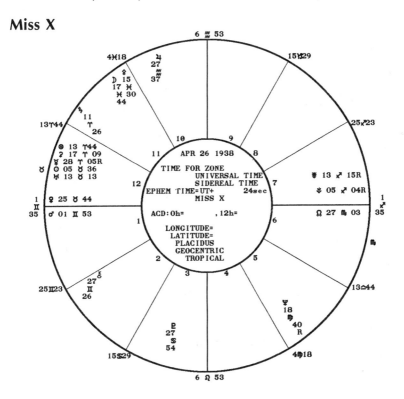

♋ 13-♈-31	? 27-♊-08	♂ 07-♓-35	♏ 11-♌-07	⚷ 15-♏-33R
⚴ 08-♓-03	♅ 09-♌-46	♀ 07-♈-01	☌ 21-♌-33	? 11-♏-15R
♍ 19-♒-01	♆ 23-♓-25	♇ 18-♒-59	⚵ 06-♏-22R	☽ 00-♉-14
AntiVertex 29-♈-02		Eastpoint 11-♉-43		

Our third chart is a woman with seven factors in the twelfth house, in addition to Pallas and the Moon in Pisces. She also has an Aries-Taurus emphasis similar to the preceding charts, a similar focus on personal and transpersonal areas of life with less concentration on the interpersonal. With Venus and one of the Moon's nodes conjunct the Ascendant, Moon on Pallas, a planet in the fifth house, two asteroids in the seventh house, and Pluto in Cancer, she is certainly likely to need some emotional ties with other people, but may try to satisfy that need through transpersonal activities. A helping profession is a common choice with such patterns. With the interpersonal factors in the chart associated with idealism, a religious career is a frequent choice. The Pallas-Moon conjunction is in Pisces. The seventh house asteroids, Juno and Vesta, are in Sagittarius; Neptune is in the fifth house, which is related to love and children among its meanings; Venus and the node are in the twelfth house. If that intense desire for a perfect relationship or a perfect partner is directed at ordinary human beings there are several possible dangers. She might never find the perfect person and just live frustrated. She might think she had found the perfect one and then be let down, or continue to see the other as superior and feel herself to be inferior. She might pick someone else looking for perfection who would reject her. She might pick someone who felt superior, acted like "God." She might pick a victim who would let her play God in the relationship. None of these dangers is inevitable, but they are all possible and are not mutually exclusive. Often individuals try several in succession, looking for a solution to the unconscious desire. When we understand the problem, the solution is obvious, but not necessarily easy to implement. One solution is a life devoted to spiritual service with some good friends who are accepted as valuable even though they are human. Or, we can form a partnership with someone who shares our goals, beliefs and ideals.

Sometimes, with a strong Aries-Taurus emphasis added to the transpersonal focus, there is too much independence to make the sacrifices required in a close relationship. As has been discussed earlier in this book, the freedom-closeness issue is a major theme in the Western world today. In this chart, the rising Mars is a strong additional indication of the need for personal independence. Uranus conjunct the Eastpoint offers the same message, and planets in Aquarius and/or the eleventh house say it again. The horoscope also, like both of the men previously described, could indicate conflict between personal rights and needs and spiritual ideals. De Chardin restrained his personal desire to promote his spiritual vision in order to maintain his tie with his Church. Buchman turned his personal morality into a cause and used what power he could muster to promote it. In effect he created his own "church," where he ruled. If our current subject is aware of the potential conflict, she can find her own compromise solution.

I have not included the name of this subject since she is not a public figure, so perhaps we can call her Miss X. She demonstrated her ability to assert her personal needs by throwing temper tantrums when young, on one occasion, throwing a pot of food through a plate glass door. However, her spiritual aspirations became increasingly intense, and she muted her own needs, softening her voice and seeking to meet the needs of others until her friends saw her as truly saintly. She did use her power successfully in the business world, providing her own security and reject-ing any dependency. As is common in a chart where the water side of the nature can only manifest as nurturance, when the fire and earth are too strong to accept dependency, she met others who were willing to ex-press the dependency for her. As is the way with projections, the "others" became excessive, leaving Miss X in the familiar Atlas position, carrying the world and wondering why no one did anything for her. She never married, but took in an older woman alcoholic whom she tried to "save." Spiritual service to humanity in a defined profession can be a healthy way to manifest Letter Twelve. Trying to save someone in a personal relation-ship that should be equalitarian is often a disaster. The "victim" rightly perceives the situation as a personal put-down and finds a way to get even. There are many ways to do this. We can criticize the savior for an inade-quate job. We can deceive, manipulate or take advantage of the rescuer. We may simply play "super victim." The alcoholic friend did them all on different occasions. The harder Miss X tried to be a saint, the more she was manipulated, and the more frustrated she became. But saints should not be angry or resentful so she maintained her composure. A pot through a glass door might have been a healthy release, but Miss X was convinced that she no longer had a temper.

Repression is a total blocking of a part of the nature so it is literally buried in the unconscious part of the mind. Mars and Aries and the first house all symbolize our right and power to fight for our own needs. When we cannot allow ourselves to assert ourselves, we may indeed become a saint and we can be a dead saint pretty quickly. Miss X developed a rash in the spring of 1975. Doctors diagnosed the problem as *lupus erythematosus*, and she was dead in less than six months. This more serious form of lupus attacks the inner organs. It is thought to be an auto-immune illness in which the body's own immune system, which is a defense against attack from outside, somehow turns against the person and destroys the body it was supposed to defend. There could not be a clearer Mars-Neptune conflict. Mars, the key to total self-will, in conflict with Neptune, the self-wipeout: "I must sacrifice myself for the good of others." If we understand the conflict, we can find a solution, a compromise between our needs and those of others, a compromise between our aspirations to be perfect and our humanness. But we completely block a part of ourselves at enormous cost. It cost Miss X her body, but if we accept rein-carnation, we assume she will have another chance to work out a compromise between humanness and sainthood. My favorite motto is "I'll be God tomorrow. It's OK to be human on the way to perfection, and remember to enjoy the journey."

Miss Y

Most of the victims of lupus are females who receive far more cultural pressure to repress their aggression and sacrifice themselves to serve others. Our next subject, whom we will call Miss Y, lacks the twelfth house emphasis but substitutes Neptune on the Ascendant. She also has the Moon on the MC, to be cast in the role of professional mother. Venus, ruler of the Ascendant, opposes it, and Mars in Aries falls in the seventh house. Different keys to an area of life in conflict with each other are a sign of conflict within that area. Any ruler of the first house, including Mars the natural ruler, in stress aspect to any other ruler of the first, represents a danger of self-blocking, of self attacking self. When the rulers of the first house are in the seventh house, we experience a confrontation of our needs and the needs of the important other(s) in our lives. We may give in, fight, or run as has been said repeatedly. Or we may learn to compromise, have healthy competition, and help people professionally. Personal relationships which are theoretically between equals should be a "give and take."

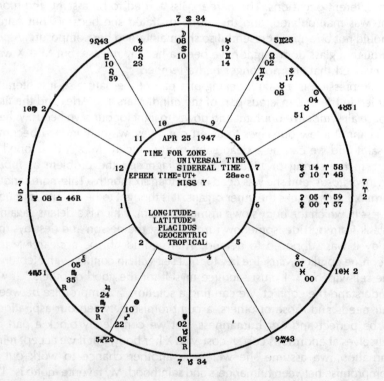

  ☊ 04-♈-05   ? 25-♈-06   ♅ 27-♓-24   ♏ 08-♍-17   ⚳ 01-♍-27
  ⚴ 09-♌-33   ♃ 28-♋-12   ♇ 05-♎-32R ♐ 26-♐-06R ? 02-♓-05
  ♅ 10-♓-21   ♆ 08-♉-35   ♅ 17-♏-49 ♇ 16-♊-28 ☽ 07-♊-37
      AntiVertex 27-♎-05   Eastpoint 08-♎-58

The preceding patterns would be sufficient to indicate a strong need for Miss Y to work on her relationships. But there is much more. Venus, ruler of the Ascendant, moved into the seventh house when she was about five years old, repeating the personal vulnerability to others. The Sun is also in the seventh house, showing ego-vulnerability to the attitudes of others. Saturn in Leo, Leo in the tenth house and Juno in Capricorn connect love and power with the danger of feeling anxious, and either trying to keep the power in her own hands or of looking for a father-figure to provide security, or of retreating from the whole thing. None of these actions will provide lasting satisfaction. The idealization of partnership said by Neptune in Libra (present in a whole generation), by Chiron and Jupiter in Scorpio and by Pallas in Pisces, opens up the same hazards discussed with Miss X. If Miss Y puts others on a pedestal, she is putting herself down or she is setting herself up for hurt when they show their humanness. If she plays Atlas and tries to save others in personal relationships, she could end as the savior who becomes martyr and hence victim. She can resolve the problem by helping people professionally, which will permit her to find her own strength and to express her idealism. Then she can keep her personal relationships human.

Unlike Miss X, Miss Y never identified with her Mars and Aries. She started life with that side of her nature projected, identifying with the Neptune in Libra that wanted to please others and always do the perfect thing. She chose a profession in which she could mother and save people, clinical psychology. At the time I saw her, she had just lost a relationship which she had highly valued, and she was experiencing pressures in her work as well. A physical checkup to discover the reason for a variety of problems produced a diagnosis of lupus. Fortunately, Miss Y had both the objective intellect and the psychological training to understand the emotional source of her illness. She confronted her feelings that her self-worth depended on pleasing others and on always doing the perfect job. She looked for new activities that she could enjoy and that would give her a sense of personal power. She was able to accept the lost relationship as a learning experience and to reach out to new friends without feeling totally dependent on them. In a few months, the lupus had quietly disappeared, and Miss Y had a new faith in herself and her ability to handle life.

Mrs. Z

Mrs. Z is included in this chapter because she also had lupus. In fact, she had a large number of fairly chronic illnesses which flared and retreated from time to time. As we can see in the horoscope, she was strongly identified with being a wife, mother and homemaker. She has Cancer rising with the Moon in its own sign in the first house, and Mars is in a stellium in Libra in the fourth house. Ceres conjunct Mars repeats

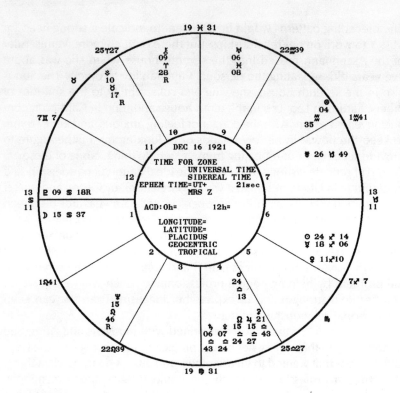

   19 ♓ 31

25♈27　　　　⚷ 09 ♈　　　⛢ 06 ♓ 08　　22♒39

    ♉　　☿ 10 ♉ 17 R　　28 ♈ R

7♊ 7

⊕ 04 ♒ 35　　1♒41

10　　9

11　　DEC 16 1921　　8

TIME FOR ZONE
UNIVERSAL TIME
12　　SIDEREAL TIME　7
EPHEM TIME=UT+　　21sec
MRS Z

ACD:0h=　　12h=

LONGITUDE=
LATITUDE=
PLACIDUS
GEOCENTRIC
TROPICAL

♇ 26 ♑ 49

13 ♋ 11　　☢ 09 ♋ 18R

13
♑
11

☽ 15 ♋ 37　　1

6

☉ 24 ♐ 14
☿ 18 ♐ 06

2　　3　　4　　5

♀ 11♐10

1♌41

7♐ 7

♂ 24 ♎ 13

♏

♆ 15 ♌ 46 R

?
Ω ♃ 21
♄ ☿ 15 15 ♎
06 07 ♎ ♎ 43
♎ ♎ 24 27
43 24

22♌39

25♎27

   19 ♍ 31

⚷ 04-♌-25R　? 02-♓-38　⛢ 07-♉-14R　♏ 28-♏-35　⚸ 12-♍-34
⚴ 05-♎-23　▽ 02-♑-35　♇ 20-♌-15R　♆ 21-♓-43　⚵ 12-♎-44
♎ 16-♈-12　⚶ 15-♑-27　▽ 17-♑-55　⚷ 26-♎-43　☽ 16-♋-34
   AntiVertex 00-♊-10　　Eastpoint 21-♊-09

the identification with her own mother and with the mother role. Juno
in Capricorn and Saturn in Libra suggest a choice of father-figure as partner. Pallas and Libra in the fourth house again tie partner to parent. She
might play parent to her partner or he might be parent to her. If they take
turns, they can establish an equalitarian relationship. If one of them is
parent all the time, there is no partnership. We have a Phyllis Schlafly
marriage with the wife as a child.

In spite of the Cancer-Libra emphasis in the chart, there is also a strong
grand trine in fire signs in earth houses. Fire and earth give us the
steamroller, and their strength may conflict with the culturally approved
submissive wife and mother. Mrs. Z was a traditional church member and
she stayed in her place. She raised a large family, took care of everyone,
and periodically was sick and let others take care of her. She worked in
her home and in volunteer service for the church, but never in an outside career, and she never knew she had any fire. The body knew it, when

the urge to assert herself turned inward into illness, but in her belief system, illness was an unfortunate accident that an expert doctor might be able to fix.

Mrs. Z might well have ended her life with one of her chronic problems, especially with the lupus. But when her last child graduated from high school, and her husband got his first good job, so that it looked as if their scrimping and saving days were over, her husband walked out. At that crucial juncture, she could have totally crumbled. Instead, she went out and got a job outside the home for the first time. She moved into her fire signs in her earth houses, and her illnesses disappeared. She didn't understand what happened, nor did her doctor. But she began expressing her fire energy outwardly instead of blocking it so that it was forced to express inwardly against her body. She found a self-confidence and vitality she had never guessed was in her. Her fire rebuilt her body instead of destroying it. She still does not know what happened or why her health improved so dramatically. If there is a choice between insight and action, the latter is more important! Insight without changed action only leads to guilt and increased frustration. When we change our action, we also change our attitudes about ourselves, and we create a new world for ourselves. Either can come first, as long as we include the action!

CHAPTER 16

What Price Faith and Hope?

As has been suggested repeatedly, our world is shaped by our beliefs. Our faith tells us what we can do, what we ought to do and what we want to do. When our faith tells us that we cannot do what we want or that we have to do what we would rather avoid, it helps if we are aware of that inner conflict. It is easier to find a compromise solution if we know the nature of the conflict. When deeply desired goals seem really unreachable and the current reality seems unbearable, a faith in something beyond ourselves is vitally necessary. When we can't meet our needs through our own power, faith in a Higher Power can reassure us. With such faith, we can keep going, trusting that things will work out in the end. With such faith, we can hold on to the hope that the future will be better.

As was done in Chapter 13, the two horoscopes to be featured in this chapter are presented first, to permit readers to make their own analyses. The charts will then be discussed astrologically-psychologically, and finally the details of the life will be described.

Chart 1 — male

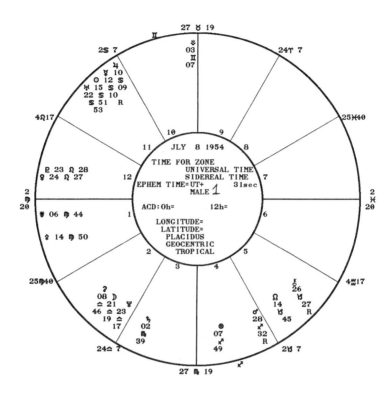

    & 16-♌-37   ? 16-♍-13   ♂ 07-♎-09   ♏ 19-♉-15   ⚸ 13-♒-43R
    ⚶ 14-♌-52   ▽ 04-♓-05R   ⚴ 11-♎-23   ☊ 20-♏-43   ⚵ 23-♏-00R
    ⚷ 27-♎-01   ⚳ 15-♈-03   ▽ 29-♒-11R   ⚱ 24-♎-06   ☽ 21-♓-18
    AntiVertex 26-♋-42   Eastpoint 22-♌-41

Chart 2 — male

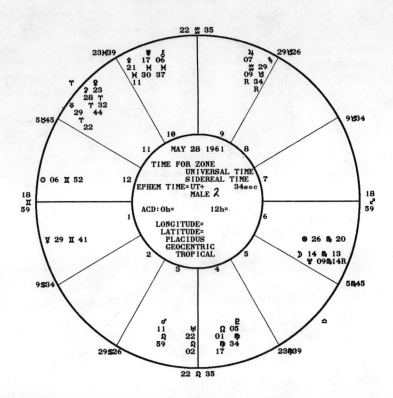

⊕ 10-♉-13	♀ 27-♏-07	♅ 10-♊-26	♏ 02-♐-52R	⚷ 08-♋-35
⚸ 05-♋-17	⚵ 21-♌-24	♯ 10-♎-25R	♓ 02-♏-03R	⚴ 07-♓-41
♆ 14-♊-42	⚶ 16-♋-17	⚳ 02-♈-32	♇ 11-♈-49	☽ 18-♏-55
	AntiVertex 10-♉-31		Eastpoint 27-♉-14	

The **first subject** is a male with a stellium in Cancer, the Moon conjunct Neptune in Libra, Eastpoint-Pluto-Venus in Leo in the twelfth house and Mars in the fourth house. A strong focus on water, planet, sign or house, appears in all of these patterns. All of the combinations except Moon-Neptune also have a fire-water mixture. An emphasis on water suggests emotional sensitivity with either strong dependency or capacity for nurturance. If the person develops the strength shown by fire and earth, the need to be protected and cared for will diminish and the individual will protect others. If the earth ability to handle the material world, to hold a job and make a living, is not developed, and if the security needs block the fire self-confidence (of Aries or Leo) and the faith in something higher (of Sagittarius), the individual may live with considerable anxiety and/or depression.

Normally, air is helpful to permit objectivity and rational detachment. The Cancer stellium is in the Aquarian house with Uranus and Mercury, the two air planets, included in the mixture. Since Mercury rules the Virgo Ascendant, and the Antivertex (an auxiliary Ascendant) is also included, there is some instinctive capacity to express both the air and the water, the conscious and the unconscious aspects of the mind. However, I have observed that often Letter Eleven represents a part of the nature that is more developed as the individual matures. To some extent it appears to represent a future goal in the early years. It is also possible for a major emphasis on air-water mixtures to be expressed as an outer passivity since the individual is living largely in the head. Development of some of the fire and earth is necessary to gain a sense of power to be oneself and power to cope with the world. Also, since both the lesson factors, South Node of the Moon and Saturn, are in water signs in air houses, there is a challenge in the combination. The lesson might involve developing more ability to see the whole perspective and to take things lightly. Or, our subject might need to do less of the air scattering; he might need to learn to focus and use his mind effectively and productively. The water lesson could be learning to handle his sensitivity. If each part of life is expressed in its own proper place, with Cancer, Moon and the fourth house, we are sensitive and vulnerable to the feelings of our family in our own home. We take friends and the general transpersonal area more superficially and casually. When the Cancer is in the eleventh house, the Moon is on Neptune, and Sagittarius is in the fourth house, we have connected all three major forms of Letter Four to the transpersonal area. We might be sensitive and vulnerable to the feelings and attitudes of everyone. If there is deep faith in a Higher Power, such a person can become a healer and helper of humanity. If such faith is weak, the individual may be thin-skinned and easily hurt by anyone.

Another potential challenge inherent in this mixture of Letter Four with transpersonal factors (planets, houses and signs) is the freedom-closeness conflict. The transpersonal side of the nature wants independence to be part of a larger scene, to remain free to do big things in the world. Letter Four wants a permanent, rooted, secure home; a nest and a family. Life should be big enough for both, but we have to juggle time and energy to integrate these very different parts of the nature. Since character puts us where we fit, and the early life is a result of the past life character, we often experience the results of our character as impacts from the world, quite outside our control. Either Mars or Sagittarius in the fourth house is often associated with changes of residence or of the people living in the home, though the individual might simply travel a lot. The point is that we tend to be conscious of one side of the nature while the opposing desire is buried in the unconscious or projected into other people around us. Since the unconscious usually wins, we keep getting what we didn't know we wanted. If we wanted independence, we feel that our family is confining us and we may run away or rebel in other ways. If we consciously wanted closeness and permanence, the home or family may be disrupted or just keep changing.

Of course, we have the same message with Uranus in Cancer (everyone born for seven years at a time will have that mixture), with Cancer in the eleventh house, and with Jupiter, as ruler of the fourth house in this chart, in the eleventh house. Anything important in the nature will be repeated again and again in the horoscope. With Letter Four a key to one of the parents, some of this ambivalence over space and closeness will be manifested in one or both parents. Venus rules the tenth house and Pluto rules the fourth house. Their conjunction in Leo either indicates parents who are similar, or one parent playing both roles some of the time. The Cancer-Leo mixture blends the warmest, most caring parts of our twelve sides of life, so there is likely to be emotional intensity in the relationships with both parents.

Both parents are also connected to faith, with Venus and Pluto in the twelfth house, Moon conjunct Neptune, and Sagittarius in the fourth house. Various expressions of the parent-faith mixture can include religious, spiritual or idealistic parents. These words carry different connotations from orthodox to personal high standards and expectations. Parents can expect too much of themselves, each other, children, or life in general. Or, the child may expect too much of the parents. If too much faith is placed in the parents, the child may lack faith in himself or in a Higher Power. If the child is never able to live up to the parents' expectations, it is hard to build a sense of self-worth. But the primary message of such mixtures of parents and faith is that the example of the parents offers us an opportunity to learn what to do or what not to do in the area of beliefs, goals, values.

It is possible to see other clues to the individual's experience of his parents. Vesta in the house of one parent suggests the Virgo theme. The parent may be very involved in work, by choice or by necessity. The parent may be critical or the child may criticize the parent or it may be mutual. Since Vesta is in Gemini, there is less danger of excessive criticism or total absorption in work. Air shows many interests and a more accepting nature. If the parent is not handling the Virgo principle, there may be problems with work or with health, personal body functioning. Since there is no way to be sure which house is which parent, I look for clues to try to differentiate. With even a small amount of Cancer in the tenth house and Capricorn in the fourth house, we may have a tenth house mother and a fourth house father. Often, it is necessary to talk to the individual to be sure, and sometimes the parental roles have been so mixed, it is necessary to read both tenth and fourth houses as both parents. In this case, Ceres and Moon are both in an air sign in an earth house, which seems to support the tenth house mother; a mother who is intelligent and practical. But as already indicated, Venus ruling the tenth house is conjunct Pluto ruling the fourth house, so the parents are very close, or are similar in some way, or one is playing both roles some of the time. We could also read Jupiter, ruler of the fourth house, in Cancer as connecting mother to the fourth house or pointing to a nurturing father. If the fourth house is primarily father, we have patterns suggesting a very emotional father, with the strong fire-water combinations. Father is a primary role model for our subject since Mars is in the fourth house, and its ruler, Pluto, is conjunct the Eastpoint. Mother is less obviously a personal role model with Mercury ruling the Ascendant in Cancer.

Saturn is usually a key to father or an alternate early authority figure, so its position in Scorpio supports the likelihood of an emotional father. The third house position of Saturn might be a father able to accept equality (father like a sibling), or a sibling like a father, or a younger sibling for whom we play a father role. Sometimes there will be another relative such as an uncle or aunt who takes on the parent role. Since the father is the primary role model, our subject is offered a chance to learn about emotions, the freedom-closeness dilemma, the constructive handling of the conscious intellect, ideals and perhaps sensuality in some form with the Pluto-Venus conjunction. Remember, role models are positive if we wish to imitate them; negative if we are trying to learn what not to do. Often there are mixtures. We want to be like the parent in some ways and to do the opposite in other areas. For example, father might be warm but too sensitive, capable but with too high expectations so he was never happy. The chart shows the principles but not the details. To get the details, we have to talk to the person.

In view of the general emphasis on emotional sensitivity in the horoscope, it is quite important that our subject be practical, be grounded. The anxiety and depression to which water may be prone can be counteracted by any of the other elements. Air detaches and sees the situation in perspective and analyzes it objectively. Fire does something exciting to satisfy personal desire. Earth works to gain a sense of accomplishment and to avoid the helplessness and dependency of water. Since the chart has Virgo rising, in addition to two asteroids in Virgo in the first house and a strong Vesta in the tenth house, part of the identification is with work. Our subject has to feel a sense of productive accomplishment to feel good about himself. We note that although Saturn is sextile the Ascendant, showing ability to work effectively and a good model from either a father-figure or another relative or neighbor, Vesta is square the Ascendant and quincunx Saturn, so there may be problems in finding his work in the world. In any counseling interview, we would emphasize the importance of his finding a job which gives him a feeling of doing something well and consequently having more control over his life. Air signs in the earth houses suggest a preference for working with ideas and people, with the conscious mind. With some of the rulers of both sixth and tenth houses in Cancer in the eleventh house, the chart again suggests work with people, perhaps in a nurturing way. Saturn is a co-ruler of both the fifth and the sixth houses, so he may have lessons in emotional relationships and in work. The Mars quincunx to the MC is another clue to possible challenges in the career. We may be pulled between home and career, or just keep changing the job or the home with the fire restlessness and reluctance to be tied down. Jupiter, Mercury, node, and Sun are all octile the MC, repeating the likelihood of challenges in the career. The Leo grouping in the twelfth house squares the MC reiterating the message again. The red flags fly especially when we see rulers of a house in conflict to factors in or ruling the house, so Mercury and Venus aspects to the MC are highlighted. But a similar pattern appears with Vesta (natural key to Virgo) square the first house Virgo, and with Saturn (natural ruler of the tenth house) quincunx Vesta in the tenth house. Our subject clearly needs to pay extra attention to finding satisfying work. Additional education might help. His Mars, ruling the ninth house of higher education, is quincunx both MC and Antivertex, a yod pattern, which suggests changes and new directions in his schooling.

In summary then, we have a young man likely to be highly sensitive and emotional, to whom friends are extremely important. It is highly important for his sense of self-worth that he find work that brings satisfaction and that lets him feel capable. He needs to learn something from parents in the area of faith, trust, values. Father may provide an example of handling or mishandling emotions. Mother may provide an example of handling the practical world. The chart suggests that he has intelligence (Mercury conjunct Jupiter and all three mental planets in the eleventh house), but he also has lessons somewhere in that mix of air and water, conscious and unconscious mind, detachment and connectedness or openness. He may have artistic talent, but the primary choice of career should probably involve working with people. He might expect too much of himself or others (Mars in Sagittarius, Pisces in the seventh house, keys to both parents in the twelfth house). He also might be too self-critical with Virgo rising. Virgo is great as long as it is expressed where it belongs, in the job. If we turn everything into a job, we lose the fun of life.

The **second subject's** chart will be discussed before the presentation of life events for both. At first glance, we receive a rather different impression than was given by the first chart. The strong Gemini suggests a light, almost flippant attitude and much verbal facility (supported by Mars in the third house in our dramatic Leo and by the Venus in Aries in the eleventh house). Jupiter in Aquarius in the ninth house adds more air and fire, the elements of humor, flowing with and enjoying life. Uranus is in Leo with Mars, barely inside the third house but really conjunct the fourth cusp. Connecting a restless fire and air mixture to the fourth house does give us one similarity to our first subject. We have another potential freedom-closeness dilemma. If he wants a rooted family and home, they may keep changing. If they close around him, he may want to run away. With the ruler of the Ascendant in the first house, and Mars in Leo, he should have some sense of his own power and feel able to go after what he wants.

On closer inspection, we note that the earth and water elements are also definitely present in the chart. One pattern shared with our first subject is a Moon-Neptune conjunction. Mother is Piscean in some way. She might be artistic, religious, idealistic, or a victim (ill, emotionally disturbed, missing, etc.). Whatever the details, Subject Two has the opportunity to learn about faith from her example.

With the nodes across the fourth and tenth houses of parents, there might have been strain or separation in their relationship. Earth and water signs are more likely to hang on, but mutables or cardinals may split. Or, one parent might be so busy working, he or she is gone a lot. Since Uranus rules the tenth house and is on the fourth cusp, we have the potential for one parent playing both roles or for the parents being similar to each other. Since Saturn is a co-ruler of the tenth house and the Moon is in the sign ruled by Pluto in the fourth house, our first guess would be a tenth house father and a fourth house mother. Virgo in the fourth house and the Moon in the Virgo house offer additional support for a fourth house mother; either a working mother, or an ill one or one with a critical attitude, or some other variation of Virgo. Jupiter as a co-ruler of the tenth house placed in the same house as Saturn, the usual key to father, is another support for a tenth house father.

In addition to the link between both parents and the issue of faith, values and goals, both parents are connected to the capacity to handle a partnership. Juno and Pallas (the Libra asteroids) are in the tenth house, and Pluto (key to mate as ruler of Scorpio) is in the fourth house. The

Moon in Scorpio and Capricorn in the seventh and eighth houses repeat the message of parent and partner. We may keep the parent as a partner, maintaining an adult peer relationship with him or her. We may consciously or unconsciously look for a partner like or unlike the parent. The chart shows the issues; we choose the detail, and may change our choice if we wish.

There might be some sort of problem with either parent, including the potential for separation, whether mental, emotional or physical. The ruler of the first in the first marks a person identified with himself rather than with either parent. Saturn quincunx Mercury in the first house, and Moon more widely quincunx the Ascendant and trioctile Mercury, show the possibility of the family pulling apart in some way. The dominant Uranus on the IC is another key to possible instability in the home or the family. Mars, another key to personal identity, is also square the Moon (mother) and opposite Jupiter (father if the tenth house is father).

We have a mixed pattern for the parents' relationship to each other. The Moon trines some of the tenth house factors, but Ceres squares Saturn very closely. Ceres conjunct Vesta repeats the Virgo association for mother, and the Aries-eleventh house placement suggests an independent mother, but Venus connected may mean pleasure or affection. Even more than mother, father is connected to ideals with Pisces in the tenth and both Jupiter and Saturn in the ninth house. The tenth house South Node of the Moon indicates a lesson to be learned from father (if we are correct in assigning that house to him). Both Saturn and South Node connect idealism and realism with their sign-house combination, so we can assume at least a part of the lesson involves integrating the dream of perfection with the limits of what is possible.

In general, a chart with strong air can accept life and flow with it. Perfectionism is not an air problem. Fire can present more of a challenge. The essence of fire is "If I want it, I have a right to it, and I want it now!" A common pattern with fire is to keep moving, looking for a new or better desire, or just hoping to find the desire in a new place. Despite the strong identification with air in the first house, our subject has a rather intense inner conflict over high expectations and his capacity to achieve them. Mars forms a grand cross in fixed signs in mutable houses, including the two planets looking for the Absolute (Neptune and Jupiter), and including the Antivertex, which carries the same meaning as Mars and the Ascendant. The whole pattern indicates a chronic (fixed signs) struggle between personal ability to do what he wants (Mars and Antivertex) and his vision of how life ought to be (Neptune and Jupiter). Mercury's quincunx to Saturn in the ninth house, and its trioctile to Moon, with Moon a ruler of the first house Cancer, repeat the theme of feeling unable to get what he wants in life; perhaps because he wants more than would ever be possible. Unreachable goals or inability to reconcile conflicting goals, when combined with fire and a strong Uranus, are the mark of some variety of runaway.

In counseling such a person, we would emphasize the need for a healthy outlet for the fire. He needs vigorous sports or games, physical activities, variety and challenge in his life. He also needs to look at his expectations, especially in relationship to his parents. It is extremely important that he have faith in a Higher Power, that he not make his parents into God. He needs to talk to his parents or to find parent-substitutes he can talk with. He needs friends. Sometimes, Aries can be a loner, or have trouble seeing the point of view of others, but his Gemini should give him the capacity to be logical and observant. He could work in a healing, helping field, or with fluids, chemicals, hidden things with his water emphasis in the earth houses. Above all else, he needs to be reasonable in his vision, willing to take small steps, to accomplish bite-sized goals, and to enjoy the journey.

If you have not yet looked ahead, take a moment to study these horoscopes once more and draw your own conclusions about how they might have handled their assets and challenges. Then, look to the next page to see what they did in their lives.

* * * * *

Both of our subjects committed suicide. The young man with Virgo rising and the Cancer stellium was highly sensitive. He had an older brother who was quite successful, finishing an advanced education and becoming a dentist. The mother was hard-working, conscientious and intelligent. The father was an alcoholic. The mother held on to the marriage until she realized it was becoming destructive to the boys, and then she got a divorce. Our subject doubted his own ability, dropped out of school, drifted through a variety of menial, frustrating jobs, tried living with his father but found it impossible. Shortly before his twenty-second birthday (July 2, 1976), he called his mother on the phone and said he wanted to return to school and make something of his life. His mother encouraged him, said she would help in any way she could, and he decided to come back, live with her, and go to college. Later that day, he had an accident in a car borrowed from a friend. It was the last straw. He felt he had never done anything right, and he shot himself.

The new asteroids add some interesting patterns to the picture presented earlier. Icarus (potentially another Sun) squares the MC from the sixth house, repeating the problems in stabilizing his work. Progressed Icarus was opposite the progressed Moon at the death, repeating the emotional conflict over ambition and security needs. Progressed Moon was also conjunct Urania (potential Uranus), another indication of possible impulsive action. Pandora was natally opposite the Ascendant, but by progression, the aspect was exact to the degree. Both of these charts had Pandora on an angle and related to Letter One (personal action) supporting the idea of action that leads to irreversible consequences. Once taken, we can't undo it. Frigga progressing over the MC and quincunx Mars might simply repeat the frustration over career and his sense of powerlessness. Progressed Urania (Uranus) and Dudu (Pluto) were conjunct the "real" Pluto. Transiting Urania was also conjunct the Leo group. Progressed Venus and Ascendant were together (saying, "I ought to be able to enjoy life") just moving in to oppose Diana in Pisces in the seventh house. If the myth of Diana is a valid clue, she could be associated with isolation, feeling cut off from people. In mythology, she is close to animals but has problems with people. But one of the most interesting patterns is the opposition of progressed Sun to the natal Part of Death (Ascendant plus eighth cusp minus Moon). I don't think that this young man had to die. With faith in his own ability to handle challenges, and faith in a Higher Power to help him, he could have confronted the problem and worked it out. Running away was no more a solution than his flight from school, home and a variety of jobs. If we believe in reincarnation, he will have another chance to learn to do the best he can and then to trust that things will work out.

The parents of our second subject divorced and he stayed with his father, who was a teacher in a boys school. During the summers, the father often taught at a summer camp, and his son accompanied him. The mother worked, and had little contact with her son. The father was interested in psychic and occult areas, and sometimes discussed them with his son. The boy appeared well adjusted and stable though he said little about his personal feelings. Neither parent had any inkling of his inner feelings of alienation and frustration until the day (August 17, 1978) that he left a despairing note, and committed suicide by tying himself inside a large plastic bag hung from a tree branch where he died by suffocation.

There are many dramatic aspects in the progressed chart, including some of the new asteroids. Progressed Mars was on Uranus and the IC, a typical runaway pattern. A grand trine of progressed Mercury-Moon, natal Neptune and progressed MC might shock traditional astrologers. It is important to remember in dealing with progressions that the current pattern shows the timing and the issues, but the natal chart shows the basic character. Unless the person has changed, the natal character will express. The natal Mercury trioctile the Moon-Neptune conjunction was mentioned as one of the clues to possible alienation from parents and too high expectations of parents and life. The grand trine and the fire (including progressed Sun, now in the first house trioctile Neptune) showed the feeling that he ought to be happy, provided with all his desires. Progressed Venus had been traveling over Vesta for several years; a good pattern for work success but often indicating problems with people. They were square Jupiter, repeating the conflict over his ideals; the frustration that life was not as he wanted it.

The new asteroids fitted into many of the patterns. Progressed Mars was conjunct natal Pandora: the irreversible action of ending his own life. Natal Pittsburghia and Lilith (two potential Plutos) fell between his Sun and Ascendant, forming midpoint structures. Progressed Pittsburghia was just approaching his Ascendant, progressed Eastpoint was on the midpoint of Pittsburghia and Lilith, with the progressed MC coming to square Pittsburghia and still conjunct progressed Hidalgo (another Saturn?). Progressed Lilith was conjunct progressed Sun in the trioctile to Neptune, and transiting Lilith was just coming up to them. Transiting Pandora was on his progressed Ascendant, another contact with Letter One, personal action. Progressed Dudu (our third possible Pluto) was opposite progressed Diana while the progressed Ascendant was trioctile natal Diana. Since he took his life in fairly wild, woodsy country, and wrote of intense feeling of personal isolation, I was curious to see if Diana would be prominent. Progressed Icarus (our fiery Sun that so often overdoes) was in Aries in the eleventh house quincunx natal Diana.

Obviously, the more factors we add to a chart, the more aspects we will find. Our search is always for the repeated theme, for appropriate aspects that fit the psychological state of the person, and the events of the life as character creates destiny. Many other patterns might be mentioned. Progressed Saturn had held its quincunx to natal Mercury all of the subject's life; a major clue to the withholding of his inner feelings and thoughts, his reluctance to be open with his father. The eighth house cusp as well as the fourth are often involved in aspects when we confront death in some form. Water marks closure, finishing the chapter. Progressed Mars on the IC has been mentioned. Progressed Moon and Mercury were opposite the eighth cusp while the progressed eighth cusp was quincunx progressed Uranus, still on the fourth cusp. The quotidian progressed eighth cusp (one of the daily angles that circle the wheel in a year) was conjunct natal Icarus (overreach) and quincunx the natal node of the Moon in the fourth house. Again, I do not believe this seventeen-year-old boy had to die. He failed to learn his lesson in faith (South Node in Pisces and Saturn in the ninth house). He was unable to trust the future to be better; to trust his father enough to share his feelings; to trust himself to get more of what he wanted if he was patient and kept on trying. Maybe next time he will work it out.

CHAPTER 17

How Many Systems Work?

This book has offered the theory that most of astrology is symbolic. If the Earth and the sky share the same order, we can see the order more clearly in the visible patterns in the sky, but that does not imply that the sky creates the order. We can call the creative power God, Life, Mind or Spirit. If we are truly "made in His Image," we share a little of that creative power. We create our own character over many lives, coming in for more growth where we fit, and changing the place we fit as we change our attitudes and actions. In Chapter 15 our ladies with lupus demonstrated that it is possible to change our attitudes and heal the body, or we can change our actions and they in turn change our attitudes and produce the same healing. Of course we can also continue blocking our own energy and stay ill or have accidents, surgery, and so on. A psychologically interpreted horoscope should help us to understand our conflicts (we all have some) so we can make peace with ourselves.

If the sky is simply a convenient way to see the cosmic (and our personal) order, there is no logical reason why one technique should work better than another. Astrology has always been pragmatic, trying out many different systems. Since we are using the sky to try to understand our more complicated Earth, it is normal to want to keep our techniques simple and easy to handle. But our models never tell all, so we keep making them more complex, or we invent new models. One will often hear or read endorsements of one model and attacks on another. Even when the models seem contradictory, somehow they all seem to work some of the time. The perennial quest of astrology is to find the most dependable systems that give the clearest, most complete answers, with the least investment of time and energy. I have suggested that the systems that work on one's own chart are likely to work on most of the people around us, since life is a mirror and we draw our own to us. But it is still advisable to try out a variety of systems before we commit ourselves to one or a few, and to keep our minds slightly ajar for the possibility of new and valuable techniques. When we think we have arrived, we stop growing, and it may take an earthquake to wake us up, to force us to reopen our options.

My experience suggests that on the big events of the life, all the systems work. The essential theme in the chart will be shown by different planet-sign-house-aspect combinations, but it will show in some way. In this chapter, a variety of charts are offered which all preceded a traumatic event in one man's life. John McCormick was a friend of many who will read this book. He was a serious student of astrology, and I think he would be willing to have his chart used to demonstrate some of the varied techniques that are currently available. A brief description of the techniques was presented in Chapter 9, so they will be simply named at this time, and the patterns will be indicated which show the repeating themes. If astrologers can see that all the techniques, all the ways that we multiply and divide the sky and equate one cycle with another, simply provide another way to see the same order, maybe we can stop thinking that "this aspect causes that event." The aspects show (not cause) the character, and the character causes the events. We can change our character, but we have to want to change. Sometimes it has to hurt a lot before we want to make the effort. Sometimes, it is too late for this lifetime.

John McCormick

Probably the characteristic we remember first about John McCormick is his sense of humor. The Sagittarius Moon, Ascendant and Mars all suggest that he started life with that humor. As if he needed any more, he also had Sun and Mercury in the Sagittarius house. Though Sun and Mercury were in the sign of Virgo, he was much more a Sagittarius: sharp, quick-witted and quick-tongued, with a twinkle in his eyes and a struggle with overweight, which wasn't helped a bit by Moon on the Ascendant and Jupiter on Venus. His letters in Edie Custer's *Mercury Hour* offered his wit to a large and appreciative audience, though occasionally the humor was barbed enough to be unappreciated by the target.

Strong earth was present also, with even more Capricorn than Virgo. He had the two auxiliary Ascendants (Eastpoint and Antivertex) in Capricorn, showing he came into life identified with career and achievement. Jupiter, ruler of his Ascendant, so again a key to instinctive identity, was placed in his tenth (Capricorn) house, as well as Saturn, also a ruler of the first house and very powerful in its own natural house. The (mean) North Node of the Moon, Venus and Pallas shared the tenth house, showing pleasure in running his own show and in doing a good job. However, since the tenth house factors were in Libra, the sign that naturally

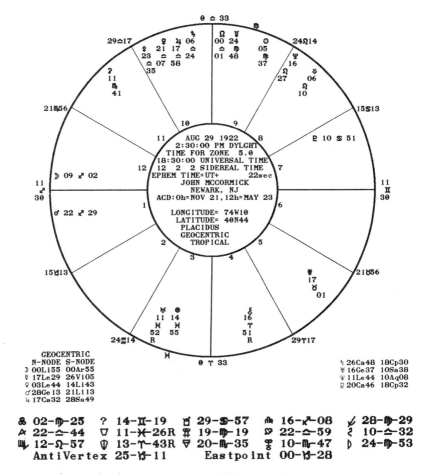

GEOCENTRIC
N-NODE S-NODE
☽ 00Li55 00Ar55
☿ 17Le29 26Vi05
♀ 03Le44 14Li43
♂ 28Ge13 21Li13
♃ 17Ca32 28Sa49

♄ 26Ca48 18Cp30
♅ 16Ge37 10Sa38
♆ 11Le44 10Aq08
♇ 20Ca46 18Cp32

⚷ 02-♍-25   ? 14-♊-19   ♉ 29-♋-57   ♏ 16-♐-08   ⚸ 28-♍-29
⚹ 22-♎-44   ⛢ 11-♓-26R   ⚺ 19-♍-19   ♋ 22-♎-59   ⚷ 10-♎-32
♨ 12-♌-57   ⚴ 13-♈-43R   ⚵ 20-♏-35   ⚶ 10-♏-47   ☊ 24-♍-53
     AntiVertex 25-♑-11   Eastpoint 00-♑-28

squares the tenth, there was a potential for conflict between career and relationships, or between control, power, dominance vs. equality, sharing and compromise.

For the most part, all the signs are in houses that square them in the natural zodiac, so wherever factors (planets, nodes, etc.) formed aspects to each other, integration was needed to harmonize the different parts of the nature. Pluto in Cancer in the seventh house, like the Libra in the Capricorn house, is a parent-partner mixture; a repeat of part of the cardinal dilemma. When we take turns being parent, we have a real partnership. Chiron in Aries in the fourth house presents the "freedom vs. closeness" corner of the cardinal dilemma, or rootedness vs. change (moving, traveling, others coming or going from the home). The nodes across Aries-Libra and the Eastpoint-Westpoint axis across Capricorn-Cancer, with all in cardinal houses (if the mean node is used), presents a very exact cardinal grand cross. So the life requires independence, closeness (dependence or nurturance), equal sharing and power. In mundane terms, the cardinals want time for personal interests, for a home and family, for a mate and for a career. The juggling act of life tries to find room for them all.

Although there are astrological planets or angles in all of the cardinal signs and houses, Letter Four is likely to be the one that requires attention. Cancer falls in the seventh and eighth houses, the area where projection is most likely, where we tend to disidentify with part of our nature and to attract others who are willing to express it for us. The repeated mixture of Letter Four and fire is another red flag. If Chiron is like Jupiter, it is fire, and it is in Aries in the fourth house. The Moon is in Sagittarius and conjunct the Ascendant, two more associations with fire. The Ascendant, as a form of Letter One, carries the fire potential of automatic, spontaneous action, and the fact that it is in a fire sign in this case is an additional statement of the principle. Yet, though the Moon is very much a part of the instinctive action with the close conjunction to the Ascendant, it is also likely to be partly unconscious on the twelfth house side of the angle. If anything, presence in a water house increases the power of that part of the nature. We do it without even knowing consciously that we are doing it. If there is conflict in the principles (as there is with fire and water), a compromise solution may be harder due to the lack of awareness of the problem. So, the tendency with such patterns is to be very conscious of the need for independence (Mars in Sagittarius in its own house is pure freedom drive), and to feel uncomfortable and to struggle against the need for emotional closeness and security.

The placement of both Jupiter and Saturn, rulers of the signs in the first house, and therefore keys to instinctive identity and action, in the tenth house in Libra strengthens these sides of the cardinal dilemma. With Jupiter, Saturn and the tenth house all transpersonal, the identification with larger issues is strengthened. People are important, with that stellium in Libra, but are likely to be sought in transpersonal areas, through the career and work for society as a whole, rather than in traditional home and marriage. Yet Letter Four is still present, with the Moon on the Ascendant expressing an intense but unconscious cry for mothering, and the bulk of the chart unable to accept it. The most common attempted solution to such patterns is to identify with playing parent and helping others through the career. But the deep need for something closer is like a burr under the saddle until the issue is resolved. We may substitute pets for people. We may cling to our home and/or other possessions as a source of the hunger for emotional roots that is never acknowledged. We may overeat or overdrink or over-smoke. But the unpacified child in us is still crying for something that is unacceptable to the rest of the nature.

The baby side of Cancer is the most difficult part of the cardinal dilemma for many people. John's Moon is square Uranus (a primary key to freedom), quincunx Pluto (a primary key to closeness in its own nature, its sign and its house), square the Sun (a key to loving and accepting love), octile the Antivertex (another form of Letter One, independence to be ourselves) and octile the Pallas-Venus conjunction in Libra (another clue to a desire for relationship). In a counseling session, we would discuss the early relationship to the mother, exploring any hurts that might still linger in the unconscious, fighting the emotional vulnerability.

The baby side of Letter Four is vulnerable, plus, if we accept it, we lose all the rest of the cardinals: independence, equality and power. But if it is part of the nature, it must be dealt with, or eventually it manifests in unpleasant ways, coming at us in forms that are beyond our control. The solution is to accept our dependency in small doses, to let friends help us, give to us, and to be able to be open and vulnerable, acknowledging emotional needs. But it is hard for someone identified with self-reliance, productive accomplishment and just "staying on top" of life to admit personal weakness in any form. We may become ill or disabled as the "baby" in us tries more and more desperately to get emotional support, and we still may maintain the stiff upper lip, the culturally approved behavior for males.

Of course in a counseling session, we would want to discuss both parents. With John's first house rulers in the tenth house, especially since one is Saturn in its own house, a father-figure would have been personal role model. But we don't know the details until we talk to the person. With the Cancer-Capricorn polarity in the first-seventh houses, or an interchange of rulers of these angular houses, a grandparent may take over the parent role. Or the parents may have separated, with the nodes across the MC-IC axis. The South Node on the IC shows a lesson coming from the home and presumably mother; Saturn in the tenth house shows a lesson coming from the father-figure. Mother is also a role model with Aries in the fourth house and the Moon conjunct the Ascendant. The struggle with dependency must have begun very early, with the exact position of the node on the angle, and the Moon reaching the Ascendant soon after birth by progression and in the second year by solar arc. Often, there will be appropriate events at both times, events symbolic of the conflict between independence and dependence-vulnerability.

Another major issue in the horoscope, connected to both parents and to John's own instinctive self-expression, is the issue of ideals, faith, values, perfectionism. Sagittarius rising and Mars in Sagittarius are forms of "I should be God" or "I am already there." The planetary form of the alphabet is the strongest. Michel and Francoise Gauquelin found the rising Jupiter in actors, politicians and Nazi leaders, who tend toward the latter expression. John took the other road, and tried to always live up to very high standards. Being God (a One-Nine mixture) is even harder than being Atlas, a danger with One-Ten mixtures. When you are trying to do both, as John's chart suggests, you are asking a lot of human nature. No wonder any kind of weakness is unacceptable! We would discuss the relationship with parents because they are connected to the issue of faith, with Chiron in the fourth house plus the Moon in Sagittarius in the twelfth house and Jupiter in the tenth house. A parent might have set too high standards for himself or herself or for John, or John might have been let down by parents who failed to live up to his expectations. Whatever the details, the parents provided an example in the area of beliefs and values. If they were reasonable, John got a good example. If they played overdrive or victim, John had a chance to see what not to do. One common form of victim involves the attitude, "If I can't do it all perfectly, I won't do anything." John has too much earth to take that path. But there is a very real danger of the common form of the mutable dilemma in which the person accomplishes a great deal but is never satisfied. It always should have been more, or better, or sooner, or easier. Moon-Ascendant, Sun and Uranus form a t-square in mutable signs and houses. Pisces and Sagittarius in conflict with Virgo typically mark the struggle between the vision of the perfect world and the limits of what is possible. Since Uranus is in the Gemini house, we actually have a mutable grand cross, indicating the need to integrate the interest in everything, the desire to do something really well, the drive to find the final **truth**, and the feeling that he should already be there, at peace with the Whole.

As with all the dilemmas, these naturally conflicting parts of life, a great many different variations are possible. One common form of the mutable dilemma, the inability to decide what we want most and to commit ourselves to anything, is less likely for John because of the strong earth, including the loaded tenth house. Another common form seems likely: the conflict between different values. The Sagittarius-Pisces part of the dilemma, said by a square between the signs and between the ninth and twelfth houses, can be a contest between truth and kindness. Fire and air let it all hang out. Water and earth restrain for security reasons, efficiency or sensitivity, and fear of hurt to ourselves or to others. I suspect that this issue was a major one. Fire tends to act (or speak) first and to think later. Uranus in the third house and the true South Node, just inside the third in Aries with both mean and true nodes moving there by progression, would tend to support that instinct. But the Libra wants to be liked, to have harmonious relationships, and the tenth house is status-conscious. And above all, the twelfth house Moon wants to mother and save the world. So there must have been struggles between the biting humor that is so associated with John through his letters in the *Mercury Hour*, and the sensitive, idealistic side of his nature. What role did parents play in his struggle with this issue? We may never know, now that he is gone.

The search for an ideal is also strongly linked to the area of relationships. Mercury, ruling the seventh house, is in the ninth house. Moon, ruling both the seventh and eighth houses, is in Sagittarius in the twelfth house. Neptune is in the eighth house. Venus and Pallas are conjunct Jupiter in Libra. Mars, ruling the fifth house, and Sun, the natural ruler of our capacity to love and be loved, are in the sign or house of Sagittarius. With the repeated theme associating relationships and ideals, we may never find the perfect person and never make a commitment. The greater the independence and commitment to career, the more likely this choice becomes. It is also possible to turn another person into an idol and refuse to consider anyone else. Or, we may choose a helping profession and pour our idealism into our work. Vesta in the eighth house, Mercury, ruling the seventh and in Virgo, and the Libra (including Venus and Pallas) in the tenth house support the attempt to meet relationship needs through work. Sometimes, with Cancer in the seventh house, Pluto in Cancer and Ceres (another key to mother) in Scorpio, the mother remains an adult partner in place of marriage. Or, the relationship with the mother remains an unresolved problem that blocks the willingness to commit to a partner. We solve the parent-partner issue by taking turns, as has been said repeatedly. But if we can't accept another person in a parent role (that anxiety over dependency), we may be stuck.

With the strong mutable and air emphasis in John's chart, he was clearly highly intelligent. A fine mind is usually able to resolve the dilemmas of life, to understand the issues and to find reasonable compromises. But it is necessary to understand the role of the unconscious in the situation. If that sensitive, vulnerable, passive, helpless part of us is totally rejected and repressed, it becomes unassimilable. It is not destroyed, but sealed in a capsule and buried, only to erupt in our lives in unanticipated and sometimes painful ways. Even a little knowledge of psychology and the unconscious may be enough to call attention to the buried or projected parts of the nature, so that the conscious intellect can begin work on integrating them with the consciously accepted parts of the character. A psychological understanding of astrology can offer the insight, and then it is up to us to work out the necessary compromises in the life.

The new asteroids echo much that has already been discussed. Four fall in Virgo in the ninth house, intensifying the focus on work and ideals; possibly on unreachable ideals. Sappho, Diana, and Psyche are all clustered around Mercury, restating the importance of the intellect. Dudu is close to the Sun, increasing the potential for willpower or for a Leo-Scorpio conflict over power and emotional desires. If Dudu and Psyche both symbolize the urge to explore the mind, the patterns certainly fit the interest in astrology. But they may also repeat the search for the ideal mate. Our other two potential Plutos are in the eighth house, offering another repetition of the importance of insight and shared power and pleasure. Dembowska in the seventh house and Hidalgo in Libra in the

tenth house connect our two possible Saturns to partnership, again calling for integration of power and equality, or marriage and career with possible fear of loss of power. Eros, on Pallas and Venus, says it again from
the other side; the asteroid and sign calling for relationship while the house
calls for career or power. Urania joined to them reminds of the need to
maintain independence, and fits the career in astrology. Amor in Aries,
conjunct Chiron, plus Frigga in Sagittarius widely conjunct Mars, reiterate
the freedom-closeness dilemma, and the association of mate and perfectionism. Icarus (another possible Sun) in Scorpio is similar to Sun conjunct Dudu: will the power be kept or shared; will it express out or be
contained? Toro, exactly conjunct Ceres, again intrigues us with the
mother. Was the relationship pleasurable, or did one try to possess and
control the other? Did the mother die, or remain so remote that she might
as well have been gone? Maybe someone knows that early story. All the
chart offers is the importance of the mother as a key to emotional security and to faith.

John McCormick was originally trained in technical skills, but the later
years of his life were devoted to astrology. He wrote two books and served
as a board member of the American Federation of Astrologers, lecturing
at the A.F.A. conferences and for other astrology groups around the U.S.
He was best known for the sense of humor that is so often associated
with Sagittarius. But behind the humor was the sincere devotion to truth
that is also Sagittarian. He was often with people, seemingly gregarious,
but there was a quality of aloneness also there. If he had personal problems, they remained private. Over the years of writing for *Mercury Hour*
and speaking at Edie Custer's Seven Hills conferences, he had formed a
strong bond of friendship. He was engaged to be married and had made
plans to move to Virginia from his native New Jersey, but he ran into a
truck while riding his moped and died in the resultant surgery on May
7, 1981. He left many friends who will miss him.

A number of different systems of current patterns are presented here
for the date of the accident and death. In the secondary progressions,
also known as the day for a year system, a variety of patterns indicate
the possibility of major action and change in the life. Progressed Mars had
held an octile to Uranus (both progressed and natal) for several years, and
it was still within the permissible one-degree orb. During the early years
of the aspect, Mars had also been octile Moon, and then Ascendant. During the later part of the aspect, Uranus had retrograded to square the Moon
within the one-degree orb.

Progressed aspects that stay in orb for years are important keys to basic
issues in the character and life. We can see the obvious freedom-closeness
issue in this pattern of Moon-Mars-Uranus-Ascendant. The latter three want
independence, risk, change. The Moon clings to security, familiarity, a
nest. The issue of ideals is also clear. With Mars in the first house,

Progressed positions for John McCormick on May 7, 1981.

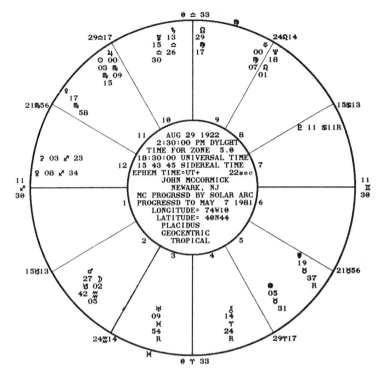

A 06-⚏-41   M 28-♏-11   X 05-✶-23   E 23-⚏-37

GEOCENTRIC
N-NODE S-NODE
☽ 27V149 27P149
☿ 26L153 07Sc40
♀ 16V147 21Sc08
♂ 16Ge28 12Sc50
♃ 19Ca49 29Sa58

♄ 28Ca53 17Cp09
♅ 15Ge37 11Sa45
♆ 12Le49 09Aq04
♇ 21Ca16 18Cp17

Solar Arc Directed positions for John McCormick on May 7, 1981.

☉ 03-♏-15   ☽ 06-⚏-40   ☿ 22-♏-26   ♀ 18-✶-46   ♂ 20-⚏-07
♃ 15-✶-36   ♄ 04-✶-02   ♅ 09-♉-30R   ♆ 14-♎-05   ♇ 08-♏-30
♟ 09-♑-19   ⚷ 21-✶-13   ⚸ 14-♋-39   ⚹ 03-♎-48   ⚶ 14-♊-30R
A 09-⚏-08   M 28-♏-12   X 22-✶-49   E 28-⚏-06

we want to do what we please immediately, and the corollary of desire is the power to do what we want. Uranus, an air planet in an air house, is clear about what is in view, the world right around us, and theoretically able to accept it with tolerance; there will be another day. Sagittarius, Pisces, twelfth house want perfection totally and now. Maybe we could find our ideals somewhere else. Mars and Uranus are ready to move at the drop of a hat. You don't even have to drop the hat. But what about that stepchild Moon? What Moon? Ignore it. Dependency, clinging, need for familiar surroundings and possessions are for other people. The South Node of Uranus conjunct the natal Ascendant for the whole life is only repeating the same message: "No one puts strings on me. I will find myself through astrology and friends."

At least progressed Mars is past its long octile to Moon and Ascendant, and it is now sextile-trine the progressed nodes of the Moon. Such a pattern marks a time for potential integration of these conflicting parts of the nature, a time to accept closer relationships as possible without totally abandoning independence. We have to remember that the current pattern shows the timing of the issue being brought to the foreground in the life, but the natal chart shows the nature of our action unless we have changed our basic character. So current aspects between Mars and Moon (or any form of Letters One and Four) show a time to acknowledge our need for both. If we have already made peace between them, we will handle the current opportunities successfully. If we have not reconciled these two parts of ourselves, we will face problems that force us to deal with the issue.

Astrologers who omit the nodes of the Moon would be left with only the "almost out of orb" octile of Mars-Uranus and a sextile of progressed Mars to progressed MC. Many astrologers would be tempted to rectify the chart to have Mars still octile the Ascendant. But if we are willing to look at alternate forms of the astrological alphabet, we will find additional Mars aspects. Progressed Icarus (our little Sun that so often overreaches) is conjunct natal Mars, and so is the progressed South Node of Vesta. Vesta is our super workaholic. When in high focus, we may neglect relationships for work, or be frustrated in work and become ill. Combined with Mars, it intensifies the difficulty in accepting closeness. Progressed Mars is also opposite the North Nodes of Vesta and Saturn for the same message, octile progressed South Uranus for more need to stay independent, as well as quincunx its own North Node and square progressed nodes of Venus and Chiron. Conflict aspects between different forms of Letter One are "self against self." Venus wants to enjoy life, so conflicts with Mars may mean we are unable to find the pleasure we want. Or our need for independence may be in conflict with our need for a mate — Venus as ruler of Libra. Chiron wants perfection, so a Mars square may mean we lack the power to attain it. The progressed South Node of the Moon (both mean and true) is also conjunct the Part of Mars (Ascendant plus Mars minus Sun), which I interpret as another form of Letter One. We are still not through with Mars. By progression, it is parallel (within one degree orb) both natal Ascendant and Eastpoint. We will leave midpoints, which have been widely promoted in astrology, for others, and mention one other Arabic Part. If John's birth time is accurate, his progressed Part of Death (progressed Ascendant plus progressed eighth cusp minus progressed Moon) had just reached the one-degree trine to progressed Mars when the accident and death occurred.

There are, of course, many other aspects in the progressed chart. Progressed Toro is conjunct the natal Ascendant, squaring Uranus and quincunx Pluto. Natally, Toro was conjunct Ceres (mother) in a grand trine to Pluto and Uranus. Again, we wish we could ask about mother as a key to being with others. Progressed Venus was conjunct the natal Moon: mother, home, mate, a frequent pattern for marriage. But is it OK to be open and trusting of others? All over the chart, the patterns were calling for relationships, for moving closer, for dealing with feelings while Mars and Uranus wanted to pull back. Amor was progressing over the South Node of the Moon, a lesson in love. Hidalgo was progressing over Pallas, Eros and Urania: control vs. caring vs. detachment. Diana was also just about to leave that mixture, while Dudu and the progressed eighth house cusp were moving in on natal Diana. I am still wondering about Diana. Is she within herself basically ambivalent about closeness, seeking self-sufficiency, self-containment, even isolation? Is she protective mother but unwilling to be mate? Either way, we have power issues connected to relationships. Dembowska has been hanging there in the seventh house opposite natal Mars and progressed Icarus. If Dembowska is like Saturn, the power and the freedom are again confronting the need for closeness. Will closeness bring loss of power, the danger of being overwhelmed? The progressed Ascendant (another Mars) is opposite natal Vesta across the second and eighth houses: my pleasures vs. ours; self-containment or sharing. Progressed Ascendent is also conjunct the heliocentric position of Mars. Progressed Frigga is on the Eastpoint, a strong desire for closeness. Progressed Pandora is on the progressed Antivertex: action with Pandora may be irreversible. Progressed Eros is on progressed Ceres: mother and love again. Progressed MC is octile progressed Saturn: the threat of losing control.

Progressed Moon is just coming to the square to progressed Sun, lacking eight minutes if we are purist about the one-degree orb. But if the whole thing is symbolic, and our goal is to find the repeated theme, we are seeing again the conflict between power and dependency though both Sun and Moon want closeness in their own right, and both in the chart are displaced into the transpersonal area. Their progressed signs now represent the fixed dilemma: freedom and closeness still, but personal vs. shared

pleasures also, or personal power vs. shared power. Since the Sun sym-
bolizes the life force, it is singularly lacking in aspects for the end of life.
Unless we resort to midpoints, obscure aspects, asteroids or nodes, both
Jupiter (Ascendant ruler) and Sun seem disconnected. But the aspects are
there if you are willing to use angles, nodes and asteroids. Jupiter at zero
Scorpio aspects the MC axis, and the Eastpoint axis as well as progressed
Vesta. Progressed Sun aspects asteroids: natal Dudu, progressed Eros and
Ceres, with a parallel to natal Ceres and a contraparallel to natal Pallas.
The themes are still mother, love and relationships. Home and familiar
surroundings can become a surrogate mother. Mars and Uranus deny any
need for shelter or reassurance. When we know we are deeply ambivalent
over our desire for closeness vs. our fear of dependency, loss of power,
criticism, rejection, etc., we can find a compromise position. When we
are only conscious of one side of a conflict, the other side of us may be
repressed into the unconscious, and may manifest in drastic events. An
accident may remove us from the closeness we didn't know we feared.
Mars triumphs over Moon-Venus.

The other current techniques being presented will be discussed only
briefly. Secondary Progressions are my preferred system for current patterns. I feel that they give a clearer picture of the long-term issues in the
nature, the aspects that stay in orb for lengthy periods. Uranus square
Ascendant and then Moon; Pluto quincunx Ascendant; Mars moving
through the midpoint of the pattern, octile both ends; these were basic
keys to the issues that needed to be faced and resolved. The MC octile
to natal and then to progressed Saturn was another major key. Jupiter moving into a water sign, aspecting the water nodes of the Moon, was calling
for a recognition of the emotional unconscious side of the nature; the
neglected stepchild. Personal counseling would have advised a long look
at the issues of dependency, perfectionism and self-assertion. A solution
would have required small amounts of closeness, willingness to be human
in need of help at times, and a healthy competitive outlet for the Mars
and general power in the chart. Making peace with the memory of mother
might have been very high on the agenda. Maybe it is happening now,
on the next level of life.

Solar Arc Directions, the technique I consider most helpful after Secondary Progressions, show highly appropriate aspects. The same planets
shown to be important by their long-term aspects in secondaries are emphatically giving notice in the directions. Uranus has moved to the quincunx to Moon and the trioctile to Mercury. (Aspects in directions are
always from a directed planet to a natal planet since the whole chart moves
at the same speed and the natal relationships do not change.) Directed
Pluto is square Moon, trioctile Antivertex and octile Pallas. Mars is trine
Venus and just short of trioctile Saturn if we stay with the one degree orb.
Ascendant is sextile Moon and trioctile Mercury. Moon is trine Saturn,

opposite Vesta and octile Mars. Jupiter is trine Neptune. Saturn is not quite at the square to the Sun, and there is no aspect from directed Sun unless we use the asteroids. Most astrologers who favor Solar Arc Directions prefer midpoints to asteroids. Novice astrologers are often dismayed that there can be sextiles and trines when an event is classed as negative, but there are always mixed harmonious and stress aspects. Often, as already indicated, the harmonious aspects will be between planets that are natally in conflict aspect. Unless that initial conflict in the character has been faced and resolved, the current pattern shows only the issues and the time, while the natal aspect shows the nature of the result. The periods for special awareness are the times when planets that were natally in stress aspect move to new stress aspects. If we understand our own inner conflict, we can handle the situations well. The occasion is much like receiving a report card at school. We have a chance to see how we are doing in our growth. Character produces destiny so we see our character out there, visible in the events in our lives.

Readers can study the alternate techniques for additional relevant patterns. I will mostly point out the focus on Mars in the different systems, since both accidents and surgery are traditionally associated with Mars. In the Tertiary Progressions (one day equals one lunar month), progressed Mars had entered zero Pisces, so was quincunx MC and North Node of the Moon, as well as octile Chiron in the fourth house. In the Minor Progressions (one lunar month equals a year), progressed Mars was just reaching the trioctile to the MC and was, in effect connected since it was in orb of trioctile the true node. Transiting Mars was quincunx natal Moon and trioctile Mercury. The Ascendant in John's Solar Return was conjunct his natal Mars. In the precession-corrected Solar Return, Mars was conjunct the return Ascendant. Mars was on the Descendant of the Kinetic Solar Return and on the Midheaven and natal Moon-Ascendant in the precession-corrected kinetic solar return. Thus, all four forms of Solar Return had Mars on an angle. The Lunar Return before the accident had Mars conjunct the MC. In the precession-corrected Lunar Return, Mars finally escaped an angle conjunction, but Vesta was on the Ascendant, and Mars was conjunct Mercury and Sun, trine Ascendant-Vesta and Neptune more widely, quincunx Uranus and opposite Juno. In the Kinetic Lunar Return, Mars squared the Moon and formed a yod (double quincunx) to Jupiter-Saturn in Libra and to Uranus in late Scorpio. The precession-corrected Kinetic Lunar Return put Uranus on the Ascendant so it joined in the yod to Mars, and Mars was also trioctile the MC. Returns are treated more like transits with wider orbs permitted.

A brief description of these various systems was presented in Chapter 9. Kinetic Returns draw the horoscope for the moment that the transiting Sun or Moon reaches the progressed Sun or Moon while traditional returns use the natal positions. Precession correction moves the planets by the

Solar Return

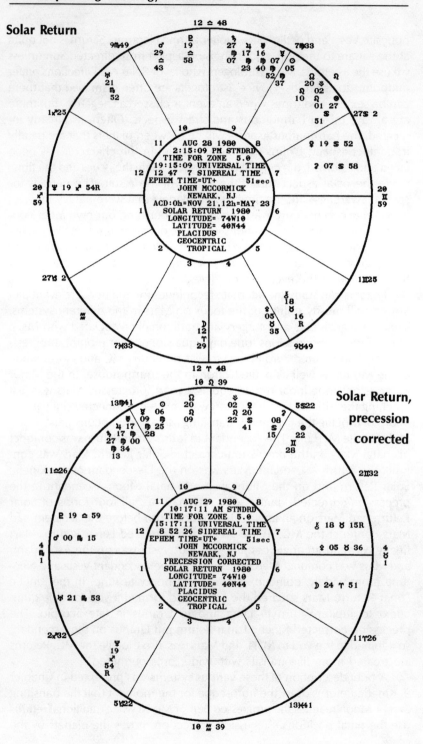

Solar Return, precession corrected

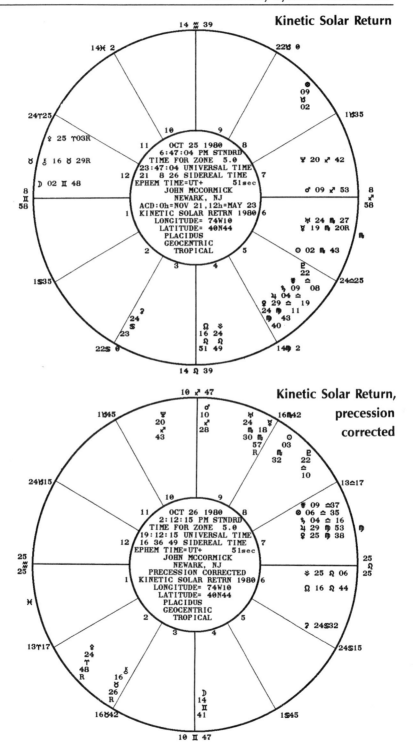

Kinetic Solar Return

Kinetic Solar Return, precession corrected

amount the solar system has moved against the backdrop of the stars, but the Tropical Zodiac is retained. Sometimes one system seems a little clearer and emphatic, and sometimes another. On the big events, they all work. In the end, each astrologer has to choose one or two systems. The charts presented here are still only a tiny part of what might be done. It is possible to spend one's life doing charts with no time left for living. The primary purpose of showing the different systems is to escape the ethnocentricity of believing that there is only one "right" system, and to point out the absurdity of thinking that one or two aspects "caused" an event. The sky is part of the order in the cosmos. Any way we look at the sky, we see the same order. The character is symbolized by all the systems in different ways. The character creates or permits the events. Our potential for making a better life lies in our capacity to change our character: to make peace with ourselves.

CHAPTER 18

A Man With Faith

Benjamin Creme (pronounced "crem," with a short "e") is an artist who has become a guru. He expounds and expands on the work of Alice Bailey, as she followed and enlarged the ideas of Madame Blavatsky, founder of Theosophy. Spiritual leaders fascinate me. As readers of this book are well aware by now, I think that our beliefs create our personal worlds. Periodically, our experiences conflict with our beliefs, and we have to decide whether we will ignore one of the two, or whether we can make an adjustment to reconcile the conflict. A firm prediction can precipitate such a confrontation. A few years ago, the Jehovah's Witnesses were predicting the end of the world and the coming of the Kingdom of God in 1975. Right up to the year before the Judgment, they were urgently advising everyone to accept Jesus and follow their path to salvation. As 1975 progressed with the normal struggles between humans and no sign of the Heavenly Kingdom, the prediction was quietly forgotten. Others who have prophesied the end of the world or promised their followers that they would be picked up by flying saucers while the rest of the earth went up in flames or floods, have tried to explain the failure of the prophesy in various ways. The favorite explanation is that the prayers of the faithful moved God to prevent the destruction.

Unlike the prophets of doom and gloom, Benjamin Creme offers a prediction of hope. In the teachings of Blavatsky, Bailey and others, God is said to periodically incarnate on earth in a physical body to offer His wisdom in a form suited to the state of humans at the time He comes. Krishna, Buddha and Jesus the Christ are said to be different incarnations of the same cosmic Soul. Blavatsky suggested that the next incarnation of this Avatar would use the name of Maitreya Buddha; that He was waiting in Shamballa in the astral realm (above the material realm) in the area of Tibet and the Gobi desert. Creme says that for some years, the current Christ (preferring the familiar Western name) has been overshadowing Creme and speaking through him. Creme has lectured often in California and in England and less often in other places, as the spokesman of the Christ. He has also written a book called *The Return of the Christ*.

In both his lectures and in his book, Creme has said that the Christ has already entered a physical body, this time choosing to materialize an adult body rather than to come as a baby. Creme states that the Christ has come because of the anguish and unsolvable problems in the world, to help humanity to bring peace and love into the world, to replace the violence, to encourage the world to share. In effect, we have gotten the world into such a crisis that we need God to come in person to bail us out. Creme has made a firm prediction that the Christ will make His presence known to everyone on earth by simultaneously being heard and seen on all radios and televisions, with each person understanding what is being said as if it were said in his or her own language. This appearance before the whole world was to happen in the middle of 1982. (This book was being written early in 1982, but is only reaching print in 1983.)

Creme's horoscope is highly appropriate for a guru. Mercury, Sun and Ceres are rising in Sagittarius and Jupiter, ruler of the Ascendant, is in the tenth house of profession while Saturn, the natural key to profession is in the Jupiter house. The search for **truth** is clearly central in the nature, as well as the potential of turning it into a career. Additional mutable emphasis further supports a life devoted to the mind. The Moon is in Gemini and the nodes of the Moon in Virgo-Pisces fall in the Gemini-Sagittarius houses. Like the rising Sagittarius and Saturn (ruling the first house placed in the ninth house), Chiron in Aries is identified with personally finding the Truth and with sharing it with others. Often, Saturn or Virgo in the ninth house, and Jupiter in the tenth house, can indicate skepticism and doubt in matters of faith. I have not read Creme's book, but have been told that he mentions his struggles with doubt and disbelief. Both Saturn in the ninth house and the South Node of the Moon in Pisces suggest a lesson connected to faith, whether the lesson involves having too much, too little, or directing it in the wrong place.

There is potential for both harmony and conflict in the area of faith. The mutable dilemma, said by the grand mutable cross of Ceres, Moon and nodes of the Moon, indicates a need to integrate the ideals and values with the everyday world of the possible, or to work out conflicts between different beliefs and values. On the harmony side, Uranus in Pisces, Pluto in Cancer and Jupiter in Scorpio form a grand trine. Water trines show psychic potentials along with the capacity to nurture and/or be nurtured. Neptune, another key to faith, forms a grand trine in fire signs with Chiron and the Sagittarius cluster around the Ascendant. The most charismatic gurus I have seen have tended to have the grand trine in fire with Neptune

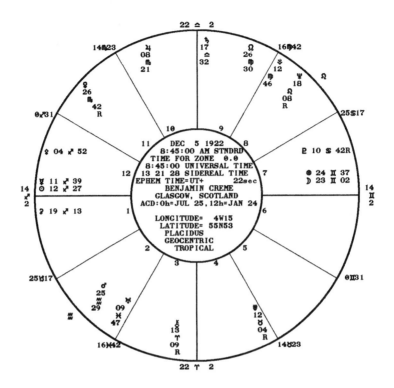

☊ 08-♎-29	⚷ 15-♊-33R	⚷ 26-♌-50	⚷ 14-♑-02	⚸ 01-♏-22
⚵ 03-♐-15	☋ 12-♓-03	⚴ 27-♎-52	⚶ 27-♐-22	⚷ 29-♎-55
⚳ 20-♍-30	⚕ 25-♓-38	⚳ 08-♑-48	⚷ 07-♑-17	☽ 11-♏-53
AntiVertex 02-♒-08			Eastpoint 18-♑-49	

or Jupiter or Sagittarius in the first house. Fire shows the self-confidence to offer our vision as Truth for the world. There is also verbal fluency with Mercury in Sagittarius conjunct Sun and Ascendant, and Venus in Scorpio is often highly magnetic. It is certainly a proper chart for a spiritual leader.

Since a chart shows issues but not details, it is not possible to measure the conviction and sincerity of Creme from his chart. Con artists and Nazi leaders may have strong Jupiters or Sagittarius. A personal contact and the evidence from the life are needed to determine the level at which a person is functioning. By these measures, Creme is absolutely sincere in his beliefs. His message calls humanity to move toward love and sharing, a similar message to the one being offered by the cosmos as Pluto moves into Scorpio in 1983. Unless we learn to share the resources of the planet in love and sisterhood (as well as brotherhood), a Scorpio period, to be accompanied by a massive focus on Capricorn (report card time), is likely to bring more than angry words. Through his life, which speaks more loudly than words, Creme clearly wants humanity to move toward harmony and happiness. The questions in my mind center not on his sincerity, but on whether his vision is accurate. We cannot specify his degree of accuracy solely from his horoscope, just as we cannot be sure of his sincerity from the chart alone. But at least we can look at some of the current patterns in the middle of 1982 to see whether they look joyous or disappointed. We can also check the current state of his mutable dilemma, to see whether it seems to be moving toward integration with the keys to faith, maintaining harmonious aspects while the natal conflict aspects are out of orb.

Progressed positions for Benjamin Creme on June 1, 1982.

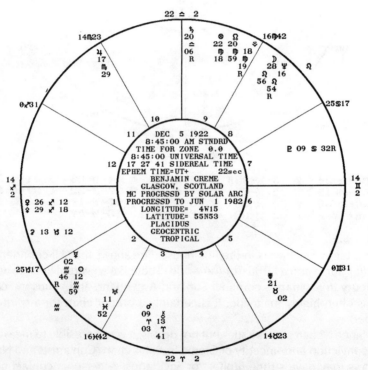

A 06-⊀-21   M 22-⊀-35   X 23-⊀-12   E 21-⊀-12

The Antivertex is represented by an X.

The long continuing trine of Pluto to Uranus is encouraging, though it might mean a devoted wife who supports his New Age interests. Pluto will eventually make the exact trine to Jupiter, another encouraging note, though this aspect might mean harmony between marriage and career, or general favorable reception by the public of his work, artistic or spiritual. Less encouraging is the long square of Neptune to Jupiter in fixed signs and houses. The spiritual work may have been pursued at a financial cost. His wife may be consciously encouraging but unconsciously resistant. There may be conflicts between different values and beliefs. But Neptune trines Ceres in the first house, suggesting success in his spiritual endeavors through his own action.

Another questionable aspect is presented by the lengthy conjunction of progressed Antivertex and Eastpoint with the South Node of the Moon. I see the South Node as a place where we first have to learn and then give something to the world. Creme is clearly giving a mystical message, a highly appropriate action for Pisces in the Gemini house. Our question is whether the Pisces intuition has been successfully meshed with the real world right around us. Or could the vision be a fantasy? Whether or not it is true, he is in action, giving it out to the media with those patterns. As usual, we will only know by the results whether the lesson of making sure the vision was realistic was mastered. If the Christ had appeared as forecast, the South Node lesson could be considered learned. Since the prediction failed, there is still a need for growth in integrating the mutable dilemma, for integration of the dreams with the reality of the world. During much of the time that the Eastpoint and Antivertex are conjunct the South Node, they are also square the seventh house Moon and the progressed MC is opposite the Moon and square the nodes. The full mutable dilemma is in action through the signs, while the first and seventh houses bring in part of the cardinal principles. The combination is basically repeating the need to integrate personal desires with those of others, and personal vision with external reality.

Additional aspects that force us to question Creme's vision involve progressed Mars. Mars has been moving through a quincunx to Jupiter, and a square to Pluto has started more recently. Any Mars-Jupiter aspect involves action and ideals or goals. With the closet-cleaning quincunx, we may change our action or our beliefs, goals and values. Creme has done that, shifting from artist to spiritual teacher and offering new beliefs to the world. But with any Mars-Jupiter stress aspect, we have to consider the possibility of acting against better judgment, and the tenth house reminds us of the test of the Law, cosmic and karmic, along with natural and cultural. The consequences will give us feedback. We can count on Letter Ten for that. The Mars square to Pluto might be friction with others who prefer to keep the *status quo*, or strain on Creme's marriage due to the time demands of his traveling and speaking. Any Mars-Pluto conflict asks us to harmonize our own will with the rights of others, to make sure we do justice to both. A fire-water confrontation may be as simple as feeling pulled between action directed outwardly, and needing time to also work inside. Mars is also approaching the octile to its own natal position, a "self against self" pattern that suggests either frustration that he cannot do what he wants, or ambivalence about what he is doing or has done.

Supportive aspects include Venus semisextile its own natal position, suggesting pleasure from what Creme is doing and the involvement with many friends, including making new friends with Venus natally in the eleventh house. He also has progressed Ceres trine natal Vesta, a good augury for work success. His Sun, in contrast, has been quincunx Vesta, another possible indication of the new direction he has taken with his work, but, especially since natal Sun squares Vesta, another form of the mutable conflict of beliefs with reality. At the same time, the progressed Sun has been sextile Chiron, a strong fire combination encouraging acting on his faith. The progressed Sun is also square Juno in the fourth house, still another clue to the problem of integrating marriage and home with his public life. Progressed Ascendant trioctile first Saturn, but now MC, could show tension between personal needs and career demands, or be another statement of faith vs. reality with the progressed Ascendant now in Pisces. Creme's birth inclinations and his present urges are spiritual, while Saturn and the MC (carrying the same meaning) are always the acid test against the laws of the universe and consequences stemming from past actions.

The patterns discussed seem very mixed, with some potential for satisfaction and public support, but some problems connected to the mutables, planets as well as signs and houses. Often, the progressed Moon will assist in evaluating the emotional state during a specified couple of months. The Avatar was to appear in mid-1982, which could mean any of the summer months. In early June, the progressed Moon moved into the last degree of Leo in the eighth house, so in early July it entered Virgo. Aspects in late Leo include trioctiles to progressed Ceres and Chiron (which are square each other). The combination does not look favorable for spiritual and work elation. In early Virgo, the Moon is octile Saturn and quincunx Mercury; again, not exactly aspects for spiritual triumph. Saturn marks feedback time. An octile in an earth sign suggests coming back down to earth; in artists' terms, "back to the drawing board." There have been new messages explaining that a personal appearance was deemed unnecessary after all; that the Christ is continuing to work but appearing only to believers. Since the Avatar did not appear to the world, Creme is still working on that South Node in Pisces and Saturn in the ninth house. When experience conflicts with faith, we need to work out a compromise. Our faith creates our world, our choices are shaped by it, and we cannot function without some kind of faith.

CHAPTER 19

Postscript: A New Chart for the U.S.

I had planned to begin and end the chart section of this book with horoscopes in which spiritual interests and faith were central issues. But I have decided to include a speculative chart for the signing of the Declaration of Independence on July 4, 1776. I spent a good many hours looking for a workable U.S. horoscope during my early years in astrology, but never found one that fit the events to my satisfaction. Some years back, I was given a photocopy of new historical information on the signing, but my time has been too limited to attempt a proper rectification. During the day on mundane astrology in our 1982 16-Day Intensive, I ran a few charts on a speculative time, and became excited when the angles started making proper aspects for some of the major events in our history. I am sure that others have also experimented with the July 4 chart, and for those who enjoy such enterprises, I am including a number of progressions for major events.

My early attempts at rectifying the chart had ranged from 11 AM to 5 PM. All historical documents agreed on the fact that the Congress met at 9 AM and worked through the day on a variety of business items. Thomas Jefferson had written that the Declaration of Independence was signed in the late afternoon, but letters written by others mentioned the morning. The new item was a letter from a committee appointed by Congress on July 4, 1776, to raise troops for the defense of New York and Pennsylvania. Paul H. Smith, historian at the Library of Congress, writes:

> The particular significance of the document lies in the fact the committee was appointed as the third item of business after the Declaration was approved, yet their letter begins; 'Gentlemen, the Congress this morning directed us to confer. . .'

If three items of business were concluded after the Declaration and before noon, we have to consider an earlier time. Another historical source had said that the decision to attempt a permanent break with England was made on July 2. The discussion on July 4 involved only some arguing over the wording of the Declaration, and it was signed and put aside to permit decisions on defense. The war with England had started the year before, and the colonies were hard pressed to find, train and provide for their troops. In light of that letter, the signing could have occurred even before 10 AM. Remembering all the astrologers who were devoted to the historically absurd chart with Uranus rising, I wondered whether it would be possible instead that Uranus was on the MC. The miracle of modern computers produced four charts complete with progressions for different major events in U.S. history. After I had looked at those charts, I started to get excited and ended up running another dozen. The chart is still obviously speculative, but it has given me more appropriate angle aspects than any other I have tried. I expect to go on testing it, but in the meantime, readers of this book can try their own systems.

First of all, does the chart itself make sense? Uranus on the MC certainly fits a statement of independence. In fact, all three of our keys to freedom are in the tenth house: Uranus, Mars and Jupiter, with the Sun just moving into the tenth. Certainly, that kind of power is stating, "No one is going to tell me what to do." Mars remained in the square to Neptune for the greater part of the war, during the desperately difficult period when Washington held the untrained and ill-equipped army together almost single-handedly. But Mars is also trine the sixth house Moon and Pallas, and trine Juno in the second house; earth houses showing the capacity to handle the material world successfully. The Aquarian Moon also speaks for freedom and democracy, and what could be more appropriate for America, bread basket to the world, than both Moon and Ceres in the Virgo house of labor and the harvest? The Cancer in the tenth and eleventh houses also mark our capacity to feed the world, while the second house Saturn manages to make a profit at the same time that the first house Neptune is presenting us as natural saviors and preachers. Jupiter in the tenth may also indicate a career as a professional savior.

The grand trine in air signs and earth houses has been noted. Vesta in Taurus in the ninth house completes a grand trine in earth signs in fire houses: the original steamroller. With Saturn in Libra and widely conjunct Juno, part of our national lesson is to learn to cooperate. We know how to play savior and bulldozer, but cooperation is another matter. In spite of all the air in the chart, Saturn and South Node of the Moon in air signs indicate that we are learning how to handle equality and acceptance. With South Node in the fifth house, and Capricorn on the cusp, we are also learning about power and sex. The mixture of puritan morals and license, seen in our traditional religious views, contrasted with pornography and

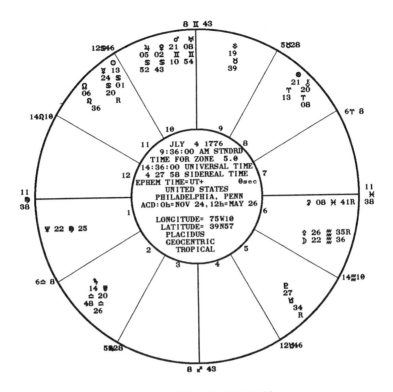

X 13-♌-20   E 05-♍-09

The Antivertex is represented by an X.

divorce certainly mark this as an area needing integration. Only a good many more hours of work can provide support for the chart, or will dismiss it as another also-ran. The progressed charts are offered for your entertainment.

Since the natal and progressed angles (MC, Ascendant, Eastpoint and Antivertex) are the primary tools for fine tuning in rectification, I am including a few of the aspects to angles that make this chart worth our consideration. The war for independence had actually begun a year before the formal Declaration was issued. A horoscope can sometimes indicate events leading up to the actual beginning of the person or organization being studied. The MC exact conjunction with Uranus would picture the existence of the conjunction for the preceding year, using the approximate "degree for a year" measure for the progressing MC. The Uranus conjunction would have continued for the chaotic first year after the Declaration, and, within a few months, the square of MC to the natal Ascendant would have begun and lasted two years. At the same time, progressed Ascendant was trioctile Pluto for approximately the first two years after the official Declaration of Independence. During the war years, the progressed Eastpoint also moved through the square to natal MC and Uranus, and the progressed Vertex sustained a quincunx to natal Sun and then to progressed Sun for a time. Of course, there were many aspects between planets such as Sun square Saturn and Mars square Neptune, but planetary aspects (except for the Moon) do not vary enough with time of birth to be very useful in rectification.

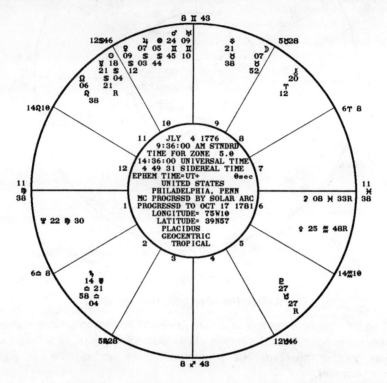

A 15-♍-56   M 13-♊-45   X 22-♌-48   E 10-♍-54

The end of the war against England, when the fledgling country had actually won its independence, was marked by the surrender of Cornwallis at Yorktown, Va. on October 17, 1781. Secondary progressions for that date show the progressed MC in the favorable semisextile to the natal Sun; progressed Mercury has finally ended the long quincunx to natal Moon; progressed Vertex is conjunct the natal Moon and quincunx Neptune; progressed Eastpoint has reached the natal Ascendant; progressed Moon has reached the ninth house and is semisextile MC-Uranus, sextile progressed Jupiter, square its own mean nodes, and trioctile Neptune. It was a triumph to win, but almost insoluble problems also faced the new nation. Probably the biggest challenge involved the need to persuade thirteen independent colonies to cooperate. Some historians believe that it would never have happened without the diplomatic skill of George Washington and the high esteem in which he was held.

By the time the Paris Peace Treaty was signed on September 3, 1783, the progressed Sun had reached the retrograding progressed Mercury, an appropriate aspect with natal Sun on the cusp of houses ten-eleven (showing the issue of independence and executive power at the time of the original Declaration), and with Mercury ruling both the MC (power) and the Ascendant (independent individual action). By the time Washington was inaugurated as our first President under the new Constitution in 1789, the progressed MC had reached the conjunction with natal Mars. The early days of the shift from a loose confederation of independent colonies to a unified nation were not easy, but the goal was accomplished. As the progressed MC trined natal Moon and squared Neptune, the Bill of Rights was adopted, guaranteeing the freedoms that we tend to take for granted but which are so rare in many parts of the world. But the freedom (desired by both first house and Aquarius) was not extended to slaves. Much later, with progressed Ascendant aspecting that Neptune-Moon quincunx, the slaves would also receive freedom through the Emancipation Proclamation.

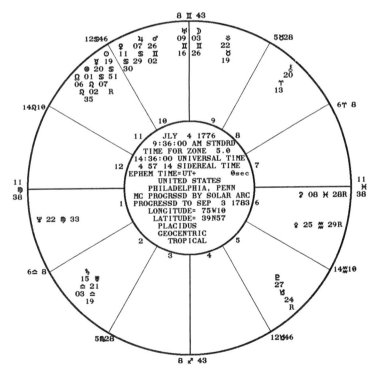

A 17-♍-28   M 15-♊-33   X 26-♌-26   E 12-♍-58

During the naval battles that led into the second war with England, the War of 1812, the progressed MC was moving over natal Sun and progressed Jupiter, and (during the period when England actually invaded the U.S. and burned the capital city) the MC squared Saturn. During this same period, the progressed Eastpoint was conjunct Saturn. The progressed Ascendant reached Saturn in time for the founding of the U.S. Bank and the enactment of a protective tariff to prevent competition that would threaten the financial interests of the young country. At the actual date of the declaration of war on England in 1812, the progressed Moon had just passed over Mars (while tempers escalated over the impounding of our ships in England's war with France) and the Moon was still in the square to progressed Neptune. The remaining angle axis, progressed Antivertex-Vertex, had moved into Scorpio and was square progressed Mercury, ruler of the natal MC and Ascendant.

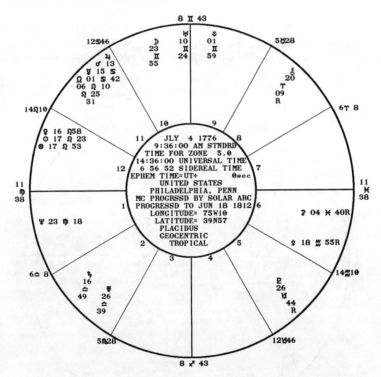

A 11-♎-21   M 13-♋-05   X 00-♏-41   E 15-♎-26

Our first presidential death in office occurred on April 4, 1841, when Harrison died of pneumonia after a month in office. Progressed MC was sextile progressed Uranus (we must remember that the quality of the natal aspect tends to occur, while the progression shows the timing). Progressed

MC was also quincunx the Descendant and octile progressed Mercury, always important because of its natal rulership of the angles. Progressed Ascendant squared the progressed mean nodes of the Moon and progressed Mars. Progressed Venus was on Neptune, usually associated with pneumonia. Progressed Moon was on natal Sun, and was just reaching the square to natal Saturn, which is always a key to an executive power figure. Progressed Sun, another key to power people, was sextile progressed Eastpoint and square progressed Antivertex.

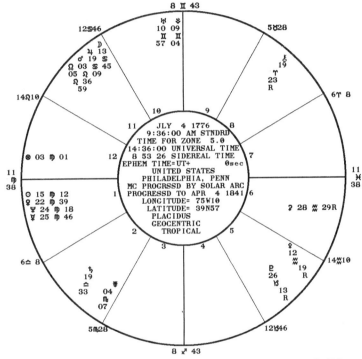

A 04-ℏ-27   M 10-♌-54   X 14-♐-25   E 15-ℏ-50

We have not begun to exhaust the aspects in this brief survey, since the local angles for Washington, D.C. are slightly different than the Philadelphia angles where the Declaration was signed, and there are also quotidian (daily) angles to consider. The Washington quotidian MC was square the progressed MC and trioctile progressed Mercury on the actual day of death. Since the horoscope of any beginning can be a useful representation of the nature of whatever was started at the time, this chart of our first presidential death in office might be helpful when we try to understand others in the series. Most astrologers have associated these deaths with the Jupiter-Saturn conjunctions, which come at twenty year intervals. Progressed Jupiter was square progressed Saturn when Harrison died, and both were octile the natal Eastpoint which fell on their midpoint.

Jupiter and Saturn also formed a t-square to Chiron in Aries. If Chiron is associated with Sagittarius, it is a ruler of the fourth house, and it is in the eighth house, completing a pattern that fits an ending. Progressed Saturn is also quincunx natal Vesta, the classical aspect of separation. The involvement of Jupiter, Chiron and the ninth house could connect the death to some kind of overconfidence or to a problem with faith. Was Harrison too old to be a practical choice for the office of President? The pneumonia developed out of a cold caught while walking to market in the early morning without a coat. He could have delegated someone to do the shopping. Was he really ambivalent about taking on the job but let himself be talked into it because his fame could secure the power for his party? The Whigs had never had one of their members elected president; the Democrats had been in for several terms of office. The campaign was a circus, won by the slogan "Tippecanoe and Tyler too," referring to Harrison's success against the Indians at Tippecanoe.

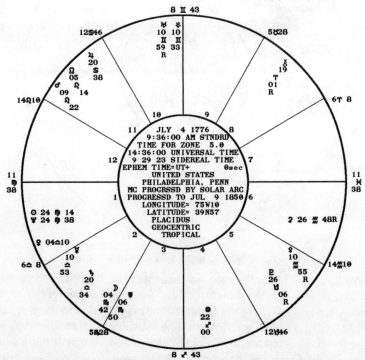

A 11-♏-32   M 19-♌-56   X 23-♐-53   E 24-♏-43

Our next presidential death in office was not associated with the Jupiter-Saturn cycle. President Taylor died on July 9, 1850, after five days of illness. The progressed MC had just reached the octile to natal Jupiter, and it was sextile progressed Saturn, semisextile progressed Jupiter, trine Chiron and square Vesta, tied to that same t-square in cardinal signs and fixed houses noted for Harrison. Even if we do not use Chiron as a co-ruler of Sagittarius, both Jupiter and Saturn rule the fourth house in this chart, and they are maintaining their mutual square and their octiles to the natal Eastpoint. In the chart for Taylor's death, progressed Ascendant was quincunx progressed Uranus and Vesta which maintained a tenth house conjunction for years. Progressed Sun was now on Neptune, (where Mercury and Venus had been at Harrison's death), with progressed Mars octile. Progressed Antivertex was square progressed Sun-Neptune and quincunx natal Mercury. Progressed Moon squared its own progressed nodes. The quotidian MC was opposite the natal Moon on the day that Taylor died.

Some fascinating parallels existed between the men who suffered these first two presidential deaths. They were both career army men who won their fame fighting Indians. They did not seek the Presidency but had it offered by their party, which used their popularity to win the office. They were the only members of the relatively short-lived Whig party to be elected President. Neither of their wives were hostess at the White House; Mrs. Harrison because of personal illness, and Mrs. Taylor from personal reluctance. A daughter-in-law acted as hostess for Harrison, and a daughter for Taylor.

At the start of the Civil War, fought ostensibly over the issue of slavery, progressed MC had been moving through the midpoint of natal Sun-Saturn, had just entered Virgo, and was still octile Saturn. Through the four plus years of war, the progressed Ascendant moved through the quincunx to Chiron and natal Mars, the opposition to natal Vesta and the trioctile to natal Jupiter. At the time of the Emancipation Proclamation which officially freed the slaves, progressed Sun was trine natal MC-Uranus and just leaving the trioctile to natal Moon. Progressed Ascendant was square natal Moon, sextile natal Neptune, semisextile the conjunction of progressed Venus and Saturn, trine progressed Jupiter and just past the quincunx to natal Mars. Progressed MC had just reached the natal Eastpoint for a change in Law and personal action and independence, and it also was quincunx the progressed true South Node of the Moon. Another angle crossing with the same mixture of Four-Ten (change of power) and One-Seven (personal action-interaction), was shown by the progressed Eastpoint crossing the IC. Progressed Antivertex was opposite Jupiter, and the Antivertex was quincunx the true North Node of the Moon. Progressed Moon was in the ninth house (law courts, moral principles), trine Pluto and octile natal Sun. Within a month, by the time the news got out, progressed Moon had reached the one degree orb of a trioctile to natal Saturn. Progressed Mercury was just coming to the trine to natal Venus.

The aspects seem appropriate. Two angle axes crossing two others simultaneously suggest major changes in the situation. Angles are always involved for overt changes. Neptune is traditionally associated with confinement or bondage as one of its many forms of being victim, but its first

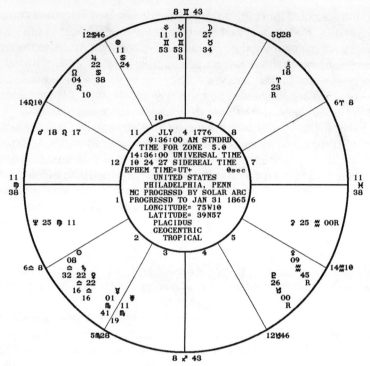

A 22-♏-22   M 04-♍-14   X 06-♑-29   E 07-♐-53

house position in the quincunx to the Aquarian Moon shows an uneasy conscience. With progressed Venus and Ascendant participating in the long-standing pattern of Jupiter-Saturn-Neptune-Moon, the boil was lanced. Slavery was an economic issue, and there were drastic economic repercussions in the South following the War Between the States, and many remained bitter to their deaths. Lincoln was elected by the Republican Party, and the permanent affiliation of the South with the Democratic Party dates to the Civil War. The results have often produced strange bedfellows when conservative Southern Democrats formed uneasy alliances with conservative Northern Republicans. As the South has prospered economically in recent years, some of the hurts have faded. But political equality has proved often illusory where there was economic discrimination. Perhaps the struggle for freedom and equality is never won, but in 1865, the U.S. took a giant step.

As the progressed Moon moved through the trioctile to Saturn, only two and a half months after he signed the Proclamation, Lincoln became our first president to be assassinated on April 14, 1865. Progressed Mercury had just reached the square to the mean nodes of the Moon. Progressed Mars was still in orb of the octile to natal Venus. The progressed angles remained as listed above.

Our second presidential assassination came in 1881 when Garfield was shot on July 2, and died September 19. Progressed MC square natal Mars and progressed Eastpoint opposite natal Mars are fitting aspects. The aspects included octiles and trioctiles to the natal true nodes. Progressed Ascendant was trioctile Chiron, just short of the quincunx to natal Jupiter. Progressed Sun was conjunct progressed Saturn, with both square progressed Jupiter. Yes, that Saturn-Jupiter square was still there waiting to be activated. Progressed Mars was quincunx Pluto. Progressed Moon was opposite natal Mars for the shooting, and quincunx natal Mercury (tenth house ruler) for the death. During the period that he fought for his life, the Moon squared Neptune. The quotidian MC on the day of his death was on the natal IC, opposite MC-Uranus.

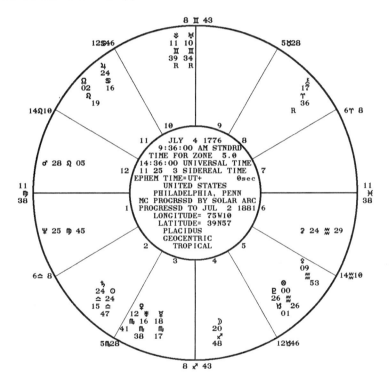

A 04-♐-26   M 20-♍-29   X 18-♑-47   E 21-♐-58

When McKinley was shot on September 6, 1901, progressed Mars was square MC-Uranus-progressed Vesta, while progressed Venus had just reached the opposition to the grouping. The Jupiter-Saturn square had finally ended but had been replaced by progressed Saturn square Pluto. Progressed MC still held a trine to progressed Uranus (remember the quality of the natal conjunction comes through), and progressed Sun was semisextile Saturn (from a natal square). Progressed Moon was sextile natal Mercury (their natal aspect was a quincunx) and at the midpoint of natal and progressed Neptune. Progressed Eastpoint was quincunx MC-Uranus-Vesta. Progressed Mercury was trioctile natal Mars and square the true nodes. The quotidian MC reached the opposition to natal Mars for the date of death, eight days after the shooting. The quotidian Ascendant on the same day was square the MC-Uranus-Vesta combination.

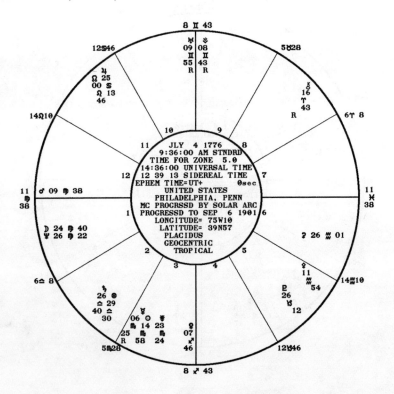

A 19-♐-48   M 10-♎-40   X 02-♒-40   E 09-♑-00

Harding's death in office on August 2, 1923, was credited to food poisoning and pneumonia, but the Teapot Dome scandal was a contributing factor. Government-owned oil reserves had been leased to private companies by two of Harding's Cabinet members; bribery was proven, and there was talk of impeaching Harding. Everything in the affair could be connected to Neptune: oil, scandal, imprisonment of one official, food poisoning and pneumonia. Progressed Mars was conjunct natal Neptune and square its own natal position. Angle aspects included progressed East-point and true node on Pluto; progressed Ascendant quincunx natal MC-Uranus; progressed MC trine Venus, and quincunx progressed Vesta in the ninth house of courts and moral principles; progressed Sun on the Washington, D.C. IC, opposite the local MC. The progressed MC had been conjunct progressed Saturn when Harding was elected, and he consistently pursued a very conservative course, favoring big business.

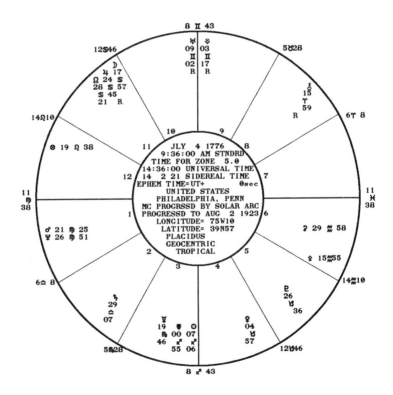

A 08-ᕝ-48   M 02-ᕬ-48   X 17-ᗑ-35   E 28-ᕝ-28

The economic crash and world-wide depression hit in the fall of 1929. October 24 is sometimes called "Black Friday," when the stock market collapsed. Aspects involving fixed planets, houses and signs would be considered most appropriate. Would you settle for progressed Ascendant square natal Saturn in the second house; progressed MC in Scorpio (joint resources, returns on investment) quincunx natal MC-Uranus and octile progressed Mars, ruler of the eighth house; progressed Venus, ruler of the second house, opposite natal Sun (natural key to investment and speculation) and headed into the square to Saturn as the depression deepened; progressed Mercury just starting the octile to natal Saturn and still in the trioctile to natal Sun; progressed Antivertex on the natal Moon, quincunx Neptune; progressed Sun quincunx natal Sun and still in the octile to Pluto in the fifth house (investment and the return on it)? Progressed Ascendant had entered the fifth house, and progressed Venus had just reached the fifth cusp. Progressed Eastpoint in the fifth was quincunx natal Eastpoint and just moving into the quincunx to natal Jupiter to form a yod as the bread lines lengthened. Progressed Saturn squared the progressed mean nodes of the Moon. Progressed Moon was just coming to the cusp

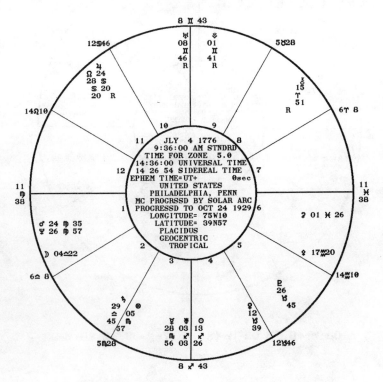

A 15-♍-01   M 09-♏-07   X 21-♒-57   E 04-♒-23

of the second house, and would be moving through it during the years of increasing financial pressure on the "average citizen." It would be years before the world economy began to stagger back toward normalcy, and Hitler was one of the costs. The war against him provided the money to produce recovery though at the cost of increasing government indebtedness. Could this scenario and this chart provide lessons for the decade of the 1980's?

Then there was Pearl Harbor, on December 7, 1941, with the U.S. precipitated into a war against Germany and Japan. For starters we have progressed MC quincunx natal Mars, progressed Ascendant conjunct the progressed mean South Node, just past Pluto but Venus is on Pluto along with the true South Node. Progressed Vesta and Neptune form long trines to the group in Capricorn; we did win, and bolstered our economy in the process. Progressed Antivertex was trine progressed Saturn, trioctile natal Saturn and quincunx progressed Mars. Progressed Moon opposed the natal Ascendant, facing the issue of partners and enemies on the seventh cusp. Progressed Mercury was weak: only a sextile to progressed Eastpoint; were we not using our intelligence? However, quotidian MC

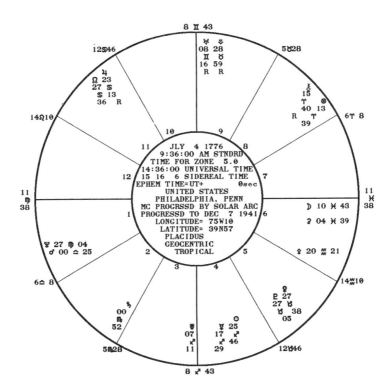

A 28-♑-42   M 21-♏-27   X 00-♓-41   E 16-♒-34

squared natal Mercury on the day of the Japanese attack, and quotidian Ascendant was on the midpoint of Mars-Neptune, on the natal North Node, while the quotidian Antivertex squared Neptune, just past natal Mars. Natal Mars was at the midpoint of the Philadelphia and Washington quotidian positions of the Antivertex.

The first atom bomb was dropped on Japan on August 6, 1945. The progressed Moon at two degrees of Taurus was quincunx progressed Mars, square progressed Venus and Ascendant, sextile natal Venus (Japan surrendered almost immediately). Progressed Venus was still barely in orb with the square to progressed Saturn, just past the trine to progressed Mars, and quincunx its own natal position. Progressed Ascendant was also within orb of the quincunx to natal Venus. Progressed MC was trine natal Mercury. Progressed Eastpoint was trine natal Mars. Progressed Antivertex was trine natal Venus. We won. It was unconditional surrender. But as the Moon moved into the ninth house, there were questions raised about ethical issues. The quotidian Ascendant had been opposite that natal Neptune the day the bomb fell.

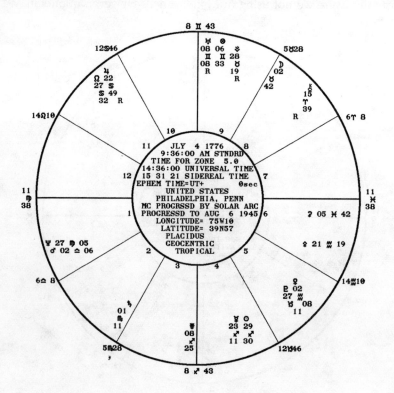

A 03-♒︎-21   M 25-♏︎-11   X 03-♓︎-24   E 20-♒︎-26

Two more events, and we'll leave it to you to judge and to carry on. John Kennedy was assassinated on November 22, 1963. Progressed MC was quincunx natal Sun. Progressed Antivertex was trioctile progressed Saturn. Progressed Eastpoint was on the natal Descendant with Ceres. Progressed Ascendant had just left the trioctile to natal Saturn and the local Ascendant was just coming to it: a midpoint flanking Saturn. Progressed Ascendant was also octile progressed Chiron which had continued to maintain its opposition to natal Saturn. Progressed Moon was square progressed Neptune from the fourth house, as well as semisextile Pluto and the South Node. Progressed Venus was quincunx Mercury, that familiar separation aspect to the ruler of the MC. Progressed Mars was trine natal Uranus and trioctile progressed Venus. Progressed Mercury was semisextile natal Moon (remember the natal quincunx). Yes, the quotidians were there too: MC opposite progressed Saturn; Ascendant octile progressed Neptune and trioctile progressed Moon; Eastpoint opposite Pluto and progressed South Node of the Moon; Antivertex quincunx Pluto.

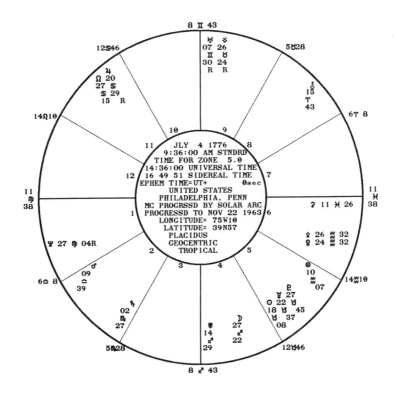

JLY 4 1776
9:36:00 AM STNDRD
TIME FOR ZONE 5.0
14:36:00 UNIVERSAL TIME
16 49 51 SIDEREAL TIME
EPHEM TIME=UT+ 0sec
UNITED STATES
PHILADELPHIA, PENN
MC PROGRSSD BY SOLAR ARC
PROGRESSD TO NOV 22 1963
LONGITUDE= 75W10
LATITUDE= 39N57
PLACIDUS
GEOCENTRIC
TROPICAL

A 00-✕-53   M 13-♐-50   X 17-✕-25   E 11-✕-00

Then there was Nixon: experiencing a character assassination rather than an attack with bullets. Some people thought he was no worse than many other Presidents, while others thought he got off lightly with a pardon and a palace by the Pacific Ocean, paid for by the taxpayers. He resigned on August 9, 1974, with progressed MC quincunx natal Mercury and square the midpoint of natal and progressed Neptune. Progressed Ascendant squared natal Mars. Progressed Eastpoint and Antivertex grouped at the opposition to the Neptune midpoint. During the episode of Watergate, the time of the great cover-up, they opposed Neptune exactly. The progressed MC opposed natal Mars during the election while the secret attacks on the Democrats were occurring. Progressed Sun was still barely within orb of the conjunction to progressed Pluto at the actual resignation, so that aspect also had been in effect for much of Nixon's period in office. Progressed Mars squared natal Sun. Progressed Moon, still in the ninth house of legal affairs and moral judgments, had been forming a grand earth trine and reached the octile to natal Sun in time for the resignation. Progressed Mercury was at the midpoint of the progressed angles, octile MC and Antivertex. Quotidians too? MC opposite

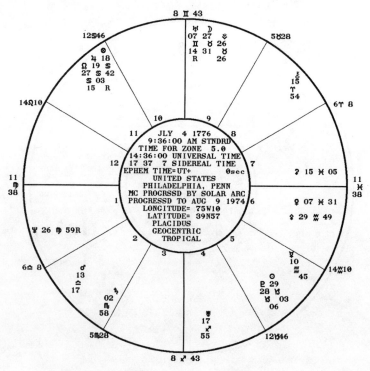

A 20-♓-14   M 24-♐-45   X 25-♓-54   E 23-♓-46

natal Mercury; Ascendant quincunx progressed Mars; Eastpoint square Pluto and progressed Sun; Antivertex square progressed Jupiter. The local (Washington) MC was also trioctile natal Uranus while progressed Venus squared progressed Uranus.

The following chart is enclosed for any readers who would like to guess the challenges the United States will be facing in late 1986 and the spring of 1987.

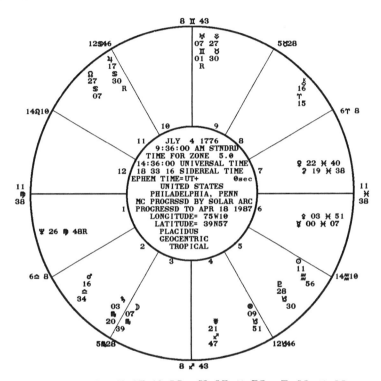

A 14-♈-09   M 07-♑-38   X 05-♈-58   E 09-♈-03

They are interesting patterns. There are many more dates in our history for which we might run charts, but that will have to wait for another book. Remember, the planets are not doing it. We choose the details among many possibilities. Where masses of people are involved, the level of insight and personal mastery is apt to go down, so in mundane work, we may see the negative potential more often than the positive. But in our personal lives, we can grow; we can make our world a better world, hospitable to love and generosity and peace. Our world is a mirror of our own nature. It only takes one light to dispel darkness.

INDEX

Bold face indicates major discussion of a topic.